Concept of Teaching and Learning Process

Concept of Teaching and Learning Process

Dr. Satpal Swami

RANDOM PUBLICATIONS
NEW DELHI (INDIA)

Concept of Teaching and Learning Process

ISBN 978-93-5111-841-1

Published in 2016 in India by

RANDOM PUBLICATIONS

4376-A/4B, Gali Murari Lal, Ansari Road
New Delhi-110 002
Phone : +9111-43580356, 011-23289044, 011-43142548
e-mail: sales@randompublications.com,
info@randompublications.com, randomexports@gmail.com

Reprinted 2025

Type Setting by : Friends Media, Delhi-110089
Digitally Printed at : Replika Press Pvt. Ltd.

Preface

Teaching is a highly professional activity. It is often said that good teachers are born. This is true that every body does not have a bent of mind for teaching. But nowadays due to mass education, teachers have to be created and trained. There was a time when some specific communities took to the teaching profession but nowadays teaching has ceased to be the preserve of the few. Individual students may be better suited to learning in a particular way, using distinctive modes for thinking, relating and creating. The notion of students having particular learning styles has implications for teaching strategies. Because preferred modes of input and output vary from one individual to another, it is critical that teachers use a range of teaching strategies to effectively meet the needs of individual learners. Sound health instruction should incorporate a variety of teaching methods intended to complement the learning styles of children. This should lead to young learners who are both intrinsically and extrinsically motivated to inquire, infer, and interpret; to think reflectively, critically and creatively; and in the final analysis to make use of the knowledge and skills they have gained by becoming effective decision- makers. This book is useful to both students and teachers, retaining its appeal as a guide to the educationists and policy-makers and a comprehensive introduction to the students at both undergraduate and postgraduate levels.

– Author

Contents

1

Concept of Learning

NATURAL PROCESS OF LEARNING

Learning is a natural process of growth or change in a person which is manifested as new modes or patterns of behaviour. This change exhibits itself as a skill, a habit, an attitude an understanding, or as knowledge or an application. Learning is a relatively permanent change in behaviour and is the result of reinforced practice through the process of "stimulus and response".This definition of learning assumes that certain conditions in the environment bring about fundamental changes in our behaviour that persist for a long time. The changes which result from learning are positive and active, not negative and inert. Learning is not directly observable but inferred from one's performance. We can infer that a person has learnt something when he does something, which he could not do before.

A person may know some thing and yet may not have learnt it. You may know how a computer works, but may not be able to operate it. Thus the distinction between learning or acquisition of knowledge and performance is an important one. We use the term 'behavioural tendency' to maintain the distinction between learning and performance. The relatively permanent change in behaviour refers to a change in performance.We can also define learning in terms of cognitive development. Cognitivists say that learning is a change or reorganisation of cognitive structures, which involves acquisition and transformation of new knowledge. Thus we may conclude that learning is a change in knowledge, skills, attitudes and values brought about through experiences and this change in knowledge may or may not be expressed in overt behaviour.However, it may be pointed that all behaviours cannot be related to learning. Some behavioural changes are due to biological development or maturation. In maturation, growth developments are independent of specific learning conditions. A child starts walking once his/her legs are strong enough to support his/her weight.The child is born with the potential to mature and at successive age levels, grasp and learn language, ways of behaving, attitudes, and values of his/her cultures he is born also with potential for reorganising and remoulding many aspects of his culture in harmony with changing conditions and needs. Thus, the child is a product of culture as much as he is of biology. Through maturation and learning, the child acquires a culture. The process through which the child is taught the cultural ways that society accepts him to follow is termed as 'enculturation'. In this process, the child adjusts his innate biological characteristics to the prevailing cultural practices in society.

CONDITIONS OF LEARNING

Gagne distinguishes eight conditions of learning, or varieties of learning, beginning with the simple forms and ending with the complex ones. Although Gagne refers to these conditions as learning types, he is primarily interested in observable behaviour and performance, which is the product of each condition.

In this condition of learning he combines a basic behaviourist thought with cognitive theory into a hierarchical model of different types of learning. Here, we shall give a brief description of the phases of learning advocated by Gagne.

VARIETIES OF LEARNING

Gagne identifies five categories or varieties of learning which include:

- Verbal information skill;
- Intellectual skill;
- Motor skill;
- Attitudes; and
- Cognitive strategies.

Each type of learning is acquired in a different set of prerequisite skills and a different set of cognitive processing is required to support the learner's cognitive processes during learning. Thus, learning is the result of interaction between a learner's internal and external events variables. In other words, Gagne attempts to synthesise the basic principles of cognitivism and behaviourism.

The varieties of learning identified by Gagne are summarised below:

- *Verbal Information Skill*: Verbal information skill provides ability to state/ recall information. This has to be developed to meet the needs of a particular subject matter.
- *Intellectual Skill*: Intellectual skills are the most important skills involving the mental operations. They include conceptualisation of environment; discriminating between things; understanding concepts, seeing relationships between things. Reading, writing and handling of numbers are the other abilities, which also come under this variety. These abilities range from the simple to the complex.

- *Motor skills*: Motor skills are physical skills. They include a sequence of physical movements.
- *Cognitive strategies*: Cognitive strategies include learner's thinking, remembering and learning the procedures we use for ordering and processing information internally. They are learned over long periods.
- *Attitudes*: Attitudes are deep-rooted in us and we find it difficult to change them. They determine our predisposition to positive and negative responses towards an object. Our attitudes strongly affect our motivation for learning.

Educational Implications of Gagne's Theory of Learning

We present here three broad educational implications of Gagne's theory of learning to teaching:

- *Prerequisite behaviour*: Gagne advocated those processes of learning that move from the simple to the complex. The learner has to develop the prerequisite capabilities before he acquires new terminal behaviour. Thus, the use of a hierarchy of learning and task analysis is an integral part of instructional activities.
- *Learners' characteristics*: Learners' individual differences, readiness and motivation to learn are the important issues to be considered before designing instructional activities.
- *Cognitive process and instruction*: Transfer of learning and the students' skills of problem solving are integral parts of internal conditions of learning applicable to the instruction. The skill of learning 'how to learn' should be developed in the learner. The emphasis should be on the individuality of the learner.

ACTIVITIES THAT FACILITATE LEARNING

A classroom teacher performs a number of activities, which are aimed at facilitating learning.

These activities are:

- *Presenting the material*: The teacher present the prescribed materials, which are available in part or some other form. The teacher is supposed to breathe life into the text and help the learner communicate with it.
- *Identifying the objectives*: The syllabus and very often, the prescribed text itself make it clear as to what educational objectives are to be achieved through a particular course. But practically, it is the teacher who identifies them and states them in behavioural terms for the learner. It is the teacher who points to what is significant and what trivial, what needs more attention, and for what purpose.
- *Motivation and learner*: To reduce distraction, the teacher provides motivation. He brings learners to a state of readiness in which learning

takes place more easily. All of us know of teachers whose very name or presence provides enough motivation for a successful teaching exercises. And then there are teachers who are demotivating in most of the situations.

- *Exploiting learner's experience*: Good teachers build on learners' experiences. One and the same concept may be brought home to rural learners with the help of their experiences and to those of urban learners with theirs.
- *Providing learning activities*: Once a new concept is taught or a new piece of information is given, the teacher promotes learning through learning activities. For example, after having taught formula, the teacher asks learners to apply their learning to work out the solution of a few problems.
- *Facilitating retention*: Just knowing about a concept, does not amount to having learnt it. The learner should be able to retain it in his memory. Good teachers use different ways and means to help their students to improve their retention through exercise.
- *Promoting transfer of learning*: Having learnt a concept or obtained any new learning, the learner should be able to transfer his learning to various issues within and across various disciplines. For example, if we have learnt about the notion of Relativity in physics, we should be able to think of a different kind of Relativity in sociology. Besides, transfer also means facilitating further learning. Used in either sense, transfer is provided by the teacher in the classroom through various means.
- *Providing occasion for feedback*: For successful teaching, two way feedback is needed from the learner to the teacher, and vice versa. The teacher provides occasion for this exchange. For example, he puts a few questions to see whether or not the learners have learnt what he taught.

It is worth noting that each individual learns as a result of his own efforts and successes. No teacher can learn anything for him. The teacher's task is to understand and encourage the child, to watch for an appropriate psychological moment when he has a high degree of readiness to learn a specific task, to guide him into making a response, and then to reinforce his natural satisfaction in his own success.

The learning that occurs in a child through experiences provided by the teacher starts from what he has previously learnt and moves in directions that are determined by the needs and interests he feels at the particular moment. A teacher is effective if he is able to identify the child's own purposes and feelings of need. It is through the identification of these keys, the teacher unlocks the doors of learning in any direction that the child can see as significant for the satisfaction of his own purposes and needs.

PROGRAMMED LEARNING

Programmed Learning or Programmed Instruction is a learning methodology or technique first proposed by the behaviourist B. F. Skinner in 1958. The purpose of programmed learning is to "manage human learning under controlled conditions".

Programmed learning has three elements:

1. It delivers information in small bites,
2. It is self-paced by the learner, and
3. It provides immediate feedback, both positive and negative, to the learner.

It was popular in the late 1960s and through the 1970s, but pedagogical interest was lost in the early 1980s as it was difficult to implement and its limitations were not well understood by practitioners. It was revived in the 1990s in the computerised Integrated Learning System (ILS) approach, primarily in the business and managerial context. Programmed learning remains popular in self-teaching textbooks. The methodology involves self-administered and self-paced learning, in which the student is presented with information in small steps often referred to as "frames". Each frame contains a small segment of the information to be learned, and a question which the student must answer. After each frame the student uncovers, or is directed to, additional information based on an incorrect answer, or positive feedback for a correct answer.

CRITICISM

Programmed Instruction has been criticised for its inability to provide adequate feedback on incorrect answers and for its lack of student instigated conceptualisation opportunities. It works best in basic courses which introduce the vocabulary of a discipline, heavily fact-based courses, and rule-based technical courses.

SIMULATED TEACHING

Normal experiential learning that leads to an expert professional in clinical practice is associated with prolonged exposure to that practice. The over-riding idea is that by simulating clinical scenarios, learning is accelerated by the debriefing/ feedback session. The expert knowledge is made explicit to the trainee and reinforced with video and verbal feedback.

Simulation training can:

- Prepare students to cope with future roles.
- Provide practice in a safe environment with no risk to patient or student.
- Test/challenge trainee's technical and decision-making skills during realistic patient care situations.
- Be an assessment tool.
- Lead to standardised teaching.

Skills that can be assessed/practiced using simulation:

- Interpersonal and communication skills.
- Critical thinking and decision-making skills.
- Practical skills.
- The use of equipment.

The Best evidence medical education (BEME) collaboration is an international group of individuals, Universities and organisations committed to the promotion of best evidence medical education. They formed a topic group in 2002 that addressed the question: "What are the features/aspects of high fidelity simulators that lead to most effective learning?"

FEEDBACK

The absence of learner feedback was the greatest single factor for ineffective simulation training.

The lack of feedback could lead to:

- Learning of the wrong learning objective.
- Not realising what the desired behaviours should be by not focusing on them.
- Not transferring skills to clinical practice.
- Spending increasing time on only one aspect of training.

PRACTICE

A lack of opportunity for practice is also associated with a poor educational outcome. This could often be attributed to insufficient access to the simulator, as training sessions are usually time dependent, and the simulator is often a hotly contested resource. In addition, each learner is different, and some learners inevitably need longer or more frequent sessions with the simulator to achieve the same educational results as their co-learners.

VALIDITY

Poor validity is associated with a lack of realism. In some simulators novices can out-perform an expert, which questions the validity of that simulation. Typically, this would also lead to a lack of correlation with other outcome measures.

FIDELITY

A common belief is that low fidelity simulation is better than high fidelity. However the group concluded that all levels of fidelity should be used based on the required outcomes.

This is discussed by Maran and Glavin, where the progression from low to high fidelity simulation is compared to the progression through medical education. Their conclusion is that the range of fidelity available is almost all potentially useful, but that many simulators are underused due simply to a lack of clear educational goals.

'SIMULATOR' LEARNING

Students learn to master the simulator rather than the task. The solution to this is to have multiple outcome measures for the task.

ASSESSMENT

There is current controversy about the use of simulators in high stakes examinations. Issues of domain specificity and itemised versus global scoring systems have bee raised. There is ongoing research into all of these factors though, and it seems certain that simulation will be included as part of high stakes assessment, along with other outcome measures.

IN SUMMARY

If you are thinking of using simulation in teaching you have to think:

- Who am I teaching?
- What am I teaching them?
- What are they expected to learn?

The simulation scenarios should:

- Be as realistic an environment as possible.
- Should involve feedback/debriefing/video sessions.
- Well prepared with a back up plan for equipment failure.
- Involve the observers by getting to make notes on teamwork, situation awareness, communication, etc.

Remember to create a relaxed teaching environment, as simulation can be a stressful experience for students. There follows a brief description of the reasons why simulation has become more popular as a teaching and assessment tool.

MEDICAL SIMULATION

The first recorded use of a medical simulator is that of a manikin created in the 17 Century by a Dr. Gregoire of Paris. He used a pelvis with skin stretched across it to simulate an abdomen, and with the help of a dead fetus explained assisted and complicated deliveries to midwives. In spite of this early start, medical simulators had not really gained widespread use in the following centuries, principally for reasons of cost, reluctance to adopting new teaching methods, and scepticism that what was learned from a simulator could not be transferred to actual practice. All of these reasons are still relevant today, however the combination of improved technology and increased pressures on educators have promoted simulation as one option to address the following problems with traditional clinical skills teaching.

An Alternative to "see one, do one"

In the past, health care professionals learnt on the job, which some still believe is the best way to gain experience. However, there are a number of barriers to this type of traditional clinical teaching.

These include:

- Humanitarian issues – practicing on patients is not ethical. We have moved into an age of where learning on patients is not acceptable if there is an alternative.
- There has been a decrease in the number of inpatients. In part due to an increasing number of day case patients and also the fact that chronic conditions are being cared for in the community. This has led to a decrease in exposure and access of the trainees to ward patients.
- The training time for postgraduate medical education has decreased and will decrease further. With the implementation of new training schemes, experience cannot be built upon over time as before.
- Some situations are so rare that to gain experience would take many lifetimes.
- Legal/litigation issues. The possibility of educational establishments being sued by patients and ex-students for not teaching and assessing clinical skills as laid down by the regulatory bodies could arise.
- Record keeping, reproducibility, assessment and validity are issues all brought to the forefront with clinical governance and revalidation. Simulation is seen as away of addressing some of these issues.
- Students learn more effectively in a non-threatening environment.
- There is increasing emphasis on multidisciplinary learning, and clinical skills' teaching is an ideal forum for this.
- The increase in workload for health care staff means there is less time to spend on traditional clinical teaching, which is compounded by the increase in student numbers.

Recent Recommendations

Simulation training extends from part task trainers, procedural training to the experience of full clinical situations. For example canulation, basic and advanced life support to high fidelity simulators.

However, they also include communication skills, how to take consent, bereavement counseling and IT skills. In 'Tomorrow's doctors: Recommendations on undergraduate medical education.' *GMC July 2002, there are lists of clinical skills that medical students have to be competent in before graduation:*

- "The essential skill that graduates need must be gained under supervision. Medical schools must assess students' competence in these skills. The curriculum must stress the importance of communication skills and the other essential skills of medical practice."

In 'Unfinished Business: Proposals for reform of the Senior House Officer grade.' A report by Sir Liam Donaldson, Chief Medical Officer for England, proposed changes in junior doctor training which were considerable. With a shortened training period and the probable division of service commitment from effective training time, the provision of effective skills training and competency-based assessment will have to be addressed.

- "An objective of the foundation programme would be to develop and enhance core or generic clinical skills essential for all doctors (*e.g.*, team-working, communication, ability to produce high standards of clinical governance and patient safety, expertise in accessing, appraising and using evidence as well as time management skills.)"

Multidisciplinary Teaching

As well as increased emphasis on clinical skill teaching, there is increased emphasis on the multidisciplinary approach to learning. Of interest during multidisciplinary teaching are human factors such as decision-making and behavioural interaction, which is thought to be of major importance in the occurrence of critical incidents.

As quoted in 'Working Together – learning Together' A Framework for Lifelong Learning for the NHS. DoH, November 2001:

- "We are taking forward work to develop more pre-registration inter professional education programmes which incorporate common learning in core skills and knowledge. As a minimum we intend to ensure that all health professionals should expect their education and training to include common learning with other professions."

This emphasises that predetermined health care groups deliver many of the skills required by patients during their care, however in the future who delivers these skills may well change. It is envisaged that simulation teaching could provide packages that any group could access and interact with other groups for relevant multidisciplinary situations.

APPROACHES AND PROCEDURES FOR TEACHING AND LEARNING GRAMMAR

If you live in a country where English is the main language used, you may have discovered that many approaches to teaching English in schools tend to sideline the structure of the language. In fact, your first meeting with the notion of grammar is more likely to have been when you were studying a foreign language. This is not, of course, the same as learning the grammar of English, as languages differ in the way they work and in the terms we use to talk about them. Consequently, if you are a native speaker of English, you may find that your knowledge of how English works is at best sketchy. This can be a particular problem for teachers of English as a foreign language because their students may sometimes know more about English grammar than an inexperienced teacher. This should not be too surprising since English language students study the structure of English in some detail. However, without the necessary background, the teacher will be at a disadvantage and may even find him/herself in an awkward situation when trying to explain a specific point of grammar.

Teachers of English need to have a good command of the grammar of English simply because our students expect to learn Standard English that will serve them in most situations. We need to remember that they are likely to be speaking to non-native as much as native speakers of English. This is not therefore a question of overly pedantic insistence on correct English, rather the emphasis is on a more pragmatic approach that ensures the English they use is not going to confuse the person they are writing or speaking to. Grammatical accuracy has recently become more important due to the rise in learners of English who need to communicate in writing. Currently, an increasing number of learners require English for Academic and Occupational Purposes (essay, dissertations and reports for example) to be as close to native-speaker competence as possible, so accuracy is a major consideration for them.

FOCUS OF ENGLISH GRAMMAR

Tense	Concerning time sequence
Person	Reference to people or things
Syntax	How parts relate to each other

USES OF ENGLISH GRAMMAR

An awareness of grammar or the structure of language can result in more efficient writing and speaking. An understanding of the mechanics or workings of language is far more useful and more easily acquired than memorizing technical terms. You can understand the mechanics of language by studying utterances and their: audience – form – function

It is useful to be able to distinguish between the more grammatical items in a statement and those, which have a mainly lexical function. The grammatical items are the working parts of the statement, whilst the lexical items carry content or meaning. There is no absolute distinction between grammatical and lexical items. However, it is possible to think of a continuum, with lexis at one end and grammar at the other.

The study of English grammar study has developed over hundreds of years. The objective has generally been to find a set of rules which accurately and comprehensively define, describe, and explain the workings of the language. In the past, grammar study was very prescriptive. Rules were laid down as to how English must be used. Many of these prescriptive rules were based on the rules of the Latin language, which historically had strong religious and cultural ties with English. Latin was regarded as the perfect language and as such was used as a model for English. However, it was a blueprint which didn't fit, and the struggle to make it fit has left us with such prescriptive rules as 'Never end a sentence with a preposition'.

In the past, the study of grammar was thought to be a series of rules and regulations:

- Rules for writing good English
- Learning to analyse sentences grammatically

The most significant development this century has been the move towards a descriptive and functional approach to understanding of the workings of English. That is to say, the emphasis currently is on observing how the language is actually operating in practice. Changes are charted and variations noted, with a neutral attitude. A language is best seen as a living organism, which is constantly in the process of evolution.

The nature of its changes reflects and affects its users. As Latin has been a dead language for hundreds of years, its imposition on English is at best interesting and at worst ludicrous.

Every language has a basic structure. This is composed of its essential grammatical features, which are its working parts. It also has more superficial features such as its vocabulary, which changes and develops in accordance with cultural and social phenomena.

IMPORTANCE OF FOCUSING ON GRAMMAR

- Without grammar, language doesn't exist.
- How can I feel confident about using grammar if I don't understand the rules?
- A solid knowledge of all the rules is necessary to speak a language well.
- The best way to learn a language is practice the correct usage.
- Good English means correct use of Grammar in English.
- Making mistakes reflect poor learning.

UNDERSTANDING ENGLISH GRAMMAR

Understanding English Grammar presents a linguistic introduction to the structure of English that is accessible to students who have had little or no opportunity to study the language.

- Familiarizes students with the essential structural characteristics of English.
- Features accessible coverage of syntax, morphology, and phonology, as well as basic linguistic concepts.

- Includes numerous examples, exercises, and an indexed glossary.
- Is supported by an online instructor's manual.

The latest and effective way to understand English grammar is based on reading textbooks and physical demonstrations. It can be done by teaching comprehension as a skill of the reader, which depends equally on the quality of the writing. Good nonfiction and most good fiction start with good grammar. The reader does not need to know technical grammar; grammar is the responsibility of the writer. Traditional phonics is designed to TEACH READING. Literacy programme researchers and teachers consider writing and its accompanying grammar to be secondary.

The way in which teachers now teach writing is an example of how standards-based curriculum impact teachers. Writing is primarily a group project in which self-expression is emphasized. Grammar is considered a restraint on expression. The opposite is true. The best way to teach English grammar is not as rigid rules. In fact grammar gives writers great latitude in emphasis and emotion while giving clarity to the text for the reader. The parts of speech are mobile and interchangeable, one part often acting as if it were another.

Sentences often contain phrases or clauses that act as a single part of speech. Grammar is not static; it slowly but constantly changes what is considered correct usage. The writer uses grammar like a symphony conductor uses the orchestra. The education of children in home school should include grammar help, and the best way to teach English grammar is as a course with coverage of, and reference to, multiple parts of speech. Good grammar helps acceptance into higher education, and home schooled children can efficiently acquire good grammar through this book.

Grammar as a course is considered a necessity for all students.

An advanced artificial intelligence and grammar engine enable the detection and correction of language errors that may damage the image you want to project. The impressive proofreading abilities of the ever-improving spell checker and smart punctuation check will prevent you from getting embarrassed in case you are not sure about the nitty gritty aspects of the English language. An English text correction features are coupled with its text enrichment database. The software algorithms constantly scan an endless number of texts, adding to the large variety of enrichment suggestions for synonyms, extra adjectives and adverbs that bring English text enhancement to a whole new level. English text enhancement also builds on remarkable online English dictionary and thesaurus, which can be supplemented by an optional Multi-Language Translator, giving you immediate foreign language translations within any dictionary entry. This genuinely makes the software adaptable for international English users. At its core, the term grammar refers to either the inherent structure of words and sentences (morphology and syntax respectively) in a language; or to the study and description of this structure, published as grammar rules in books about the language. Other approaches include more topics under the term grammar: orthography (spelling, punctuation and capitalization), semantics, phonetics and phonology (sounds) and pragmatics.

We unconsciously use grammar all the time when we use language for speaking, listening, reading and writing. If we want to improve our English language abilities, there is no escape from addressing grammar issues.

Grammar explains how the language should be structured, using various categories. Number refers to formation of singular and plural nouns and other parts of the sentence that have to agree with number (e.g. child Vs. children) whereas Gender, a category hardly existent in English, but alive in German, regards the differences between masculine and feminine or even neuter nouns and how these affect other words in a properly phrased sentence. Tense and aspect treat the formation of verbs, from the English I write - She writes; We write - We are writing distinctions, all the way to far more elaborate verb conjugation systems of other languages. A grammatical category or element never stands alone as it influences all other parts of the structural system of a language.

Grammar topics are usually sorted in books into word grammar and sentence grammar. Word grammar sections are further divided according to the different parts of speech - content words, containing verbs, nouns, adjective and adverbs; and structure words, containing determiners, pronouns, prepositions, conjunctions and interjections. Sentence grammar relates to the construction of phrases, clauses and full sentences, all the way up to paragraphs and full texts.

ENGLISH GRAMMAR: THEN AND NOW

Nowadays, there are modern approaches to grammar, which bring it alive and relate it to our real life, outside of outdated grammar books containing endless lists of grammar rules. The older prescriptive grammar approach, used to have students theoretically analyse sentences for correctness in literary and religious texts, as if they were training to become linguists. This was based along the lines of the traditional approach to the instruction of ancient Latin and Greek, which were not even used in speech in the Middle-Ages onwards. The purpose was preserving the formal standard usage of these languages while treating grammar as a theoretically isolated area of study. This is now supplemented by the descriptive approach that looks at how people actually use grammar in real life conversations and texts using modern living languages. It acknowledges language change and various styles as acceptable, resulting in more than one way of saying things. Pedagogical grammar for language learning purposes teaches only those grammar rules relevant to successful practical communication themes like shopping, looking for a job or opening up a business.For example, the uses of the present perfect for indefinite past events or events going from past to present are geared towards speaking about former work experience either during a spoken job interview or in a written letter of job application. Alternatively, perfect modal forms are used for a hypothetical discussion of alternative consequences to past actions or the expression of regrets on what may/should have been.

Grammar is therefore now seen, not merely as theory, but as an enabling tool for authentic language practice. As some rules still need to be taught formally, a balanced combination of all the approaches is the solution for using grammar effectively. For improving your English writing, It is not to be understood that grammar is less important today than how it may have been perceived before.

Whereas spoken language or literary dialogue may tolerate numerous grammar mistakes as part of a person or cultural group's individual style, written language of expository articles, business documents and of course academic texts must adhere to conventional grammar and style.

Generally speaking, written language is more formal in both form and content than spoken language. Consequently, "She doesn't want to do nothing" may qualify for informal coffee table chats, but will not for a written letter of complaint about a worker or service provider. The conventional practice of avoiding double negatives in writing would therefore call for "She does not want to do anything."

RULES OF UNDERSTANDING

In order to understand and learn English Grammar you need to understand its basic rules which are described as follows:

Agreement

Agreement in a sentence refers to all of the parts of the sentence corroborating with each other. For example, you wouldn't say "John have two pieces of toast and has three." You would instead say, "John has two pieces of toast and have three." The subjects and verbs need to be in agreement. Without sentence agreement you have all-out civil war in your sentence and no one knows what is going on.

If your sentence parts don't agree with each other you will have to jump in and mediate, causing hard feelings all around. Errors in agreement are the most common mistakes made in writings. To avoid this, just follow the simple rule: A singular subject requires a singular verb, and a plural subject requires a plural verb.

Wrong: Identification of these goods have been difficult.

Right: Identification of these goods has been difficult. ('Identification' is the subject here)

Wrong: The best way to keep your children happy are to give them enough responsibilities.

Right: The best way to keep your children happy is to give them enough responsibilities. (Use a singular verb if the subject is a phrase or clause) *Awkward:* Neither John nor I am interested in this project.

Better: John is not interested in this project; nor am I. (If you write an awkward sentence, consider rewriting it)

Exception: Use a singular verb if a compound subject refers to the same person or thing.

Example: Milk and breads is a typical breakfast for many people.

Tense

Tense refers to time. Tense is used to show the relation between the action or state described by the verb and the time, which is reflected in the form of the verb. There are two basic tenses in English; the present tense and the past tense. The present is like the base form, although the third person singular adds -s. Regular verbs add -ed or -d to show the past tense, while irregular verbs change in many different ways, or not at all in some cases.

One of the forms which a verb takes by inflection or by adding auxiliary words, so as to indicate the time of the action or event signified; the modification which verbs undergo for the indication of time. What time is it in your sentence? Whatever time it is it should remain consistent throughout your whole piece of writing.

If it was last week you are talking about, stay there. Tenses in English Grammar are basically Verbs that can take various forms, depending on whether they refer to the present or the past, and on the temporal relationship of one event to another. These forms are the tenses.

Examples: Every day we watch television for an hour or two. [simple present, here used for a routinely repeated action] While I was watching the news, the phone rang. [1: past continuous, denoting an action that was continuing; 2: "rang" is simple past, for an event that happened while the first (watching) was going on] Are you watching the game on Saturday? [present continuous, here used for the future].

You have been watching too many thrillers. [present perfect, denoting an action that has occurred in the past and continues to occur in the present.This tense causes particular difficulty for adult learners of English. It seems to have no equivalent in other languages, which instead have structures like "You are always watching too many thrillers" and "I am standing here since seven o'clock"].

Different linguists give these tenses different names; the names above are representative, but not definitive. There are quite a few more tenses in English, but the above demonstrate the function of tense.

There are three tenses in writing, past tense, present tense and future tense. Here is an example of writing with mixed tenses: "Carrie wondered how she is going to finish in time, but Joe will help her." This sentence contains all three tenses, past in "wondered", present in "is" and future in "will Here is an example of writing with mixed tenses:

Wrong: John wanted to know why Rebecca is sad, but she will not tell him.

Right: John wanted to know why Rebecca was sad, but she would not tell him. Present tense, Past tense and Future Tense each has the following four forms. The examples below will help you understand that:

Past Tense

Simple Past: I spoke

The simple past expresses an action in the past taking place once, never, several times. It can also be used for actions taking place one after another or in the middle of another action.

Form of Simple Past

Positive	Negative	Question
no differences I spoke.	I did not speak.	Did I speak?

For irregular verbs, use the past form. For regular verbs, just add "ed".

Exceptions in Spelling when Adding 'ed'

Exceptions in spelling when adding ed.

Example:

After a final e only add d love – loved.

Final consonant after a short, stressed vowelor l as final consonant after a vowel is doubled admit – admittedtravel – travelled. Final y after a consonant becomes i hurry – hurried.

Use of Simple Past

- Action in the past taking place once, never or several times.
  Example: He visited his parents every weekend.
- Actions in the past taking place one after the other.
  Example: He came in, took off his coat and sat down.
- Action in the past taking place in the middle of another action.
  Example: When I was having breakfast, the phone suddenly rang.
- If sentences type II (If I talked, ...)
  Example: If I had a lot of money, I would share it with you.

Signal Words of Simple Past

- Yesterday, 2 minutes ago, in 1990, the other day, last Friday
- If-Satz Typ II (If I talked, ...)

Past Continuous: I was speaking.

Past Perfect: I had spoken.

Past perfect continuous: I had been speaking.

Present Tense

Simple Present: I speak

Simple present is also called present simple. The simple present expresses an action in the present taking place once, never or several times. It is also used for actions that take place one after another and for actions that are set by a timetable or schedule. The simple present also expresses facts in the present.

Present Continuous: I am speaking.

Present Perfect: I have spoken.

Present Perfect Continuous: I have been speaking.

Future Tense

Simple Future: I shall/ will speak.

Form of will Future

	Positive	*negative question*
no differences I will speak.	I will not speak.	Will I speak?

Use of will Future

- A spontaneous decision.
  Example: Wait, I will help you.
- An opinion, hope, uncertainty or assumption regarding the future
  Example : He will probably come back tomorrow.
- A promise
  Example : I will not watch TV tonight.
- An action in the future that cannot be influenced.
  Example : It will rain tomorrow.
- Conditional clauses type I
  Example: If I arrive late, I will call you.

Signal Words

- In a year, next ..., tomorrow.
- *Vermutung:* I think, probably, we might ..., perhaps.

Future Continuous: I shall/ will be speaking. *Future Perfect:* I shall/will have spoken. *Future Perfect Continuous:* I shall/ will have been speaking.

Double Negatives

Two negative words create a positive meaning, which may be just the opposite of what you have intended to convey.

Wrong: I don't have nothing to say.

Right: I don't have anything to say.

Wrong: Tom couldn't hardly believe what Jack said.

Right: Tom could hardly believe what Jack said.

Spelling

One of the most important things, and without it, you can kiss your credibility goodbye. Spell checkers are poor substitutes for knowing how to spell and can leave behind more errors than you realise. There are many different forms of words and your spell checker does not know which form you wanted to use. For example, "When Mark washed they're care, he forgot too putt on the wax."

Run-On Sentences

A run-on sentence is one that is just too darned long! Not only is it too long, it is incorrect. Usually, a run-on sentence can be made into two or more sentences with a little punctuation and style. An example of a run-on sentence might be: "We walked over to the commissary to get something to eat but it was closed so we didn't know what to do so we kept walking until we saw a restaurant and decided to go in and get something to eat but Andrew didn't want to eat there so we kept going for another mile." This sentence could have gone on for another mile too! Break up the sentence into smaller, more coherent parts.

Punctuation

It is very important to know your punctuation, even if you never plan on using a semicolon for the rest of your life. The most important thing to learn is where to put your commas, a common mistake among writers. Commas are used to separate parts of sentences that stand alone, such as those that are parenthetical. For example "There were too many flowers, not that I minded, but they took up most of the room." Avoid using commas after conjunctions like "but" and "and."

Usage

If you are going to use a word, you really ought to know how to use it. Some writers think big words look impressive but actually the reverse is true if the word is used incorrectly. Words don't have to be big to be misused, consider its vs. it's. If you are going to use a word, you must know how to use it. Use simple words. Many people have the tendency to use big, difficult words while writing. Avoid fancy words and phrases when simpler ones convey the idea. Omit unnecessary words.

A piece of writing, containing long words strung together in complex sentences, turns out to be poorly written and not impressive. You will have fewer chances for grammatical errors if you can cut a word out which can be cut out.

Stuffy: I will make modifications in the document.

Simple: I will change the document.

Capitalization

Words at the beginning of sentences aren't the only ones worthy of capital letters. Always capitalize proper names such as people and places. Titles of all kinds deserve capital letters and so do acronyms.

Point of View

The point of view refers to whoever is telling the story or "speaking." When you write a letter you are writing in "first person" which includes I, me, my, we and our. Second person writing occurs when we talk about you and yours and third person includes he, she, they and theirs. In third person writing, the author does not interject himself into the story.

Sentence Fragments

A sentence fragment is an incomplete sentence that does not include both noun and verb. An example of a sentence fragment might be, "Really dumb." Make sure your sentences reflect a complete thought unless you are writing dialog.

Wasted Words

A big no-no. Sometimes we throw in words just to round out our sentences, or we over-describe something, like, "The really ugly puke-green dress was hanging on the wall." Do we really need to point out that a puke-green dress was really ugly? Economize your words and you will have fewer chances for grammatical errors. There are several reasons why you might want to improve your understanding of the rules of grammar. For example:

- Without good grammar, clear communication is nearly impossible. Proper grammar keeps you from being misunderstood while expressing your thoughts and ideas.
- Writing and speaking correctly gives you the appearance of credibility. If you're attempting to build a reputation as an expert in your profession, this is extremely important.
- Other people consider good grammar to be a mark of intelligence and education. Don't allow strangers to form a negative impression of you based on your poor communication skills.

Unfortunately, there is no shortcut to learning English grammar. While there are many spelling and grammar check software programs available, a computer can't fully grasp the intricacies of the English language. In some cases, a computer grammar check will even suggest incorrect alternatives when attempting to fix common errors. Unfortunately, remembering all the rules can be a rather daunting task and consulting authoritative grammar handbooks becomes a necessity. Since many writers have difficulties with "run-on sentences," this post will address the topic of fused sentences and comma splices.

FUSED SENTENCES AND COMMA SPLICES

More commonly known as "run-on sentences," fused sentences and comma splices are independent clauses that are incorrectly joined. An independent clause is a group of words that can stand on its own as a sentence. When two independent clauses appear in the same sentence, they must be joined in one of the following ways:

- With a comma and a coordinating conjunction (and, but, or, nor, for, so, yet)
- With a semicolon (or occasionally a colon or a dash)

According to Strunk and White's The Elements of Style, there is an exception to the above grammar rule. It states that a comma is preferable when the clauses are very short and alike in form, or when the tone of the sentence is easy and conversational. They offer the following examples:

- Man proposes, God disposes.
- The gates swung apart, the bridge fell, the portcullis was drawn up.
- I hardly knew him, he was so changed.

Fused Sentences

When there is no punctuation mark and no coordinating conjunction between independent clauses, the result is a fused sentence. The following is an example:

- I would like to pursue a career in journalism I am taking a course in English Grammar and Composition.

Comma Splices

When independent clauses are joined by a comma without an accompanying coordinating conjunction, the result is a comma splice. The following are examples:

- I would like to pursue a career in journalism, I am taking a course in English Grammar and Composition.
- I would like to pursue a career in journalism, therefore, I am taking a course in English Grammar and Composition.

In the second example, "therefore" is a conjunctive adverb, not a coordinating conjunction. It must be preceded by a semicolon.

Correcting Fused Sentences and Comma Splices

- Use a comma and a coordinating conjunction (and, but, or, nor, for, so, yet). For example:
  I Would like to pursue a career in journalism, and I am taking a course in English Grammar and Composition.
- Use a semicolon (or, if appropriate, a colon or a dash). A semicolon may be used alone; it can also be accompanied by a conjunctive adverb

or transitional phrase. For example:
I would like to pursue a career in journalism; I am taking a course in English Grammar and Composition.
I would like to pursue a career in journalism; therefore, I am taking a course in English Grammar and Composition.

- Make the clauses into separate sentences. For example:
- I would like to pursue a career in journalism. I am taking a course in English Grammar and Composition.
- Restructure the sentence. For example:
  As I would like to pursue a career in journalism, I am taking a course in English Grammar and Composition.
  Keep in mind that if you are writing a sentence with two short independent clauses and there is no danger of misreading, the comma may be omitted before the coordinating conjunction. For example:
  The car drove up and I got in.

SENTENCE COMBINING: BUILDING SKILLS THROUGH READING AND WRITING

THE EFFECTS

In reviewing the state of research on writing less than a decade ago, Sherwin was able to cite only three studies concerned with transformational sentence combining (henceforth SC), concluding cautiously that the approach was "a promising way to help students toward greater skill in writing." Research since then has strengthened—and perhaps begun to make good—that promise. A number of recent experiments involving primarily elementary and secondary school children have produced impressive evidence that SC practice, whether oral or written, indeed enhances students' syntactic maturity. The results of these studies not only verify the normative data that Hunt and O'Donnell et al. have established for syntactic maturity at various grade levels in English, but also strongly support Hunt's insight that by stimulating elaboration and expansion *within* sentences, SC exercises can actually accelerate the students' syntactic growth and thus enable them to write on developmentally higher levels of syntactic fluency.

Nevertheless, in spite of its repeatedly confirmed effectiveness in building certain types of syntactic skills, SC was bound to remain largely irrelevant to the ultimate concerns of the composition class as long as it failed to produce corresponding gains in overall writing quality. It was therefore a crucial step forward when O'Hare was able to demonstrate for the first time, even if on a limited scale, that growth in syntactic maturity correlates significantly with subjectively judged gains in writing effectiveness. O'Hare's findings were later confirmed for the same grade level by Combs and Pedersen.

Because of its far-reaching implications for the teaching of composition in general, the evidence that has emerged from all these studies invites further extensive corroboration. The substantial experimental study on which the present paper is based fits into and expands this context of inquiry. It was intended to test the effectiveness of SC further as an approach to the teaching of writing, especially by seeking answers to a number of curricular and pedagogical questions left open by previous investigations.

Above all, we were interested in how well SC worked on the college level, specifically in the freshman English class, which has so far been entirely bypassed by significant SC research. The normative figures that Hunt reported in his two pioneering monographs show a syntactic abyss separating twelfth graders from skilled adult writers, a gap about as wide as that dividing twelfth graders from fourth graders.

Since Hunt's data suggest that normal syntactic development continues beyond high school into adulthood, we hypothesized that even for college freshmen intensive SC practice should effectively stimulate and accelerate growth. In the process, as a side benefit, we would obtain normative data for this age group not currently available in the published literature. More important from our point of view, if increased syntactic fluency has proved to correlate with a significant improvement of writing quality in, say, seventh grade, we intended to test whether such a correlation could also be demonstrated for college freshmen. These, in essence, amounted to the two major hypotheses of the experiment.

Perhaps our most substantial departure from past experimental procedures involved the status of SC itself within the total composition course. In previous experiments, and apparently in some nonexperimental writing programs that incorporate SC, such practice has been treated as an adjunct or supplement to more conventional components of the course syllabus and as such used only for limited portions of the writing class.

But no one seems to know for sure how much SC per day or per week is sufficient or optimally effective, and indeed every recent experiment appears to have followed a different arbitrary formula. In the present study, SC was *the* course. The experimental group consisted of genuine SC classes where students approached all questions of writing—rhetorical as well as syntactic and stylistic—exclusively through exercises calling for the judicious manipulation and synthesis of sentences.

We emphasize "rhetorical" because most of these exercises invited the students to consider the contextual demands of the total discourse. (We found, in fact, that you can effectively and pleasantly put across just about any aspect of writing by discussing SC options—thesis, organization, coherence, emphasis, tone, rhythm, problems of grammar and punctuation as they arise, even diction.) A typical SC exercise would ask the student to combine into an effective whole—

generally a paragraph or a short essay—a series of basic kernel sentences taken from William Strong *Sentence Combining* or supplied by the researchers. Such "open" exercises, in which no specific instructions for the combining were given other than that the final product ought to be "effective," alternated with semi-open, patterned types, which lent themselves to the use of certain free modifiers such as absolutes, appositives, and participial phrases.

The emphasis throughout the course was on the students' *active* involvement in the writing process, on the one hand by producing from day to day the "best" possible version that they could come up with for particular combining sets, and on the other by participating in an intensive discussion and revision in class of their own and their peers' responses to the same task, learning in the process to weigh the syntactic, stylistic, and rhetorical consequences of given options. "Signaled" exercises calling for specific grammatical transformations, though widely used in previous experiments and common in SC texts, were altogether avoided in this course, and—in contrast to Christensen's Rhetoric Program, for example —the use of grammatical terminology was minimized; one of our implicit goals was, in fact, to test the well motivated claim that SC can be effective without requiring students to be trained in formal grammar.

Furthermore, unlike the control classes, which followed the traditional local syllabus and used *The Harbrace Reader* and McCrimmon *Writing with a Purpose*, the experimental sections did not engage in the reading and rhetorical analysis of essays by accomplished writers. It is a prevalent but as yet untested traditional asumption that the analytic-interpretive skills students may develop through the reading and discussion of model essays somehow directly and significantly transfer into active expressive skills, that is, into control of formal linguistic devices required by the writing process. Even if such transfer did occur, we argued, it was likely to be significantly less productive and of less direct practical benefit to the students of composition than controlled experience in syntactic and rhetorical decision-making in their own writing. But would not the experimental group, then, doing no reading at all as part of the course, fall behind in reading comprehension, as one might charge—even though it might register gains in some parameters of writing, possibly at the expense of that decline?

In fact, we made a much stronger claim: that, as Stotsky and others have speculated, intensive practice in putting sentences together would actually enhance the student's ability to take them apart and thus to interpret passages. Accordingly, we hypothesized that SC practice would have a positive effect on reading comprehension. In short, since the respective syllabi followed by the experimental and control groups were unambiguously different, we expected that the results of this study, if significant, would suggest a clear choice between the two approaches to composition.

In other than the dependent variables just outlined, the two groups were entirely comparable, with all major independent variables carefully controlled. The total experimental population consisted of 290 freshmen controlled at Miami University in the fall of 1976, randomly assigned by computer to twelve sections of the required freshman writing course; these were evenly divided into "experimentals" and "controls."

Neither in SAT/ACT scores nor in the reading and writing pretests did the two groups show any statistically significant difference. The instructional staff for the project was selected with special care. Rather than adopting O'Hare's procedure, for example, who had the same two teachers (including himself) teach both the experimental and control classes, we chose for each group volunteer instructors who were committed to and enthusiastic about their respective approaches, and would have been more than gratified to see their own approach proven best.

To see whether the relative experience and maturity of the teacher made any difference—whether, in fact, instructors with little or no teaching experience could cope with SC in the classroom—we had half of the experimental classes taught by faculty members and the other half by graduate assistants. These were meticulously matched on the control side, with the cooperation of the department chair and the director of freshman English, in terms of rank, years of teaching experience, and degrees of demonstrated teaching effectiveness.

Furthermore, both groups wrote the same number of compositions during the term (both in and out of class), including a two-hour pretest and a two-hour posttest, each taken under identical conditions for all classes. Each test yielded approximately 600 to 700 words, generally considered adequate for syntactic analysis. Two similar topics were used for the tests, with one-half of each group writing on one topic on the pretest and the reverse topic on the posttest, each subject thus producing an essay on both topics. Since the mode of discourse elicited by a question could affect the syntactic characteristics of the resulting paper, each topic was carefully constructed to prompt an expositiory paper—the type of writing most emphasized in both the experimental and control sections of this program, and in freshman English classes in general. Both topics, however, lent themselves to narative and descriptive detail, which tend to make writing more concrete and more substantial.

The assessment of the experimental treatment involved both quantitive and qualitative procedures. The former consisted of a detailed analysis of preand posttests for words per clause, words per T-unit, and clauses per T-unit, according to by now well-known procedures, by a team of graduate students fully trained for the purpose.

On the other hand, the procedures for the subjective rating of writing quality used in this experiment substantially exceed the scope of those employed in previous SC research, and—we believe-surpass them in validity, accuracy, and reliability.

These qualities are to a large extent a function of having available a sufficient number of qualified raters to evaluate a sufficient number of writing samples a sufficient number of times in a sufficient numer of different ways—although one would be hard pressed to define sufficiency itself other than by assuming that better raters and more ratings will produce more accurate results.

In research of this sort three modes of rating have been common: (1) the holistic or impressionistic method (used by Mellon, for example); (2) the forced-choice technique (adopted by O'Hare and by Combs); and (3) the analytic approach (employed by Pedersen), each of which in and by itself has certain limitations.

But all used together, applied to the same corpus of writing, as in this experiment, could be expected to yield optimally accurate and reliable results. The ratings were performed by a team of twenty-eight judges—some local, some from neighbouring universities, all with advanced degrees in English, and with an average of thirteen years of experience in teaching composition.

The team stayed on the Miami campus for an entire week, working full time in a single large room each day, with appropriately spaced breaks to counter fatigue. Pre- and posttests from the control and experimental sections, all written on the same type of theme tablet, had been Xeroxed (on the same machine), assigned random numbers and secret codes, and then ordered by random number, so that it was impossible for a rater to discover the identity of a paper.

The critieria for the holisitc and analytic ratings were explained in a detailed rubric given to each rater, and reviewed periodically during the tightly supervised rating sessions; they included six categories—ideas, supporting details, organization and coherence, voice, sentence structure, and diction and usage. Each paper was read four times holistically and four times analytically, each time by a different rater, and assigned scores on a scale of 1 through 6.

In the forced-choice rating, ten different judges, were to choose the "better" paper within each of 134 pairs, where each pair consisted of one experimental and one control posttest from students with identical or near-identical holistic scores on the pretest. The results of this experiment strongly confirm the claims advanced for SC in recent years: SC clearly helps accelerate syntactic growth even among young adults, and it is significantly more effective than the conventional essay analysis approach in increasing the overall writing skills of college freshmen.

Among quantitative measures of syntactic maturity, in the subordination ratio (clauses per T-unit), posttest differences between the two groups remained not significant, as they were on the pretest. But in mean clause length (words per clause), which Hunt claims is the syntactic factor that best differentiates adolescents from professional writers, the experimental group gained.89, nearly one whole word (up from 8.75 to 9.64), whereas the control group dropped.13 (down from 8.80 to 8.67).

This difference is statistically significant at and beyond the.001 level of confidence. Note that in fifteen weeks the treatment group increased its clause size by almost half of the growth experienced, according to Hunt, in the previous *eight* years of normal development. The same group showed a nearly as impressive.74 word gain in T-unit size (words per T-unit), up from 15.31 to 16.05, in contrast to the.05 word drop (from 15.00 to 14.95) by the control group.

The posttest difference between the groups, 1.1 word, is again significant at better than.001. The growth, then, is precisely in the direction that Hunt leads us to expect—a relatively stable subordination ratio (the index in which at about this age a young writer's development has just about reached the ceiling set by the language), and a vastly exploding clause size, which also jacks up T-unit size, as students learn to add details and hence substance to their sentences.

But, undoubtedly, the major thrust of this study is in the evidence it has yielded for a significant correlation of these syntactic maturity gains with improved writing in free compositions, no matter how writing quality is measured. In the holistic rating, which best reflects the overall quality of a paper, the experimental group registered a posttest gain of.53 on a scale of 6 (up from 3.20 to 3.73), in contrast to the gain of.21 by the control group (up from 3.16 to 3.37); again this posttest difference is significant at.001.

The experimental gain of.53 is perhaps comparable to a veteran baseball player boosting his batting average 53 percentage points in half a season—no trivial accomplishment. The forced-choice rating gave similar results: experimental papers were picked as better at a ratio of almost 2 to 1 (79 to 42, with 13 ties), again statistically a staggering difference.

With the superiority of the experimental group clearly established, it was instructive to see which components of writing were responsible for the qualitative gains. The posttest scores showed no significant difference in only one factor: organization/coherence. It is noteworthy that even in this one category SC practice did not have a negative effect, nor did the control group register significant gains.

On the other hand, the experimental papers came out on top in posttest scores in the rest of the analytic categories: diction and usage (at.05), ideas (at.01), sentence structure (at.01), supporting details (at.001), and the category of voice (at.001), which we had defined as the individuality of a paper—the qualities that make it different, unique, memorable, and to that extent interesting.

It appears, then, that these five of the six analytic qualities were responsible for the favourable overall judgments that gave experimental papers the significant edge in holistic and forced-choice ratings. It is interesting that not only did those qualities stressed in the SC class—sentence structure, supporting materials, and voice—appreciably raise the general effectiveness of writing; sentence combiners significantly outgained control students even in the one quality most cultivated in the conventional class—ideas.

Recall Christensen's claim that "solving the problem of *how to say* helps solve the problem of *what to say*." O'Hare came to the same conclusion—that perhaps indeed "knowing how does help to create *what*." Incidentally, the class-by-class breakdown of the results shows that while, as expected, classes taught by those with more teaching experience generally scored higher on both sides, relative lack of experience did not prevent an instructor from using SC procedures with success. In fact, the effectiveness of the method generally *overrode* the lack of experience.

On the holistic rating, for example, one experimental graduate assistant registered higher gains than any instructor on the control side, and all graduate assistants in the experimental group gained more than any but two instructors of the control group (one of them a graduate assistant). Or in the forced-choice rating, all experimental instructors had a higher percentage of winning papers than any but one control instructor. Thus, in general, not only did the two sets of experimental instructors consistently outscore their control counterparts, but in many rated categories experimental graduate assistants, though with little teaching experience, outgained experienced faculty in the control group.

While the results of this experiment convincingly demonstrate and emphatically support previous claims for the beneficial effects of SC practice on writing skills, it is somewhat difficult to try to isolate those ingredients of the experimental treatment that really did the job and to link them directly to these results. We can—and do—say to our colleagues: "Here is good evidence that SC works in the freshman English class. Why not try it yourself?" But it is not at all clear why SC *should* work. For example, among others voicing reservations about the SC method, Marzano has questioned O'Hare's claim for a significant correlation between syntactic maturity growth and writing quality gains on the ground that a correlation does not necessarily *prove* causation. Our study unequivocally supports O'Hare's findings, but again it can establish only a reasonably high probability for the cause, not invincible proof.

Indeed, no one seems to be absolutely sure why students who practice intensive SC generally become more skillful and effective writers. Does SC tap some deep cognitive skills, enhancing their growth? Or are the benefits primarily psychological perhaps increased control over the available linguistic choices simply makes writers feel more confident, giving them the incentive and the courage to use their growing repertoire of options in novel and interesting ways? Perhaps the increased control over form does encourage invention and help generate ideas; the strong showing of our sentence combiners in the latter category seems to support this assumption. In attempting to interpret the impressive cumulative results of recent SC research, bear in mind that since its "modern" inception—indeed revival—a little over a decade ago, SC has noticeably eased away from its initial linguistic orientation.

When in 1965 Hunt first suggested the use of "sentence-combining transformations" (thus, in quotation marks) to help build structural depth and complexity into student writing, he explicitly linked them to "recursive" processes "operating on the strings underlying 'kernel sentences.'" But more recently, as SC has gained ground in educational research and its underlying principles have become attractive to nonlinguists, it has shed much of its linguistic jargon and formalism in favour of emphasis on the general principles themselves and on their most effective classroom annlications.

Viewed in this light, SC may be a refinement of exercises "long in use in grammar textbooks" and referred to by Sherwin as "plain," as opposd to "transformational," sentence combining. If, as it appears, this distinction corresponds to the one between "open" and "signalled" SC exercises, i.e., those without and those with explicit transformational instructions, then our experimental classes may indeed have utilized a rather traditional "device for structuring the process of composing a sentence."

Of course, they went far beyond that, using the device for structuring the *total* process of composing. The point is that, while allowing for and encouraging almost unlimited creativity in syntactic form, SC is basically a device—perhaps one of several devices—providing *controlled* experience with writing. As such, it may be as old as it is significant. Indeed, upon learning about our work, colleagues occasionally exclaim: "But I've been doing that for years—without knowing what it was called!" At the same time, we have found that the *idea* of SC as a way of teaching writing frightens some people in the profession—the term seems almost stigmatized, still suggesting to some dull and mechanical transformational exercises calling for a fancy linguistic terminology or for odd signalling symbols, to others something too empty to be suitable as the methodological principle of a composition course.

The favourable results of the Miami project flatly refute these fears. Perhaps what scares some people is that SC seems so simple, say, in comparison to a secure, bulky handbook on rhetoric—which, of course, in a way, it is. In some sense it takes you "back to the basics"—and yet, as Strong points out, it takes you far beyond them. Day in and day out, we observed how SC leads students to discover and use in novel and creative ways the complex linguistic knowledge that most are unaware of holding in their heads. And they seem to enjoy this discovery. At the end of the course we asked all experimental students to tell us about their experience in and attitude toward SC.

Did they like it as an approach to writing? Did they feel that such practice for a semester helped them become better writers? On a scale ranging for a low of 1 to a high of 7, the responses averaged about 5 points. Would they recommend such a course to a friend? Exactly two-thirds of them responded favourably. Perhaps one respondent's terse complimentary comment about the SC class best summed up the feelings of many: "For a frosh comp course," he said, "it ain't bad."

STRATEGIES

This section will provide suggestions as well as a description of the combining technique. Generally, a pair of sentences will be provided which include a transformational rule. The rule may consist of a word, phrase, or punctuation mark which can be inserted into the sentence. Teachers of the elementary grades may find this technique helpful for several reasons. First of all, this technique can be used to illustrate the manipulation of sentences to achieve greater expression of thoughts and experiences.

Secondly, the teacher can prepare the student for complex sentence structures in their textbooks and outside readings. Third, teachers can relate the use of the rules of grammar to students' actual writing without the drawbacks of the text.

Teachers have the option of employing this technique during a reading, English, or Language Arts class. It is recommended, however, that teachers set aside time preceding or directly following the exercises for oral and silent reading. The readings could be teacher-developed or taken from the reading material appropriate for the student's reading level. Students with learning disabilities may benefit from choral reading of the exercises, but may find the written exercises difficult. Evaluation of student mastery can be measured by correctness of daily worksheets or weekly texts which require the combining process.

An elaborate form of evaluation may include a composition wherein the student uses the technique to include complex sentence structures. It is suggested that the composition be descriptive or expository. The teacher should look for examples of sentence combining, and more specifically the use of subordinate clauses. The number of combined sentences may indicate mastery of this technique.

Ideally, teachers should develop a compositional program which would include many writing assignments and a check list of writing skills to be mastered during the course of the school year. The sentence-combining technique could be only one aspect of the compositional course. Students, therefore, should be able to incorporate this technique as a supplement to already established writing objectives. Such a technique would provide a syntactically mature writing sample.

Of course, students write more proficiently with time and practice and sentence-combining enhances that growth process; yet it is unreasonable to expect the type of expansion associated with older and more able students.

Research has shown that as students mature, their writing form becomes more complex. Sentence-combining can have an immediate effect on student writing performance when coupled with a thoughtful reading program which provides contexts for the use of the language and illustrates the use of complex structures by accomplished writers. The following is a list of rules which can be used to teach students the mechanics of sentence-combining. All of the different types of exercises should be worked out orally first and then transferred to paper after students become confident with the technique.

Initially, teachers should teach the constituent parts of a sentence (i.e., doer, action, receiver of action, or subject and verb phrases). zsimple sentences by matching the subjects and predicates. For example: NP = Noun Phrase + VP = Verb Phrase.

John + hit the ball = John hit the ball. Once students are able to see the constituents that make up sentences, they are able to move on to the next step. (*Note:* Teachers may use the parts of the unit which aid in the development of specific writing skill objectives.) Students should be given practice in combining subjects (NPs) and predicates (VPs).

For example: 1) John lived in that house. 2) Mary lived in that house. 3) John and Mary lived in that house; or 1) Mary fixed the engine. 2) Mary changed the oil. 3) Mary fixed the engine and changed the oil. The rule in these sentences may be either one of the connecting words found to be most appropriate. A more advanced example would be: 1) John is tired; 2) John cleaned the garage; 3) John is tired, but he cleaned the garage. The referent pronoun *he*, and conjunction *but* are employed. One of the easiest ways to combine sentences is to put them together with a joining word between. The joining word establishes a relationship between the two constituents of the entire structure. The relationships usually are: 1) cause-effect, 2) time, and 3) comparison or contrast.

Here is an example: He was pleased *because* his work was completed.

He was pleased *when* his work was completed.

He was pleased, but somehow disappointed.

Note that a comma is used before the conjunction which can be stressed as a rule applicable to the completion of each item in the exercise. In addition, the semicolon is a punctuation mark which can be used to establish a relationship and connect two base sentences, yet reveal no particular relationship.

For example: He was pleased; his work was completed. Other connecting words are before, although, after, just when, as soon as, if, and since. The mechanism for including any of the various mentioned here is quite simple. The rule will be seen as a mere instruction to insert that word/words at the end of the first sentence, or beginning of the result or second sentence.

For example: The men went back to work.

The lunch break was over. (When)

The men went back to work *when* the lunch break was over.

Or students can be taught to put the connecting word before the base sentence, then add the result to the end of the first sentence.

For example: When the men went back to work, the lunch break was over.

Note the comma which was inserted after the base sentence.

Teachers may find it helpful to the student to include as part of the rule, the punctuation mark in addition to the connecting word (when,).

Another example using *if* as a joining word is as follows:

1. I am crying. (If) (,)
2. Something is wrong.
3. There is a problem. (;)

If I am crying, something is wrong; there is a problem.

Note the semicolon is used before the final phrase and that a comma is inserted after 'crying.' The comma could just as easily be inserted as a rule after the second sentence.

Just when

1. He makes his foul shots.
   They are important. (Just when)
2 He makes his foul shots just when they are important. *Once*
   - You are aware of all literary devices employed by writers. (Once) (,)
   - Reading poetry is more appreciable.

Once you are aware of all literary devices employed by writers, reading poetry is more appreciable.

When / Long before

1. Rain clouds appeared. (When) (,)
   We ran into the house.
   It was time to end the cookout. (Long before)
2. When rain clouds appeared, we ran into the house long before it was time to end the cookout.

The rules -ing and with

The -ing technique involves changing a word to its -ing form and inserting that word at the beginning of the base sentence. *For example:* Terry kicked the door off the hinges. (ing)(,) Terry was able to go in and put out the fire.Kicking the door off the hinges, Terry was able to go in and put out the fire. Note that 'kicked' was changed to 'kicking' and it began the base sentence. Also, the word 'Terry' was left out in the second sentence.

Teachers may find it helpful to the student if some notation (i.e., circle, underscore, italics) were used to point out the word/words to be omitted in the combining process. Another means to accomplish this result would be to underscore the part of the base sentence which will be transformed. For example: Terry kicked the door off of the hinges.

The line indicates that 'Terry' is not to be used in the combining process. Another example of the -ing can read as follows:

1. The chunky football player *pounced on the loose ball.* (ing) (,)
2. The chunky football player jumped to his feet, and was quickly tackled.
3. Pouncing on the loose ball, the chunky football player jumped to his feet, and was quickly tackled.

Note that a comma is used before the conjunction *and.* This is standard practice and should be covered at the outset, otherwise it will be necessary to insert the rule.

The with rule does two things in these sentences dependent upon the sentence it follows. Look at these examples:.

1. She was an intelligent student.
2. She received good grades. (With)
3. She was an intelligent student with good grades.

Note that the words 'she' and 'received' are omitted. Again notation may be included to advise the student to omit those particular words. Here is another example of how *with* can be used:

1. His feet *were* implanted in the mud. (With)
2. He found it was impossible to catch the frog.
3. With his feet implanted in the mud, he found it was impossible to catch the frog.

Here, *with* is at the beginning of the sentence and the form of *be* (were) is omitted because it is not needed.

Day One: Objective Students should be able to combine a noun and verb phrase to create a sentence.

Materials: blackboard, chalk, eraser, composition paper, pens

Procedure: The teacher provides the student with noun phrases and verb phrases. The student is taught to combine both phrases to create a complete sentence. This activity should be a group exercise.

The teacher must specify a rule is to be used to join the phrases together. A means to convey this idea would be to give them a basic math problem where they add two numbers to form a greater number. The rule is dictated by the size which indicates the operation. Similarly the + can be used as a rule to have students add the two phrases. *Rationale*: The students should draw an analogy between the precision of math and the precision required in the combining operation. This exercise should facilitate the development of basic understandings essential for later use of this technique.

Reinforcement: A homework assignment can be a means of reinforcing this basic operation. Also, it may be helpful to make signs which forces students to distinguish the who or what's from the what happened's. Another student can be the rule and another the output or complete sentence. This activity should stress the concept of adding to form synthesis.

Day Two: Objective Student should be able to join compound subjects.

Materials: blackboard, chalk, eraser, paper and pens

Procedure: Students should be given a list of words that can be combined to make new words. The teacher should point out the fact that these words can stand alone and still be considered as words. Once students recognize these new words as compound words, the teacher constructs sentences which have the same verb phrases but different subjects. Students should also be aware of the ways of joining together subjects. (and) This joining word serves as the rule.

Example: John hit the ball. (and)

Mary hit the ball. (+ rule)

Result: John and Mary hit the ball.

Rationale: This operation should serve as a means of exposing students to the possibility of sentence manipulation. Students should be able to recognize verb phrases which describe the same actions yet contain different subjects.

Reinforcement: Homework consisting of similar examples or/and worksheets which contain these type of combining operations. Students can role play a sentence where different students commit the same action to enable students to see that a more concise description of the action would include a joining word and one sentence.

Day Three: Objective Students should be able to write sentences containing compound predicates. Materials: blackboard, chalk, eraser, paper and pens *Procedure*: Students should be given examples of sentences which consist of the same subjects yet different verb phrases. Their task is to combine the sentences and retain the subject.

Example:

1. The fox jumped over the fence. (and)
2. The fox raided the chicken coop. (+)
3. The fox jumped over the fence and raided the chicken coop.

Rationale: Hopefully students will see that once the verb phrase is the part of the sentence to be combined, they will be able to spot sentences to be combined in their writing which may contain exact subjects but different predicates. Also, this operation should familiarize them with the use of the rule and the combining technique. *Reinforcement*: Homework, or in class worksheet which contains this type of operation. The activity described in the previous lesson could serve to illustrate that one sentence and a joining word could be a concise way of expressing a thought.

Day Four: Objective Students should be able to combine two sentences. Materials: blackboard, chalk, eraser, pen, paper, oak tag and magic markers *Procedure*: The teacher makes posters of oak tag which contain sentences to be combined. Also the teachers makes three separate posters which contain the conjunctions *and*, *but* and *or*. The teacher provides the class with two signs which contain the sentences to be combined along with access to the three conjunction posters. Students should be able to combine the sentences using the appropriate conjunction. At this point the teacher may want to introduce or insert the comma as a punctuation mark which should precede the conjunction in the sentence to be combined. Examples of this operation can be demonstrated on the board and similar exercises can be worked out as a group activity.

Ex. Red Marker: John likes chocolate. (conjunction) He eats it all the time. (+) Conjunctions Blue marker, including punctuation mark *Result:* John likes chocolate, and he eats it all the time.

Rationale: Students should receive a gradual bit of information each day. They should become aware of the lengths of words which can be combined as well as the words which can be employed to complete the process as well as specific structural clues.

Reinforcement: Activity described above is helpful and worksheet and homework assignment which involve the operation.

Day Five: Objective—The student should be able to combine noun phrases and verb phrases as well as sentences, given the rules. Materials: chalk, erasers, blackboard, paper and pens *Procedure*: This lesson will consist of having students combine noun and verb phrases as well as sentences. The teacher may allow students to construct sentences or/and phrases to be combined. The class can be divided and each group will send a representative to the board. The teacher writes two phrases and the rule. The team which completes the task first is awarded a point. The same procedure can be used with sentences.

Rationale: This is an evaluative lesson as well as a means of reinforcement. The teacher should be able to observe the effectiveness of instruction or spot weaknesses in students' grasp of combining operation.

Reinforcement: Teacher should help students who have particular difficulties. It may be necessary to have a student who understands the technique tutor a student who needs assistance.

USEFUL GRAMMAR IN SCHOOL SUBJECTS

IN SCHOOL SYLLABUS

The same evolutionary processes which make it possible to construe experience, by transforming it into meaning ... also provide the means with which to challenge the form of the construal. When experience has once been construed, it can be reconstrued in a different light. The language of schooling was described in general terms focusing on the many commonalities in the linguistic features of the texts and tasks of different academic disciplines. This chapter extends this grammatical analysis to examine two subject areas of schooling, science and history, to show how the register features are realized in different ways in different disciplines, and to show what the linguistic features common to those disciplines reveal about academic registers more generally. Science, history, and other subject areas present major challenges to students, and a great part of the challenge is linguistic. Language differs in the discourses of different subject areas due to differences in the epistemologies of the disciplines as well as differences in methodologies and pedagogies. Each subject area of schooling has its own expectations in terms of the genres that students will read and write, and each genre is constructed through grammatical resources that construe the disciplinary meanings. Developing facility with new genres involves learning new lexical and grammatical strategies to fit new tasks and contexts.

While each genre has its own register characteristics, each discipline as a whole can also be characterized in terms of the linguistic choices that are typical and pervasive. This chapter presents some genres that are typical of science and history and explores the register features that characterize these disciplinary discourses more generally. The chapter then shows how these registers are functional for realizing the kinds of meanings that are typically made in schooling. Although these registers are sometimes criticized as too abstract, dense, or distanced, without these linguistic resources, it is impossible to make the kinds of meanings that the different disciplines call for. At the same time, the grammatical and lexical choices that realize academic registers do sometimes obscure meanings, and they construct a world view or ideology that may be hidden from students' conscious understanding if they have no tools for uncovering and revealing the view that the grammar naturalizes. It is important to understand both the functionality and the challenges that academic registers present as students try to make disciplinary meanings in their writing and to get meaning from reading academic texts. Both reading and writing issues are addressed in this chapter, with examples of student writing illustrating the challenges in science and examples of history textbook passages showing the challenges for reading.

Making Meaning

Martin's analysis of middle-school science and history texts identifies some general differences between the ways that science and history draw on features of academic registers. Broadly speaking, he shows that science discourse is technical, while social science discourse is abstract. This is because the language of science builds experience of the world, while the language of history builds interpretations of social experience. These differences, reflected in the different ways these subject areas draw on lexico-grammatical resources, are explored here. In the discourse of science, the focus is on grammatical metaphor and the role it plays in realizing technicality and structuring texts. In the discourse of history, the focus is on the grammatical resources that realize historians' interpretations and perspectives.

In both cases, the focus is on the pedagogical recontextualization of meaning in classroom assignments and textbooks. The discourse of professional scientists and historians is not the same as what students work with, but the recontextualization of the discourses for pedagogical purposes does reflect the values and ways of thinking of the disciplinary communities.

Science: Theorizing Experience

Learning science means developing new ways of thinking about the world through investigations that predict and control natural phenomena. Students learn to reason in ways that are considered logical as they come to understand and reproduce the same framework of meanings that scientists or other specialists understand about an issue. An important aspect of this is using vocabulary and grammatical forms effectively to construe scientific meanings. Controlling the discourse of science requires mastering the grammatical features of the language that construe science knowledge as well as the reasoning, values, and assumptions of the discipline. Lemke points out that "the language of science teaching is 'expository' or 'analytical' most of the time... used to express relationships of classification, taxonomy, and logical connection among abstract, or generalized, terms and processes. The language of other subjects, notably literature and history, tends to be more 'narrative' in character, ... used to express relationships of time, place, manner, and action among specific, real or fictional, persons and events".

These genres are not always realized as discretely different text types, and the names and descriptions are only suggestive of some features that are commonly found in the texts of science schooling. Looking at the different genres provides a broad view of the ways that language constructs texts of different types. In actual classrooms, these genres may not occur as separate text types, and in any case, elements of one genre often occur in another (a procedural description as part of a larger report, for example). School science has developed these genres because they enable presentation of the kinds of meanings needed to do science and to understand scientific reasoning. They are not the genres of the professional or academic scientific community, but the four genres can be seen as a recontextualization that forms a kind of pathway into scientific knowledge that has both gatekeeping and learnability functions. The first genres that students encounter if they do "hands on" work are *procedures* and *procedural recounts*.

Students often begin learning a science topic with observations and experimental activities, so the texts they read for this purpose contain a series of instructions about what to do, the *procedure*. In constructing a procedural text, imperative clauses are clearly functional for outlining a series of steps. When students write about their experiments, on the other hand, their writing typically recounts the experience or procedure as a first step in documentation.

This constructs a different genre, the *procedural recount*. Here the mood is declarative, with past tense verbs recounting the experience the student has had. In *procedures* and *procedural recounts*, experience provides a concrete basis for organizing the knowledge the students are writing about. As students move into reading and writing more advanced genres in science, the text itself takes a primary role in shaping knowledge.

In the *science report*, for example, students organize scientific information in texts that set up taxonomies and classifications, presenting and sharing knowledge in more generalized ways. Reports use timeless verbs in simple present tense and relational clauses with technical terms as participants. *Science explanations* describe how something occurs, explore cause—effect relationships, and construct theories about scientific phenomena, with the grammar enabling a logical organization and sequencing as it draws on grammatical metaphor to structure clauses in ways that enable the accumulation of information.

Of course there are many other kinds of texts that students work with in the context of science, including *descriptions, comparisons, definitions*, and *syllogisms*. Each of the genres in Veel, for example, describes a variety of explanation genres, including *sequential explanations*, which show how something takes place and describe observable activities, and *causal explanations*, which describe how and why something occurs. *Factorial explanations* deal with the combination of a number of factors, and *theoretical explanations* introduce and illustrate a theory. Veel also discusses *exposition* and *discussion* genres that enable students to challenge science by arguing and persuading others, the level of linguistic proficiency needed for innovation and critical scientific literacy.

Each of these science genres has its own development, with more rudimentary realizations at lower grade levels and more developed realizations as students gain proficiency with the science concepts and the language that construes them. These genres become increasingly challenging, lexically dense, nominalized and abstract, as they move from temporal organization to logical organization. For example, the move from *procedural recount* to *explanation* requires a shift from the specific retelling of an experience to the general description of a scientific process. Students have difficulty producing the more advanced genres; for example, students may just recount the steps in a lab procedure when they need to discuss causes and effects.

Students need to learn the different genres of science, but the features of each genre vary according to the expectations of teachers in particular classrooms and contexts. For purposes of understanding the linguistic features of science language more generally, it is useful to focus on the register features of the more advanced science genres. This section, then, explores some grammatical features of the *report* and *explanation* genres. Martin calls *reports* "the major genre in science textbooks", and *explanations* "the main source of extended writing for students" in science. The language of science is often represented as abstract, objective, and information-oriented. Scientific style is described as avoiding first-person pronouns with a tendency to use the passive voice and avoid conjunction. Kinneavy calls science "thing"-oriented, suggesting that in scientific language, assertions must exclude personal feelings and persuasive or literary effect.

Martin describes how science texts organize the world into "things" and into "processes. " Reports, the "thing" oriented texts, organize information by classifying elements or listing their properties. Explanations, the "process" oriented texts, classify processes or explain them through step-by-step explication. The linguistic features that construe the context of science at a general level enable the display of knowledge through technical terms in relational processes that often suppress agency, which, along with objective modality, also contributes to the authoritativeness expected in the construal of evaluation in science texts. Thematic progression enables the accumulation of information required for structuring scientific explanations and theories. All of these register features participate in *grammatical metaphor*, a resource that pervades science writing and draws on all these features in the construction of valued texts. Introduced grammatical metaphor as a process by which concepts are construed in a grammar which is *incongruent.*

This means that grammatical metaphor takes semantic notions which are more congruently expressed in one linguistic form (e.g., *explore* as a verb) and reconstrues that notion in an incongruent way (e.g., as *exploration*, a noun). The evolution of grammatical metaphor in English was stimulated by the context of scientific inquiry. This section demonstrates the pervasiveness of grammatical metaphor in the construction of science texts and shows how it enables the presentation of science concepts and the construction of scientific theories.

When processes are reconstrued as nominalizations through grammatical metaphor, agents of the processes disappear. Using *explore* as a verb in a clause requires a subject, so someone has to be named as the one who *explores*.

Using *exploration*, on the other hand, does not require an agent, as the process itself can serve as the subject of a clause. Scientific text presents processes in the abstract, with the focus on the process itself, not on the human parties who may be involved with the processes. This removes the agency and makes the language of science highly grammatically metaphoric. A focus on the relational process reveals how grammatical metaphor operates.

The six process types that underlie the semantics of the clause: *material, behavioural, mental, verbal, existential*, and *relational. Material* (action) processes are common in science texts, as they enable description of natural phenomena, as are *relational* processes that construe relationships among entities. Complex nominalizations participate in both types of processes to construct science explanations. Relational processes are common in science reports and explanations, as the many definitions and technical taxonomies in science discourse create a context of high lexical density and grammatical metaphor.

The grammar of relational processes is complex and has been highly elaborated within systemic functional linguistics, but here, focused on understanding the grammar of science, a key distinction can be made between relational processes that indicate how one thing is a sub-class of another and relational processes that indicate how a part relates to a whole, as these two types of relational processes construe the classification and composition that are basic to science explanations. The grammar used to classify has relational clauses which are typically reversible, as in (1):

1. Solutions are mixtures that ... = Mixtures that ... are solutions.
   The grammar of composition, used to describe how one thing is a part of another, does not have reversible clauses, as in (2):
2. Animal cells have a membrane but not Membranes are had by....

These two types of relational processes, the *identifying* and the *attributive*, are used to define technical terms that participate in two fundamental semantic relations: *a* is a *kind* of *x* (*hyponymy*) and *b* is a *part* of *y* (*meronymy*). These two processes in science are also different grammatically. The differences in the grammar reflect differences in the underlying semantics of these two kinds of clause.

Technical terms are very important for constructing science, as they condense information so that an analysis and theory can be developed. The grammar uses resources such as noun compounding, expanded noun phrases, and nominalization to create the technical terms common in scientific discourse. Technical terms are not just abbreviations, but new meanings that help construct scientific theories by participating in the explication of processes. Scientific explanations draw on technical terms to develop a chain of reasoning in which each step leads to the next. Grammatical metaphor is a key resource for this, as nominalization enables the creation of technical terms and their participation in building explanations.

Science texts rely on grammatical metaphor as a resource for construing the abstract and technical meanings and logical reasoning that science requires to structure texts so that they move from familiar to new information. Grammatical metaphor enables writers of science to be flexible in presenting information and structuring texts at the same time it realizes the technicality and interpersonal stance that are valued in science writing. This section looks in turn at the construal of technicality, reasoning within the clause, and the structuring of text that grammatical metaphor enables. In these three roles, grammatical metaphor participates in the construction of the ideational, interpersonal, and textual meanings that construe science discourse;

demonstrating that these metafunctional meanings are simultaneously realized in register choices. The examples in this section come from students' writing in a university chemical engineering course. The students are reporting on an experiment they conducted in which they used Stefan diffusion tubes to determine the diffusion coefficients for three solvents in air. Each report has seven sections: Abstract, Introduction, Theory, Experimental Method, Results, Discussion, and Conclusions. Each section has its own demands related to the genre that underlies it (the *Experimental Method* section, for example, has features of the *Procedural Recount*). Here examples from the *Theory* and *Discussion* sections of students' reports show how the technical meanings are enabled through grammatical metaphor and other resources of the grammar.

Grammatical metaphor contributes to the development of technicality through nominalization. Sentences written by two different writers are compared at (3) to show how this resource participates in clause structure:

3. Writer A: D_{AB} has a *temperature dependence*.

   Writer B: Diffusion coefficients among other things *depend largely on temperature*.

   (Note that D_{AB} = diffusion coefficient)

Writer A uses a technical term, *temperature dependence*, a grammatical metaphor that presents a process, *to depend on temperature*, as a nominal element. As a nominal element, it can then participate in a relational process as an attribute of the diffusion coefficient. Writer B, on the other hand, using the congruent *depend*, "says the same thing," but does not draw on grammatical metaphor to construe the process as a technical term. Nominalization through grammatical metaphor is an academic register feature that is highly valued in this genre because it enables the creation of technical terms and the construction of densely structured texts. The dense structure emerges from a second role of grammatical metaphor. Besides construing technicality, grammatical metaphor also enables reasoning *within* a clause rather than *between* clauses. This is illustrated at (4), which again compares how a similar notion is expressed by two different writers:

4. Writer A: The three temperatures of acetone that were investigated produced calculated D_{AB} values which increased *with increasing temperature*.

   Writer B: The diffusivity is higher *when the temperature is raised*.

Here Writer A uses a clause structure where two complex nominal groups (*The three temperatures of acetone [that were investigated]; calculated* D_{AB} *values [which increased with increasing temperature]*) are linked with a verb, here a material process, *produced*. Both nominal groups are expanded with embedded clauses (marked with brackets above). The point that Writer B uses two clauses to make, that diffusivity is higher at higher temperatures, is made by Writer A in an embedded clause, *which increased with increasing temperature*. Writer

A's highly information packed sentence also identifies the substance she investigated (acetone), and refers to both her own activities in the experiment (*calculated* D_{AB} *values*), and the experimental process itself (*which increased*). Grammatical metaphor and other reduced clausal structures enable a writer to incorporate many concepts into one clause, constructing the lexically dense texts that present scientific information efficiently and concisely.

The examples at (4) also demonstrate how grammatical metaphor enables a causal explanation without conjunctions, a characteristic of academic registers more generally. Writer A takes the notion *raise*, realized in a verb by Writer B, and realizes it as a quality of the temperature in the participial adjective *increasing*. Grammatical metaphor enables Writer A to present the causal explanation of temperature's effect, then, in the prepositional phrase *with increasing temperature*. While Writer B depends on the grammar of time sequence to realize the causal link, using *when* to link the clauses about the effect of temperature, Writer A presents the conjunctive relationship of cause in a prepositional phrase which itself is embedded in a relative clause within an expanded nominal group, creating a denser text.

Writer A manipulates the resources of the grammar in sophisticated ways that enable her to pack a lot of information into each clause. Writer B, on the other hand, in a way that is typical of many students who do not yet control the resources of academic registers, uses a more congruent way of making the causal links, drawing on an informal style of explanation that is causally explicit but typically less highly valued than the nominalized grammatically metaphorical style.

Grammatical metaphor helps structure a clause in ways that allow more information to be incorporated and greater conciseness to be achieved. Grammatical metaphor is also a resource for structuring a text beyond the clause, as the shifts in grammatical realization that it allows (e.g., from verb to noun, as in example (3), or from conjunction to preposition as in example (4)), enable manipulation of thematic elements in the clause in ways that allow for more options in the structuring of the information in a text.

This is illustrated in (5), where Writer A presents the assumptions that guided her experiment (elements that realize assumptions are underlined):

5. For the analysis, these systems will be considered binary. Air will be treated as a singular compound. The error introduced by this simplification is assumed to be negligible (cites two sources).... The subscript A will be used to represent the diffusing vapour, while B, the assumed stagnant air.... When eq. (1) is combined with the species continuity equation, assuming no chemical reaction, ..., and the diffusion process considered one dimensional (z direction), (equation) Eq. (3) results. Here it was also assumed that $N_A >> N_B$. This assumption depends on B having negligible solubility in A. The

accumulation term can be neglected if one assumes a quasi-steady state condition. An order of magnitude analysis will show that this is a valid assumption when (equation) ...Assuming eq. (4) holds, ... This is taken to be the gas-phase concentration ... Equation (6) has been modified from the original with the assumptions of ideal gas and M_A on the same order of magnitude as M_B ....

This writer uses a variety of verbs, including *consider, treat, assume*, and *is taken to be*, in the clauses where assumptions are presented, demonstrating control over a range of lexical resources. In addition, she is able to draw on grammatical metaphor to use the notion *assume* in a variety of word classes, including verbal, nominal, and adjectival forms that participate in a variety of clause functions. She can construe this process as a quality (*the assumed stagnant air*), as a nonfinite predicator (*assuming no chemical reaction*), or as a clause participant (*this assumption*). In using the nominal form, the writer is able to use *assumption* in a variety of positions in her clauses; for example, in sentence complements (*this is a valid assumption when*) and in prepositional phrases (*with the assumptions of Y*).

Drawing on this variety of ways of presenting the same lexical meaning gives the writer a flexibility that enables her to construct a text which links from clause to clause in cohesive ways, elaborating on the set of assumptions she adopts for the experiment. This is illustrated in the sentences from (5) presented at (6):

5. Here it was also assumed that $N_A >> N_B$. This assumption depends on B having negligible solubility in A.

The first clause presents $N_A >> N_B$ as new information, with *assume* used as a passive verb; a construction that allows the new information to be highlighted at the end of the clause. In the following clause, use of the nominal form *this assumption* as theme/subject enables the writer to begin the clause by referring to this information and then go on to qualify the assumption appropriately. By drawing on incongruent forms of *assume*, the writer is able to employ a wide range of options for text construction and development.

The nonfinite clauses with *assuming* also contribute to text structuring, as Writer A includes additional assumptions where appropriate (*When eq. (1) is combined with the species continuity equation, assuming no chemical reaction*, ...), or uses the non-finite clause as the starting point for her next statement, introducing as background an assumption that is a condition for the next equation she will present (*Assuming eq. (4) holds*, ...).

By controlling the resources that enable her to use the notion *assume* in grammatically different ways, this writer is able to bring texture to her report, managing the flow of information effectively as she develops her explanation. In addition, she projects an authoritative interpersonal stance by adopting impersonal ways of presenting her assumptions that draw on passive and nonfinite verb forms. This demonstrates how construing interpersonal meaning in ways that appear objective also depends on the resources of the grammar. Interpersonal meanings, like ideational and textual meanings, are inevitably construed in every clause, and failing to construe these meanings in ways that are valued and expected can have negative consequences for the student writer.

The kinds of interpersonal meanings that are presented in lab reports, as in other kinds of academic writing, include how explicit the writer wants to be about where her assessments are coming from, how subjective or objective she wants them to appear, how definite they are, and so on. Examples of each of these types are shown in (7):

7. Objective (explicit): *It is obvious* that these results are in error.
   Objective (implicit): *Clearly* these results are in error.
   Subjective (explicit): *I believe* that these results are in error.
   Subjective (implicit): These results *must* be in error.

In science discourse, objective presentation enables the construal of authoritativeness as it puts the individual writer in the background. The evaluation is construed as fact, rather than as opinion, and the responsibility for the evaluative comment is not individuated. With subjective presentation, it is always clear that the evaluative comment is the interpretation of the writer alone, rather than emerging from the experimental results. The explicit subjective presentation, as in *I believe that these results are in error*, is a form that students need to move away from as they learn to present their views in the more highly valued objective ways.

The examples at (8) show how Writer A draws on the objective options to construe evaluative meanings:

8. Objective (explicit):
   - Given the error bounds on the calculations, *it is not possible* to draw any firm conclusions about this from the data.
   - Having said this, however, *it is difficult* to draw any firm conclusions from the results about the dependability of the Stefan diffusion tube method for measuring diffusivities. Objective (implicit):
   - A large molecular size *is expected* to retard the compound's rate of diffusion.
   - *A great degree of uncertainty* is attached to these results.
   - *Perhaps* a variation in experimental design and not a large degree of variability in the length measurements is to blame.

This writer realizes the modal responsibility for her statements as something objective rather than using a subjective modality such as *this may be* or *I did not expect* or *it might be wrong*. The explicitly objective realizations at (a) and (b) include evaluation (*it is not possible; it is difficult*), in structures which construe possibility and ability as facts for which she is not the apparent source. The implicit evaluations also do not individuate the student writer. At (c) she presents generalized *expectations* and at (d) she construes the reliability of her results as *uncertainty*, a nominal element that presents this as an objective "thing." She often realizes implicit objective modality in the use of *perhaps*, as at (e), where she draws on implicit objective construal of possibility to suggest an alternative interpretation related to the discussion of possible error in the experiment. This implicit objective presentation is a useful device that construes modal responsibility as something outside the author and enables the presentation of options that the author does not have to be completely committed to.

These grammatical strategies realize authoritativeness in these laboratory reports, but developing writers tend to draw heavily on the subjective options in construing inter subjective meanings, either through the explicitly subjective forms with *I* or through reliance on modal verbs. In (9), a student writer construes implicit subjective modality in modal verbs (modal verbs highlighted):

9. There were a lot of assumptions associated with this experiment which *could* cause some discrepancy in the final results. It was assumed that the temperature at the interface was the temperature of the liquid and this *may* not be the case. This assumption *could* have some effect on the final result because as stated earlier, the diffusion coefficient is a function of the temperature. It was also assumed that air is an ideal gas and single species, and that *may* not be the case because air is a mixture of different species. This also *may* affect the final results.

This writer uses the implicitly subjective modals (*could, may*) to suggest that some assumptions of the experimental procedure might not have been valid. However, without control of the verb tense that would situate these possible effects in the context of the experiment (e.g., *could have caused; may not have been*, etc.), the text appears to locate the uncertainty more in the writer than in the result.

This writer's authoritativeness is also diminished because the modals appear in conjunction with other features of interactional, rather than academic, registers, including lexical choices (*a lot of*) and clause chaining with *and* and *because*. All of these features together realize a less authoritative presentation than can be achieved in grammatical choices that realize the scientific meanings in the more condensed register that construes the objectivity that is valued in science texts. Evaluation pervades scientific discourse, where there is no sharp distinction between fact and evaluation.

Reports on experimental results incorporate assessments related to the reliability and validity of the findings, and the report and assessment are often realized in the same clause through grammatical resources that enable evaluation. This section has highlighted in general terms the register features that construe scientific meanings. These include technical terms and expanded nominal groups, often realized in grammatical metaphors that participate in material and relational processes as theories and explanations are constructed. These processes suppress expression of agency, which contributes to the "objective" construal of authoritativeness. Objective realization of modality, both explicitly and implicitly, also contributes to this authoritative stance. Grammatical metaphor also enables the kind of thematic progression typical of science discourse, where nominalization enables a linking from clause to clause as new information is reconstrued in a nominal group that serves as the theme of a succeeding clause. The display of knowledge in science in the classification and explanation that build theories, and the authoritativeness of science discourse in presenting conclusions in objective ways, emerge in texts constructed so that information is accumulated and presented step by step. These are the situational expectations that constitute the context of science discourse, and the grammar is the resource that enables the scientific meanings in the language of schooling.

GRAMMAR AS RESERVE FOR EDUCATION

RECOGNIZING GENRES

To effectively help all children develop competence with the registers and genres that are powerful for learning in school, teachers need to recognize, build on, and expand the language resources students bring to school to help them develop new ways of using language to think about the world. Both language and thinking develop through meaningful participation in tasks that promote new ways of thinking and using language. This means that the cognitive development that accompanies particular academic tasks depends on the way those tasks are embedded in their social contexts and the purposes to which the new skills are put.

Language is the central tool for cognitive development in school. Teaching should be seen as what Christie calls a "deliberate" act of instruction to achieve a set of goals. Fundamental to teaching is the notion of scaffolding—what Martin calls "guidance through interaction in the context of shared experience". Scaffolding requires a *visible* pedagogy that provides teachers with expertise and makes the criteria for success explicit to students.

For scaffolding to be effective in promoting language development, teachers need to be aware of what they are scaffolding and what they are aiming to achieve. From a linguistic perspective, recognizing that particular texts are valued in particular social contexts, such as schools, suggests that schools need to provide opportunities for students to develop an understanding of what those valued texts achieve and how the social meanings they make are construed in grammatical and lexical choices.

Too often, however, students experience an *invisible* pedagogy, where teachers manage classroom tasks and interaction without being clear about the content to be learned and the criteria for success. Invisible pedagogies do not push students to move beyond what they already know.

For example, Christie describes a language arts curriculum where students are expected to read literature and adopt a position that is their "own" in response to it, without any explicit analysis of the texts they are reading that would reveal the many and varied embedded cultural meanings.

Such an implicit pedagogy puts at risk all but those students whose socialization has prepared them to relate to the embedded meanings, those students who have opportunities outside of school to engage in the kind of discussion and critique that prepares them for such tasks in school. Explicit pedagogies foreground the patterns and relationships in the language and practices being taught. It is not enough just to have "standards" that students need to meet.

Teachers need to be informed about the linguistic challenges of those standards and have tools for unraveling the linguistic complexities that they represent. Without explicit instruction and clear criteria for success, when students fail, the failure is easily placed on factors such as ability, family background, or motivation. Students may lack experience with school tasks on several levels.

They may not understand the goals and purposes of the tasks, or they may not understand what the school values in its expectations for language use. Even when they understand the goals and purposes, they may not understand how such goals and purposes are relevant to their lives. Knowledge develops in particular contexts related to particular purposes, and the specific context and purpose shape the knowledge, and linguistic resources to construe that knowledge, that students develop. For that reason it is especially important that instruction in language be contextualized through authentic and purposeful activities.

Australian researchers have promoted a genre-based pedagogy that takes an explicit approach to literacy instruction with a goal of providing equal opportunities for all students to read and write the genres that allow them to participate successfully in school, in science and technology, and in other institutions of society.

Cope and Kalantzis characterize this approach as "being explicit about the way language works to make meaning ... engaging students in the role of apprentice with the teacher in the role of expert on language system and function ... [with] emphasis on content, on structure and on sequence in the steps that a learner goes through to become literate in a formal educational setting". The functional grammar described in this book and in other work on systemic functional linguistics grounds the genre approach in linguistic elements that realize the genres, so that they are not taught as formulaic text types but as social processes that are realized in certain language choices.

Students need knowledge about the social purposes and the linguistic features that realize those purposes in different genres. Because each discipline has evolved a way of using language that interprets the world in its own terms, students need to learn the language of the different school disciplines if they are to be effective in doing school-based tasks.

This means they have to engage in producing a range of genres from the early years. Children can be introduced to factual writing from the beginning of school if effective contexts are developed. Factual genres have their roots in language whose function is to explore the world, so the capacity to read and write such genres needs to be developed in contexts where students are developing knowledge about unfamiliar concepts. Ability to write factually or analytically will not develop in the same contexts in which personal writing develops. This means that students need social experiences that engage them meaningfully in activities for which reading and writing a range of factual and analytical genres is called for. Teachers also need to learn to recognize when factual genres are appropriate, as students are sometimes encouraged even to write about scientific topics from a personal perspective. Christie, for example, reports on how a teacher in a science class asks students in early primary grades to write a "story" about the hatching eggs that have been the students' project. The instruction to "tell a story" misleads the children into a narrative genre which is inappropriate for making meaning in this context.

When writing book reports, too, students often write in a narrative rather than analytical genre. Much of students' early writing experience, then, fails to prepare them for the genres that will be expected of them later. If students are to develop the range of genres expected in school tasks, the challenges in the development of the language resources needed to accomplish those genres must be addressed in the school context.

Each genre represents a different cultural use of language and each has its own roots in different cultural experiences. In order for students to learn to use and manipulate each genre for their own purposes, they need to share in the cultural experiences that genre helps construct.

Truly understanding and accepting that students need to share in those cultural experiences has major implications for how language can be taught and learned. Students need to be able to participate in the social purposes of the texts and tasks of schooling so that they understand the goals of the tasks they are asked to do and the texts they are asked to create.

Analyzing Language

In order to effectively scaffold the development of different genres, teachers need a clear understanding of the goals of the assignments they give and a means of helping students learn how to write texts that meet those goals. The context of any particular school task is not the same for every student. Schleppegrell demonstrates, for example, that when asked to write descriptions in science class, some students write incipient reports, drawing on grammatical resources that present themselves as knowledgeable experts who are authoritatively providing information for a non-present audience, while others write texts that construe more personal contexts as they comment on what they see or what they like.

Anderson also found register differences in the way deaf and hearing college students responded when asked to write about how they felt about writing. All hearing students responded in a similar way, beginning their texts with themselves (*I*) as theme/subject, foregrounding themselves as writers. They all used *it/writing* in the clause rheme. The responses of the deaf students were much more varied in their grammatical choices.

Only about half chose *I* as the theme/subject of the first sentence, and many of them expanded their initial clauses hypotactically and paratactically, foregrounding related or unrelated topics. These differences demonstrate the power of register and the need to address attention to grammatical and lexical features, especially with students who may not have experience with academic registers.

The point is not that every student must make the same grammatical choices, but when students' choices do not enable them to accomplish assigned tasks in ways that foreground the meanings in focus, they can benefit from attention to other options available to them. Students' grammatical choices construe different conceptualizations of the tasks they are assigned as they create different types of texts; texts which are not all valued in the same way.

For teachers, understanding the genres they are assigning and the register features that construct those genres can enable them to see writing tasks as processes through which students can express their individuality at the same time their knowledge and opinions are also presented in ways that are valued at school and in society.

Recent second language research also suggests that a focus on form can be important for students' language development. Informed by a theory of language that is discourse and meaning-based, a focus on language can be brought to learning even as new content is introduced. Students can learn how the close interaction between grammar and discourse organization enables them to create effective texts and develop the diverse voices they need to produce texts for different contexts and situations.

By making the lexical and grammatical expectations for academic assignments explicit, teachers can help students make more effective choices in approaching different writing tasks. With an understanding of the genre and register features of academic tasks, teachers can focus on grammar as a resource for the construction of texts and help students use new resources of the grammar. Information about grammar can be incorporated into writing instruction so that as students follow a process of drafting, revising, and editing, they can be made aware of the features that are especially important for construing meanings in that writing task.

Such focus on form shows students how their grammatical choices contribute to the effectiveness of their texts and helps them gain control of their writing and more confidence in their choices. Rothery, for example, shows how functional grammar can be used to teach students to write scientific explanations. As students read procedural texts that laid out the experiment they were involved in, they identified imperative verbs and sequencing markers and analyzed how referents were tracked.

Rothery points out that when the students first wrote reports on the experiments, the texts they produced were procedures, not explanations. It was only when they focused on the linguistic features of explanation that they began to write about how the process worked rather than how to do the process; learning to structure text in a new way. Rothery notes that it is not easy for teachers to facilitate such learning.

"Teachers do not have technical knowledge about the language system, the relationship between text and context, or of child language studies which document the adult's guiding, scaffolding role in adult/child linguistic interactions, a role which is crucial to children learning language and learning through language".

Without such knowledge, as suggested before, teachers may locate the literacy problem in the students' cognitive abilities rather than in the pedagogy. Lessons can also help students understand how linguistic choices make texts the kinds of texts they are. School textbooks are often constructed in ways that do not make the meanings explicit, and students need to be able to work with dense and difficult language in order to understand such texts.

Explicit analysis of the linguistic structure of texts can help students understand how language construes particular contexts and ways of thinking. The grammatical and lexical elements that are functional for creating texts in school contexts can become an explicit focus of teaching and students can engage in deconstruction of the texts they read to help them understand how the authors have constructed the text to incorporate ideational, interpersonal, and textual meanings through their lexical and grammatical choices.

A functional analysis of language can also inform educators as they prepare texts for students to read. For example, Unsworth demonstrates that it is possible to identify and specify the features that make a middle-school science textbook explanation about sound waves effective. He shows how the types of clauses selected, use of grammatical metaphor and conjunctive relations, and choice of theme in the presentation of information contribute to clear and effective text. He demonstrates how an ineffective text distorts an explanation of sound waves and creates ambiguity because it does not draw on the constellation of grammatical features that enables an explanation at increasing levels of abstraction. Knowledge about the role of grammatical resources can help educators create texts that better achieve the purposes of schooling. A functional analysis of grammatical resources also provides a framework for analyzing students' command of language and identifying the areas in which they need further development.

Explicitness about the textual expectations for academic writing is the only means of providing access and achieving fairness in assessment. Unfortunately, this is seldom done. As Rothery and Stenglin note about English as a subject area, "the goals ... are left implicit, or even misrepresented, and ... students are given virtually no tools for achieving them, [so] it is not surprising that success in English is achieved mainly by students from the middle class who bring with them a rich cultural capital of literacy, field experiences and mainstream ethical positions which they constantly draw on in the classroom". Tools for linguistic analysis are "precisely the resource which enables learners to develop the means of reflecting on language".

This capacity for reflection is an important aspect of developing critical thinking and higher level knowledge. Learning the registers that construe school-based social practices gives students tools for adapting those registers to their own social, cultural, and political interests. The values and hierarchies related to academic genres and registers are not obvious or evident without explicit instruction.

By implementing an active pedagogy that teaches about the language of schooling, educators can overcome the labels that separate students into different categories and social groups and enable a focus on the common agenda of helping students gain control over the texts that have the power to shape the future that they share.

Grammar and Writing Development

Students typically draw on the resources of the language they already know, the language of informal interaction, as they learn new ways of organizing and presenting language through writing. The academic register features described emerge gradually in children's writing, with the information-packed clause structure characteristic of academic registers only developing fully as children move into adolescence. Children's early writing appears very much like their oral language, as they first construct chained clauses, using *and* and other generalized conjunctions of informal spoken discourse, before they learn to use the grammar and organizational structure typical of academic written texts.

Research on children's writing development from a grammatical perspective has focused on the movement from this chained, coordinated clause structure to the more condensed clausal structure typical of more mature writing. In this process, children first use only coordination, but then begin to incorporate dependent clauses, vary their sentence structure, and expand their vocabulary.

Hunt's experiments in sentence-combining show these strategies developing as children's writing matures. Hunt contrasts the writing of fourth-grade students and adults in terms of how they use conjunctions to combine six simple sentences into more complex structures. Representative examples of how the six sentences were combined by writers at different ages are shown in (1):

1. 4th grader: Aluminum is a metal and it is abundant. It has many uses and it comes from bauxite. Bauxite is an ore and looks like clay.
   Adult: Aluminum, an abundant metal with many uses, comes from bauxite, a clay-like ore.

The fourth grader uses *and* to connect each pair of the six sentences into a coordinated structure. The adult, on the other hand, combines all six sentences into one that has no conjunctions at all.

Hunt concludes that "successively older students can consolidate a successively larger number of simple sentences into a single T-unit". They do this by reducing sentences to phrases or single words, using strategies of condensation which, are typical of academic registers. The first clause combining strategy Hunt describes in children's writing is coordination of T-units and predicates, starting at about fourth grade. He observes that fourth graders rarely transform predicate adjectives into prenominal adjectives, but as they gain experience, writers increasingly do this (e.g., *metal is abundant* becomes *abundant metal*), until, at about eighth grade, writers in his study use more prenominal than predicate adjectives.

Young writers coordinate predicates, but coordination with ellipsis of subjects is rare at fourth grade, and increases with experience (e.g., *it has many uses and it comes from bauxite* becomes *It has many uses and comes from bauxite*). Eighth graders also use relative clauses (e.g., *There was a man and he was a singer* becomes *The man who was a singer*, ...) and begin using appositives (e.g., *The girl next door, Staci* ...) and nonfinite participles (e.g., *Carved from a pumpkin, the jack o'lantern* ... or *Coming through the window, the burglar* ...).

Although he does not use the notion of *grammatical metaphor*, Hunt reports that it is only older writers who are able to readily make syntactic category shifts such as transforming predicates into modifiers (e.g., *The horse galloped* becomes *The galloping horse*) or transforming clauses into prepositional phrases (e.g., *an ore that has many uses* becomes *an ore with many uses*).

Children's narrative and argumentative writing also shows significant decreases in causal and temporal conjunctions as they mature. Crowhurst finds that twelfth graders are more likely than sixth graders to use the kinds of conjunctive signals that signpost the development of an argument (*first of all, next, for one thing, all in all, finally*) and are more likely to use adversative conjunctions (*however, but, whereas*). Nelson finds that older students use fewer conjunctions because they express ideas more efficiently using verbs. As students adopt the registers of schooled writing, they also learn to present their opinions and attitudes in ways that are more authoritative, as the grammatical features of the academic registers enable a more reasoned style of argument.

As Crowhurst describes it, "whereas much of the best writing at age 11 reflects the conventions of speech—as indeed, does weaker writing by 15-yearolds—able 15-year-olds have learned a good deal more both about written argument and about the text-forming devices of language. They have a variety of linguistic means at their disposal for conveying urgency and emphasis and have less need for the passionate personal statements and rhetorical questions of younger children".

A distinguishing feature of weak writing is the presence of hedges, redundancies, restarts, vagueness, or ellipses that are acceptable in conversation. Developing written academic registers means learning to make different lexical and grammatical choices than those that come naturally in interactional registers. All of this research indicates that academic writing development involves movement away from the paratactic, clause-chaining syntax of speech, and toward the reduced clauses and high propositional content of the academic registers.

Writers learn to pack more information into each clause as their writing develops. As successful children learn to write, they gradually become competent in adopting the structural and semantic properties of academic registers, coming to understand how language is structured differently when it is used in school-based tasks. They learn to compact clauses, expand their vocabulary, and present logical relationships in new ways, making the register choices that present them as effective academic writers.

This enables them to meet the discourse demands of the later years of education, which require the adoption of more academic ways of writing. Perfetti and McCutchen suggest that older children need to develop "productive control of lexical and grammatical devices". They point out that "it is not until writers reach a certain level of maturity that they even attempt to express many ideas... within a single sentence.

It is that complexity, and the sophisticated syntax that it requires, that proves so problematic for many older writers". They describe students who attempt to respond to the discourse demands of written language, but are unable to, because they are not able to draw on the grammatical features that express what they intend. As students are asked to accomplish more difficult and complex tasks, they have to draw on new grammatical and lexical resources.

When lexical and grammatical development does not keep pace with school expectations, students are unable to meet the reading and writing demands of disciplinary learning. Many of the students who have difficulty developing their writing to meet these academic register challenges speak English as a second language or second dialect. Students whose community language is a nonstandard variety of English have been shown to draw heavily on oral language features in their writing, as have second language writers.

It is difficult to generalize about second language students, since they come from a variety of backgrounds, have begun learning English at different ages, and have different experiences of literacy in their mother tongues. The structure of their first languages and differences in their experiences also contribute to the variability of second language writing.

However, a review of 72 research reports comparing the composing processes and written text features of ESL and non-ESL writers finds that, in general, adult second language writing is simpler and less effective than first language writing. "L2 writers' texts were less fluent (fewer words), less accurate (more errors), and less effective (lower holistic scores)".

Second language writers' sentences included more but shorter T-units, fewer but longer clauses, more coordination, less subordination, less noun modification, and less passivization. Second language writers also evidenced distinct patterns in the use of cohesive devices, especially more conjunctive and fewer lexical ties, and less lexical control, variety, and sophistication overall. These are the same features that are typical of the less developed first language writer.

Similar conclusions are reported in Hinkel, who compares 68 linguistic features of texts by university level second language writers with those of native speakers in first year composition courses. She describes oral features in second language writing, including more use of conjunctions, especially causal conjunctions, exemplification markers, and demonstrative pronouns for establishing text cohesion, with few lexical ties.

She links this functionally to her finding that second language writers provide personal stories rather than evidence for arguments in their essays, and concludes that these students "have a shortfall of syntactic and lexical tools to enable them to produce competent written academic text". For those students with academic language experience in their first languages, it can be very frustrating to be unable to express themselves in English with the complex syntax and lexis that they can draw on in their first language.

An even greater challenge faces the many immigrant children in today's schools who have not had the opportunity to develop academic registers in their first languages. Even when they have achieved a good level of fluency in spoken English, they may have difficulty with academic language tasks. Similar challenges face speakers of nonstandard dialects of English, in learning the ways that academic registers construe meanings. Of course these different types of learners also differ in the challenges they face. Recently arrived second language learners have to learn a whole new grammar and lexicon, while immigrant students and speakers of nonstandard dialects may already control the spoken registers. The length of time that students may need to gain control of the surface grammar may also vary based on many factors, including first language, literacy background, and social experience, but on the whole, similar issues in writing development face second language learners, second dialect speakers, and other students without sufficient experience with academic contexts for language use.

For all students for whom the notion of an academic register is not already familiar, learning to write is a great challenge, and a major aspect of that challenge is linguistic. Although the studies just reviewed do not take a functional linguistics perspective on the features they analyze, their findings support a functional interpretation.

Using the tools of systemic functional linguistics, Christie, for example, points out that use of adverbs emerges late in students' writing, and suggests that this is because adverbs of manner and modal adverbs such as *nearly* and *constantly* are involved in the expression of judgments that develops as students mature. Christie describes the new aspects of literacy that are learned as students move into the more complex demands of secondary school, identifying the grammatical features needed for more advanced writing.

She demonstrates how the use of embedded clauses and other means of expanding nominal groups is important for advanced literacy development because the kinds of texts that students are asked to write call for expanded nominal elements as themes that help to structure texts. The features of academic registers also enable students to construct the abstractions and generalizations needed for analytical writing.

Christie points out that the features she analyzes, including control of grammatical metaphor, "create the capacity in the successful writer, to handle the building of generalisation, abstraction, argument, reflection upon experience". But Christie notes that these features are slow to develop, and that "development of control of many aspects of written language is a feature of late childhood and adolescence".

Christie's research provides functional explanations for the findings of the other research reviewed here. Both structural and functional analyses suggest that to write in advanced literacy contexts, students need to draw on a constellation of grammatical and lexical features, including clause-combining strategies that rely less on conjunctions and finite clauses and more on embedded clauses and nominal and verbal expression of logical relationships. The functional analysis demonstrates how these developmental changes enable students to mean new things, construing the new kinds of knowledge that come out of the disciplinary demands of later schooling. In order to understand these disciplinary demands, it is important to recognize the different types of texts that teachers typically ask students to read and write. The new knowledge and new ways of meaning that students are developing are realized in the particular *genres* of schooling.

Grammatical and lexical features can effectively be a focus of attention only in the contexts of the texts in which they occur. Each subject has its own favoured text types. The next sections review the genres of schooling in general terms, and then focus on how academic registers are typically realized in one valued genre, the expository essay.

Genres of Schooling

Genre is a term used to refer to particular text or discourse types. This section presents an overview of some genres of schooling in order to provide a framework for discussion of the key register features of academic texts. The description of the genres themselves should be seen as merely suggestive of the text types, as these are social constructs that are enacted in a diversity of ways. While the naming and description of a genre is in that sense arbitrary, as each genre may have infinite manifestations and is always changing and evolving, it is still useful to think about the properties of the prototypical texts that are associated with schooling contexts.

Language always construes both the commonality and the individuality of our social experiences, so the actual realizations of any genre are highly varied. At the same time, looking at texts from the perspective of the different genres they represent helps us understand the variability and development that is expected of students as they gain control of academic registers.

Genres come into being to serve specific social purposes, so ability to realize the genres that are characteristic of particular social contexts allows participation in and mutual understanding of those contexts. Because school is a culture with its own expectations for particular ways of using language, students need to learn about the genres of schooling and the purposes for which they are useful. They need to have experiences that engage them in activities for which different genres are expected if they are to gain a realistic understanding of their value and purposes. In addition to such experiences, however, students often need to focus explicitly on how those genres are typically constructed with the lexical and grammatical resources of the language if they are going to be successful in participating in such construction. Defining the features of particular genres is problematic, as any one instance realizes the genre in ways that are not comprehensive or definitive of the genre as a more abstract notion.

Genres respond to the cultural contexts in which they achieve their purposes, so their realizations vary and evolve as they are created in new ways in different contexts. But to understand the challenges of schooling, it is important to recognize that there are text types that students are expected to write, and that those text types are constructed with lexical and grammatical resources that are functional for making it the kind of text it is.

Analyzing some genres that have been identified as relevant to schooling reveals the lexical and grammatical challenges. Creating an instance of a genre means using language to move through a series of stages that are particular to that genre. The narrative genre, for example, has been characterized as including the stages Abstract, Orientation, Complication, Evaluation, Resolution, and Coda as optional or obligatory elements.

Expository texts present a thesis and support it with arguments. The language used to realize these different kinds of texts can be analyzed to reveal what the linguistic challenges are in reading and writing the different genres of schooling.

Three categories proposed by Martin; *Personal, Factual*, and *Analytical*, to summarize the purposes and grammatical features of seven prototypical school-based genres: *Recount, Narrative, Procedure, Report, Account*, *Explanation*, and *Exposition*. The three categories refer to the general purposes of the genres: those that report on or create personal experience, those that present factual information, and those that analyze and argue.

The social purpose of each genre and indicates some of the grammatical features that research studies have found to be functional in realizing the genre. Different register features are functional for the realization of different genres. Each of the three categories of genres has its own sequence of development, and within each of the categories, there is an increasing demand for more academic register features as students move, for example, from writing recounts to writing narratives, or from writing procedures to writing reports, or from writing accounts to writing explanations and expositions.

The increased grammatical demands emerge from the more complex stages that the more advanced text types include. Christie proposes a developmental path in students' ability to write in these different ways. She suggests that in the early primary grades, students typically write recounts, an early step toward the development of narrative. Recounts are re-creations of personal experience that are characterized by their use of personal pronouns and material processes to talk about activities and the participants in the activities; frequent use of conjunctions, especially additive and temporal conjunctions, to link clauses; and use of the past tense. (2) is an example of a rudimentary recount, written by a first-grade nonnative speaker of English:

2. One day I played with my friends outside to played soccer. When we done to play soccer we cleaned up the house together. The house was beautiful. When we finish we go outside again to play soccer. I liked the fun day.

This text uses personal pronouns (*I, we*), material processes realized in past tense verbs (*played, cleaned*), and *when*, a temporal conjunction, to build the sequence of events in the text. Two evaluative clauses (*the house was beautiful, I liked the fun day*) point toward the assessment and evaluation that will develop in this writer as he gains skill in writing more complex narrative texts. Christie notes that as students develop, they begin writing texts that not only recount an experience, but also draw implications from the experience.

This requires a grammatical advance in order to make the link from the recount to the implication (using expressions such as *and that shows*, etc.), and a shift from past to present tense for the presentation of meanings that are timeless, not part of the recount of events. These developments prepare students to write full *narratives*, texts that include problematic events and their outcome, with a complicating action that results in an overall point to the story.

Here a variety of verb tenses helps students move between various time and perspective changes, with a pattern of participant role changes and a variety of conjunctive relations and evaluative lexis. Christie demonstrates the grammatical developments that occur as students move from simple recounts into the more complex narratives that draw on elaboration of circumstances, adverbs of manner, and use of grammatical metaphor to build experiential information in incongruent ways as writers incorporate complication and evaluation phases into their stories.

Procedure is a factual genre which is often written in the early years of schooling. It typically directs the actions of others through a set of steps. Giving directions, for example, creates a procedural text, often using declarative mood with present tense verbs to talk about generalized actions (e.g., *you go to the top of the stairs and turn right* ...). Procedures may also use imperative verbs to direct the actions of others. In middle and secondary school, students write *reports* where they need to classify and describe. Here present tense is functional as writers make generic, rather than specific references. Text (3) is a description of a picture written by a middle school student that shows some features of the *report* genre:

3. The egret is very large and slendar. It fishes for food so his eyes in the picture look determined. The egret lives in the rain forest because it looks like that in the background of the picture. The egrets live on the Long Island coasts's. They use there long stiff beaks and legs to hunt there prey.

The writer of (3) begins her text with a nominal group that introduces what she is describing in a way that is generic (*the egret*) at the same time it refers to the specific picture she is describing. The clause themes maintain the focus on the generic egret, constructing the text as a report on egrets in general, with information about this bird presented in the clause rhemes. But the student also refers to the picture she is describing (e.g., *in the picture* and it *looks like that in the background of the picture*), so the text has features both of a report with a more distanced stance and a description more situated in relationship to the picture. It is common to see features of different genres and registers in the same text as students struggle to move into more academic ways of writing.

As students move into analytical writing, they write *accounts, explanations*, and *expositions. Accounts* are structured temporally, like recounts and narratives, but they also incorporate causal reasoning, as writers tell not only what happened, but why. A further step is *explanation*, where a phenomenon is presented and explained (*How our government is structured*, for example) without temporal sequencing.

Instead, some kind of logical structure has to be developed in an effective explanation (*There are three branches of government*). Explanations draw on relational processes, technical language, and varied conjunctive relations. Expansion of nominal groups and more frequent use of circumstantial information goes along with these developments, making the control of a variety of types of clause themes important. In addition, a more authoritative voice emerges as the writer adopts consistent use of the third person.

Moving beyond explanations, students write expository texts in which they argue for a position or weigh different views. The writer expands nominal groups and creates abstractions in order to name points to be developed and argued. A greater facility with clause organization strategies helps the writer reason with grammatical metaphor, a key resource for expressing causal relationships and attitudes in more condensed and objective ways.

Modality helps to construe possibility and necessity, and logical and attitudinal connectors (*however, nevertheless*) are often used as themes to scaffold the argument. The next section of this chapter takes up these points in greater detail to describe how all these features together contribute to effective exposition. The genres within each category share some features. The personal genres, for example, share the characteristic that they are temporally organized and report on specific events. This means that less organizational expertise is needed for personal writing such as recount or narrative, because the events themselves create a structure for the unfolding text. The factual and analytical genres also include types that are organized temporally; in the case of factual genres, the *procedure*, and in the case of analytical genres, the *account*. But as students move on in schooling, they need to organize texts logically, rather than temporally, in order to present information or make claims and support them with judgments and evaluation.

The genres of schooling become increasingly demanding in terms of the grammatical expectations that underlie them. In order to move from time-ordered, narrative modes of presentation, students need to be able to make changes in both the clause-level choices and discourse organization of their writing. Creating a text that presents and supports a thesis requires use of nominalization, internal linking, and other more advanced grammatical strategies.

Of course there are different ways of naming and describing these text types; terms like *argument, discussion*, and *summary* are also used as names of schoolbased genres. These genres are not presented here as templates, but as general descriptions of culturally expected ways of writing that are recognizable in the context of schooling. Some of these genres also appear as stages in other genres.

In expository writing, for example, recounts of personal experience or reports of general information may form stages of the developing exposition. As students proceed through the levels of schooling, the kinds of genres they are expected to produce become more complicated, with exposition a target genre that is typically expected of the competent secondary school graduate.

Because expository writing is such a key genre for success in schooling at advanced levels, the following section explores the expectations for expository writing in more detail and presents some issues that face inexperienced students in accomplishing this genre.

RECENT GRAMMATICAL CHANGE IN ENGLISH

Writing-system, phonology and even lexicology are fairly well defined categories of linguistic analysis. Grammar, however, is a more nebulous category, and this has left its mark in the confusion which sometimes marks its definition in the literature; for some scholars, grammar refers to the whole range of linguistic activity, with the exception of lexicography, for others, it has a narrower meaning. In this book, the term is used comparatively narrowly, to refer to *syntax* and *morphology*. Syntax is concerned with the way in which words combine to form clauses and sentences; morphology-referred to briefly at the beginning is concerned with word-form.

In other words, grammar is to do with such matters as element-order and inflectional variation. There is a fuzzy area between grammar and lexicology, and some areas traditionally considered the realm of grammar have been discussed (e.g. some aspects of word-formation, the development of gender-systems with reference to pronoun-forms).

This fuzziness should not be seen as too problematic; it is worth remembering that our categories of analysis are attempts to order complex things in as economical a way as possible, and it is therefore not surprising that these complex things do not always fit our necessarily clumsy attempts to force them into neat categories. Indeed, it is arguable that one of the characteristic faults of linguistics, especially as practised over the last thirty years or so, has been to try to force the complexities of linguistic behaviour into strictly formal categories which are unable to comprehend the diversity of natural languages. The reason for the fuzziness of the division between grammar and lexis is that both are carriers of meaning, and it must be expected therefore that meaning is carried differently in different states of language. Such differences are clearly shown in diachronic study. For instance, the Present-Day English clause *I had loved,* consisting of subject-pronoun, verbal auxiliary and main verb, was expressed in Old English by the clause *ic lufoder* (literally 'I loved formerly'), to be analysed as consisting of subject-pronoun, main verb and adverb. Both *I had loved* and *ic lufoder* are attempts to express the 'same meaning', but one uses an auxiliary verb (traditionally seen as a category to do with grammar) and the other uses an adverb (traditionally seen as to do with lexis).

This interface is seen most characteristically in the process known as *grammaticalisation* (sometimes *grammaticisation*). In essence grammaticalisation is to do with the shift of an item from lexical to grammatical categories; its reverse, *lexicalisation,* was touched upon on page 134 above.

Once more, the history of the auxiliary verbs supplies a good example of the process, with the history of the form 'will'. The history of 'will' and its related verb 'shall' is of some interest for the study of the role of prescriptivity in the history of English. In Old English, *wille* etc. had a volitional sense 'want to', whereas *sceal* etc. meant 'must'. 'Shall' retains an obligatory sense in Early Modern English: thus the force of *Thou shalt not* in the Authorised Version of the Ten Commandments; and it retains this meaning in some, especially formal, varieties of Present-Day English (cf. *You SHALL go to the ball, Cinderella!*).

However, the form is generally dying out in present-day varieties, either altogether (as in Present-Day Scots or in US usage) or retained only marginally through prescriptive or formalised use. In the eighteenth century, 'shall' was reinterpreted by the prescriptivists as the future auxiliary appropriate for government by first-person pronouns, and it is still taught as such. Augustan grammarians such as Bishop Lowth put forward the interesting pragmatic argument that 'shall' is appropriate for first- but not second- or third-person use because to state obligation for the latter can be-to use a twentieth-century expression-a 'face-threatening' act. By the early twentieth century, these pragmatic arguments for usage seem to have been generally forgotten.

In an Old English clause, therefore, such as *Ic wille þone hlford ofsl–an* 'I want to kill the lord', *wille* is a lexical verb which implies *volition* as well as *futurity*. In Present-Day English, the reflex of the one-time lexical verb *wille* is an auxiliary signalling future tense, grammatically bound within the verb-phrase, and the semantic component *volition* is no longer salient. In other words, the verb has become grammaticalised. Thus *I will kill the lord* does not *necessarily* signal volition, and another Present-Day English verb, *want,* has to take its place if volition is to be signalled strongly. The key fact, of course, is that the Old English word *wille* 'want' necessarily has within its variational space the connotation of futurity, since 'to want' is to desire something not yet in one's possession; it is this connotation which has become the conceptual or focal meaning of the word. The word which has replaced 'will', 'want', had itself undergone a change of meaning, from 'lack' to 'desire'; this change has presumably itself been motivated in turn by the shift of the focal meaning of 'want'. The older meaning of 'want' survives only in a few fossil expressions, such as *found wanting,* and (of course) in biblical language, where Early Modern English usage has been retained.

Grammatical Variation

It was observed how contact, systemic regulation and variation interact to produce phonological and lexicological change. In this chapter, the focus shifts to events which are traditionally assigned to the category of grammatical change; the aim of this chapter is to show how outcomes which are traditionally assigned to the category 'grammatical change' are the result of dynamically interacting intra- and extralinguistic processes.

At the level of phonology, it was observed that allophonic variation was the key to phonological change. Something similar can be distinguished at the level of grammar. One source of allophonic variation is, to do with levels of emphasis: thus variants arise through emphatic or relaxed usage. In grammar, the equivalent sources of variation are similarly to do with formality or emphasis; thus, for instance, Classical Latin distinguished between *ego amo* 'I love' and *ad Romam ire* 'to go to Rome' (emphatic) and *amo, Romam ire* (relaxed).

Over time, with the obscuration of unstressed syllables in the Romance languages, inflectional distinctions in the relaxed register became unclear, and the emphatic alternative, where the pronoun *ego* and the preposition *ad* were available to express the relationship between words, was preferred in all environments. Thus in Present-Day French the sole equivalent to *Romam ire* and *ad Romam ire* is *aller à Paris*.

Other sources of grammatical variation are the result of analogical and phonological pressures. The forces of analogy put pressure on inherited or borrowed forms which are perceived as irregular, for example strong as opposed to weak verbs. It is for this reason that, in Present-Day English, only the weak-verb paradigm is still productive, and many verbs which were historically strong have joined the weak set; for example, a recently coined verb such as *jive* has been assigned to the weak paradigm (past tense *jived* as opposed to *jove*), and the originally strong verb *help* (Old English *helpan* 'help', past participle *holpen*) is now weak (cf. the Present-Day English past participle *helped*).

Phonological pressures in English have been to do with the reduction of stress on, and concomitant loss of distinctiveness of, inflectional endings; this development, as we shall see, has resulted in systemic pressure for grammatical change.

The interface between grammar and lexicon also introduces variation, in the development of periphrastic formations. A good example of this sort of thing is the appearance of the *do*-periphrasis at the end of the Middle English period, as an alternative mode of expression to signal causation or past tense. Finally, as with phonological and lexicological change, there is an additional source of variation: contact with other languages. It is no coincidence that, in the history of English, inflectional innovation has been earliest advanced in the area of the country where English came into closest contact with varieties of Scandinavian. There is evidence that Scandinavian and English were, throughout the Anglo-Saxon period, to some extent mutually comprehensible; many lexical items occur in both Old English and Old Norse, since both are Germanic languages, and the pre-Viking connections between Old Anglian and Old Norse have already been touched upon in various places.

Norse certainly supplied English with a number of inflectional features which have since become standard, for instance the *-s* ending on third-person present-tense verbs. There are also syntactic loans, some of which, such as the phrasal-verb constructions, have entered the standard language, whereas others-such as the tendency to ellipsis of the definite article, represented by the much-parodied Northern usage *t'mill* 'the mill', which probably derives from interaction between native and Norse prosodic and grammatical patterns-have had a more restricted currency.

As we have come to expect from discussions, these innovative pressures do not act in isolation; they act in combination across the whole linguistic system, the dynamic interaction between them producing change. The importance of interaction in the history of grammar is underlined when innovations are compared in terms of success or failure, that is, how long they continue to be a living part of the language. In the remainder, we shall first examine innovative failure and then innovative success. The chapter will then conclude with a history of the *do*-construction, an interesting innovation which at first 'succeeded' and then 'failed', the 'success' and 'failure' both being the result of interaction with other parts of the linguistic system.

Incipient Systems of Nominal Inflection

In Old English the relationships between and within noun-phrases were expressed by the use of formal case and grammatical gender respectively. That this system was breaking down in the Late Old English period is well attested. A good example of the kind of problem which was beginning to arise appears in the Old English poem *The Wanderer,* which survives in the Exeter Book, a manuscript copied, probably at Exeter, where it still remains in the Cathedral Library, in the second half of the tenth century. In the standard edition of this poem, line 102 reads *hrîð hrçosende hrûsan bindeð* 'a falling snowstorm binds the ground'.

However, in the manuscript the line actually reads *hrið hreosende hruse bindeð*. Old English *hrkse* 'ground' is a weak feminine noun, and it is a reasonable editorial intervention to replace the 'mistaken' nominative form by the more 'correct' *-an;* such emendations are constantly (and quite legitimately, given the intended readership) made by editors of Old English texts. But the printed text misleads if it suggests to the linguist that *The Wanderer* was copied in a more normalised Old English than actually existed.

As Dunning and Bliss point out, such 'mistakes' may not be mistakes at all, but rather examples of the obscuration of inflectional distinctions in Late Old English, that is, the loss of distinctive case-markers. That this levelling had been under way for some time in the development of the Germanic languages is illustrated by the history of the weak-noun declension. In Old English, the weak masculine and feminine declensions were.

The Germanic ancestor of the *-an* ending which is so marked a feature of both these paradigms was much more confined in extent, however. The equivalent, and more archaic, Gothic paradigms, which demonstrate a much greater variety of endings, might be compared here. It will be observed that, in comparison with Gothic, the merging of case-distinctions ('syncretism') has been much more thorough in Old English.

The syncretism which marks Old English is, incidentally, shared by other contemporary Germanic languages, for instance Old Saxon has *tunga* (nom. sg.), *tungun* (acc., gen., dat. sg.), *tungun* (nom., acc. pl.), *tunguno* (gen. pl.), *tungun* (dat. pl.), with syncretism even of the dative plural. In both cases it is possible to speak of an obvious linguistic tendency towards the merging of case-endings.

During the transition from Old to Middle English, the original Old English noun-system underwent further analogical shifts. Old English had strong, weak and minor noun declensions, and by Present-Day English the strong system has become, almost everywhere, generalised; forms which in Old English were weak (e.g. *çagan* 'eyes', *naman* 'names') or The Old English strong masculine declension irregular (e.g. *b–c* 'books', *suna* 'sons') have conformed analogically to the strong paradigm. Only a few common relicts remain in Present Day English, for example *oxen, children, feet, mice*. The Old English strong masculine declension was as indicated.

	Singular	**Plural**
Nominative	cyning 'king'	cyningas
Accusative	cyning	cyningas
Genitive	cyninges	cyninga
Dative	cyninge	cyningum

Even in Old English there are indications of the reorganisation of this system. In the manuscript of the poem *Beowulf*, dating from the end of the tenth century, forms such as the tribal names *Heaþo-Rmes* (where the sense demands an accusative plural with *-as,*) and *Heaðo-Scilfingas* (where the sense demands a genitive singular with *-es,* line 63) may be early examples of later developments, and the process may have been encouraged by a developing tendency towards syncretism (i.e. disappearance of formal distinctiveness) between dative and accusative which has been detected, for instance, in the process of revision of Ælfric's *Homilies,* composed around the year 1000. This process culminates during the Middle English period. Thus, for the Old English paradigm given, the usual Middle English pattern consists of *kyng* for nominative/accusative/dative singular, and *kynges* for the genitive singular and nominative/accusative/genitive/dative plural, from which pattern derives the common Present-Day English noun-paradigm.

There is, however, evidence that an alternative generalised system was being developed in the post-Old English period. In the 'AB-language' of *Ancrene Wisse* and related texts, it is possible to detect a paradigmatic pattern which differs from that described above. This variety of post-Old English was conservative, and attempted to maintain a distinction between weak and strong declensions, although there were some reassignments and a decay of irregular forms (thus AB-language has *bokes* 'books' for Old English *b–c*).

The borrowing into English of French nouns, which in their native form were marked for plurality by *-es,* may ultimately have helped favour the choice of the Old English strong paradigm as the model for future developments. But, in AB-language, French loanwords were assigned to both paradigms, for example *patriarchen* (beside *patriarches*), *barren, trussen,* beside *ententes, beastes, leattres.* It appears that a semantic principle was at work:

There was...a tendency to associate the plural *-es* with nouns denoting persons or classes of persons irrespective of the form of the nom. singular, and the plural *-en, -n* with nouns (denoting inanimate things) ending in a vowel in the nom. singular, irrespective of the [Old English] plural or gender.

This principle was even extended to words of Old English origin; thus a form such as *wrecche* 'wretch' (derived from the Old English weak masculine noun *wrecca*) is assigned to the strong declension in AB-language, whereas, for example, *bruche* 'fragment' (cf. the Old English strong masculine noun *bryce*) is assigned to the weak declension in AB-language. An incipient restructuring of the system of declension, different from that which has survived in Present-Day English, seems to have been under way in this variety.

Incipient Restructuring of Case-systems

A similar incipient restructuring can be seen in the development of the Old English markers of grammatical case in the Late Old English and post-Old English periods. In Old English, grammatical case, as has been stated above, provided a useful syntagmatic tracking device, marking the functions of noun-phrases, and relating determiners and adjectives to nouns at a time when element-order was more fluid than in Present-Day English. However, although the system has survived in Modern German, it largely died out in English during the Early Middle English period and, with the exception of the genitive in 's' and the singular/plural distinction, is no longer a feature of Present-Day English. The breakdown of the Old English system is well illustrated in the language of the *Peterborough Chronicle* Continuations, a text which has been referred to on a number of occasions already. One especially controversial area of the language of the First Continuation has to do with the reflexes of the Old English determiners *sç, sço, þœt* etc. (often referred to for convenience, if somewhat inaccurately, as the definite article), and also with the system of adjectival agreement.

In this portion of the *Peterborough Chronicle,* the Old English distinctions of grammatical gender have almost completely disappeared. However, there is evidence in the First Continuation that an attempt has been made to retain and reorganise the interphrasal tracking device, that is, the case-system. In the Anglian texts from the Late Old English period, there is evidence of an incipient restructuring of tracking-devices which, in Samuels's careful words, 'would have provided a remodelled paradigm for pre-modifiers'.

The pattern is illustrated with the Late West Saxon equivalents for the sake of comparison; the masculine accusative singular ending *-ne* appears in originally feminine and neuter contexts, the masculine/neuter genitive singular *-s* appears modifying historically feminine nouns, while the feminine dative singular *-re* is used to modify masculines and neuters. Such patterns appear in the First Continuation of the *Peterborough Chronicle,* for instance *on þone mynstre* 'in the minster', *to þœre mynstre* 'to the minster', where *mynster* is an historically neuter noun.

The system has obvious advantages, not least because the selection of forms can be accounted for as being based on phonetic distinctiveness. A comparison of the incipient Early Middle English system with that of Late West Saxon suggests that selection of forms was based upon the singular/plural distinction; thus *þre* has been dropped as the feminine singular genitive because of overlap in form with the similar genitive plural *þâra,* whereas *þm* has disappeared in the masculine and neuter dative singular because of overlap with the dative plural form.

Feminine *þâ* was dropped in the accusative because of overlap with the plural form; the selection of *þone* rather than *þœt* seems most probably to be because *þœt* was beginning to perform a number of other useful functions, notably as a relative marker. The system can be paralleled in the adjectives. Thus in the Northumbrian *Durham Ritual* of the early eleventh century we find masculine adjective endings applied to an originally feminine noun, for instance *ðerh allne woruld,* and this pattern is found as late as the thirteenth-century Caligula manuscript of Laamon's *Brut,* where 'predictable variation within the same paradigm' is to be found in *hæfden muchelne care* 'had much sorrow' (object) beside *mid muchelere care* 'with much sorrow' (prepositional). That this system was beginning to break down even in the First Continuation of the *Peterborough Chronicle* is, however, indicated by Clark, who lists a number of 'false' (i.e. unhistorical) case-forms which deviate from the incipient paradigm, for example:

þurh se Scotte kyng 'by the action of the king of Scots', Annal 1126 (with nom. *se* for the expected acc. sg.);

þone eorles sunu 'the earl's son', Annal 1127 (for gen. sg.; cf. Late West Saxon *þæs eorles sunu,* although it has been suggested that a different agreement pattern might have emerged);

þone abbotrice 'the abbacy', Annal 1127 (in subject position, and thus for nom. sg.; however, the expression *þone abbotrice* happens to be extremely common in object function in the annal for 1127, and its use here in subject position may be a simple slip).

As Clark points out, 'Statistically, false case-forms may be few; but their occurrence is none the less significant'. By the time of the Final Continuation, the determiner was invariably *þe,* whatever the historical case required, and Clark has suggested that the scribe of the First Continuation was attempting to maintain a system which was not part of his living language: If in his [i.e. the scribe of the First Continuation's] speech stressed [þe] [*sic*], unstressed [þ] [*sic*], corresponded to West Saxon *se,* then he might have substituted *se* for his own form...the orthography of the First Continuation suggests that the scribe, aware that by the standards of the *Schriftsprache* [i.e. the Late West Saxon standardised written language] his own usage was both provincial and new-fangled, was trying to palliate his own provincialism and modernity.

In other words, the scribe of the First Continuation occasionally hypercorrected; his usage may be taken to represent a compromise between the (now extinct) incipient restructured system, the system that became widespread and appears in Present-Day English, and the West Saxon system found in the standardised written language.

The Impersonal Construction

Old English had a number of impersonal verbs, that is, verbs without an expressed subject but with an accompanying pronoun in the accusative or dative case, for instance *m– þinceð* 'it seems to me', archaic *methinks*. The origin of such constructions has been much debated, and remains uncertain. Analysis shows that many fall, into a fairly restricted range of semantic fields, and this might suggest one way in which they may have originated; a number of them, for instance, seem to be to do with physical and mental affections. By not including as impersonal those verbs governed by formal 'it', such as Old English *hit sniwð* 'it is snowing'. These usages seem to me to follow a different and distinct path in the history of English, witnessed by the fact that, unlike the impersonal verbs without any expressed subject, the construction is still used in Present-Day English, and has even taken over from what I would regard as 'true' impersonal constructions; cf. the Present-Day English translation offered for *me þinceð* in the previous paragraph.)

The interest of the impersonal construction lies in the process whereby it first became common but was subsequently replaced. The impersonal construction has been discussed by D. Lightfoot; during the course of the Middle English and Early Modern English periods he detects a shift from impersonal to personal constructions, deriving from the 'rigidification' of Subject-Predicator word-order. The process seems to be one of analogy, whereby forms in the expected subject position ultimately conform to that position.

Following O. Jespersen, Lightfoot exemplifies the change as follows: *þœm cyninge l+codon þeran* '! *The king liceden þears* '‡*The king liked þears* > *He liked þears*. As Lightfoot points out, 'If a language learner was confronted with the sentence "the king liked pears", there would be a tendency to analyse it as [Subject-Verb-Object]; this would conform to the canonical patterns of the language'.

The example, however, is perhaps not a good one, because the Old English verb *l+cian* means 'pleased', not 'liked', and the plural used here, *l+codon,* is not therefore a true impersonal verb, but rather a verb governed by a perfectly regular nominative subject, *þeran*. Perhaps a better example would be *þ m cyninge l+code wel þœt þk him þ bMc geaf* 'It pleased the king well that you gave him the book'-although, again, it could be argued that the subject of this sentence is simply the subordinated clause *þœt þk...geaf*.

Thus far, the process of change follows an analogous pattern we might expect. However, there is a problem with this straightforward description, which is that the number of impersonal verbs actually increased during the Middle English period. Millward suggests that this increase is to do with language-contact, notably with French.

If this is the case, then we are reminded that contact can interfere with patterns; that the change was not sustained, however, suggests that the contact-induced development did not cohere with other features of the language. It is an interesting fact that even in the Middle English period a 'dummy' subject *it* became frequent (e.g. *hit þe likede* 'it pleased you') beside more prototypically impersonal constructions such as *me thristed* 'I was thirsty'.

By Early Modern English times, the form without *it* had largely disappeared; only *methinks* and *methought* appear commonly in, for instance, the works of Shakespeare, and, as Millward points out, Shakespeare never uses *himthought, usthinks, youthinks* etc. It seems that, by Shakespeare's time, *methinks* was simply a fossil expression rather than a reflection of a still-productive usage.

Non-teleological Directionality

There are at least two points worth making about the failure of the incipient innovations discussed:

1. They are evidence that linguistic innovation is non-teleological. If there were some ultimate goal for linguistic development, then such innovations as these would not have taken place. The appearance of these incipient systems shows that innovation can occur which may ultimately lead nowhere-rather like biological mutations which are not reproduced.
2. On the other hand, they are not evidence that linguistic change is non-directional; the distinction is an important one which has not always been understood clearly. These incipient restructurings did not succeed because there were other innovations-the fixing of element-order, for instance, or the generalisation of one system of nominal inflection-which were, it would appear, more in tune with the overall 'drift' of the language, that is, the ultimately successful system will be that which coheres best with developments of other neighbouring systems. Such 'success' in innovation will be pursued next.

'May' and 'Might'

It is argued here that innovations can succeed when they cohere with other developments. The success of an innovatory pattern can be seen on a grand scale in the development of the auxiliary verb-system in the Middle English and Early Modern English periods, where lexis and grammar interacted in interesting and complex ways and-even more importantly-in the shift from synthesis to analysis. (In what follows, the forms 'may', 'might' etc. are used, for ease of reference, in preference to Old English *mœg, mihte* etc. and their various Middle English reflexes.)

Proto-Indo-European seems to have had no fewer than five formally expressed moods: indicative (for statements or questions of fact), subjunctive (expressing will), optative (wishes), imperative (commands) and injunctive (unreality). Germanic languages retained the indicative and parts of the imperative, but the subjunctive, injunctive and optative were merged to form a new category, known (in English) as the subjunctive mood, whose semantic range may be summed up as to do with hypothesis, potentiality and possibility.

In Old English, the subjunctive was formally distinct from the indicative: thus *h+e bundon* 'they bound': *h+e bunden* 'they might have bound'. However, in Late Old English, the obscuration of unstressed syllables meant that this formal distinction was no longer made consistently, and *-an*, *-on, -en* are all used where the meaning of a passage would seem to require a subjunctive mood.

In Present-Day English, only a few fossil formal subjunctives remain, such as *God save the king, If I were you* etc.); the usual pattern is to express subjunctivity through the use of the auxiliary verbs *may* and *might*.

It seems fairly clear that the shift from Old to Present-Day English usage relates to the obscuration of unstressed syllables; since inflectional endings were no longer effective in signalling subjunctivity, other means had to be found for the purpose. It so happened that other Old English verb, *magan,* overlapped semantically with the subjunctive mood. The usual translation offered for Old English *magan* is 'can', 'could'.

Present-Day English *can* includes a semantic component indicating possibility, potentiality, hypothesis etc., and this plainly overlaps with the range of meanings covered by the formal subjunctive. When the formal subjunctive became indistinguishable from the indicative, it is therefore not surprising that another verb, whose variational space overlapped with it, should have taken over its functions.

Subsequent to the grammaticalisation of *magan,* the semantic slot it had previously occupied was taken over by another verb which itself overlapped with it: *cunnan* 'to be able', 'to know how to'. The shift in meaning of these verbs can therefore be seen as a 'chain-reaction', the result of an initial inflectional merger. The whole process, which might be termed the Modal Shift, is expressed in diagrammatic form. The potentiality for the Shift was only activated, and thus became a grammatical change, when the merger of inflectional endings had taken place. The changes in the use of such verbs, in both 'modal' and 'premodal' usage, has been the subject of a study by D. Lightfoot which, although couched in generative terms, is in its essentials highly traditional and along the lines suggested here. Lightfoot shows that the development of 'may' and 'might' to their Present-Day English use was completed quite suddenly in the fifteenth and sixteenth centuries; such 'sudden' completions of linguistic changes are fully explicable within the 'snowball' model which has been developed here.

This shift must have been encouraged, moreover, by a formal factor; *magan* was no prototypical verb, being a member of the so-called 'preterite-present' verb-set. This difference suggests that, like other irregular verbs, *magan* was already on its way to becoming what it has ultimately become, viz. a grammatical auxiliary rather than a lexical verb; this, perhaps, is to be expected, given that *magan* at least in part overlapped semantically with a grammatical rather than another lexical item. Hints of this shift in usage appear even in Late Old English; B. Mitchell notes 'the use of *magan* in the Northumbrian Gospels as an auxiliary in the translation of the Latin subjunctive, e.g. Matt 12.14, *huu hine mæhtes to lose gedoa,* Latin *quomodo eum perderent'*. It may be significant that this usage is recorded earliest in the North of England, where inflectional innovation is most advanced.

From Synthesis to Analysis

It has been indicated already that 'failure' in grammatical change, like 'success', is to do with the way in which an innovation correlates with the larger contextual drift of the language. The major grammatical contextual drift during the history of English has been the steady shift from synthetic towards analytic structures, that is, from a language which marked relationships between words by special endings to one which used a comparatively fixed word-order and separable morphemes such as prepositions. It is time to see how and why this major development took place, and how it relates to the triggering of the specific phenomena described above. Three related grammatical changes are relevant here:

1. The obscuration and loss of inflectional endings;
2. Developments in the use of prepositions;
3. Changes in element order.

Through an examination of the interaction of these three processes, it is possible to trace the shift in English from synthesis to analysis. Of course, the terms 'synthesis' and 'analysis' are relative, and are really the poles of a cline; Old English was much less 'synthetic' than are (for example) Present-Day Finnish or Present-Day Zulu, and Present-Day English is much less 'analytic' than, for example, the varieties of Present-Day Chinese. Nevertheless, there has been definite movement along this cline between Old and Present-Day English, and the three sets of changes here illustrate the processes involved.

1. The first of these phenomena, the obscuration and loss of inflectional endings, has already been touched upon at several points in earlier discussion. It has been observed that obscuration of inflections is a characteristic of a number of the Germanic languages. This development probably originates in the shift to fixed stress which took place during the Proto-Germanic period, that is, soon after the birth of Christ. Before this shift took place, stress was mobile; after it, stress was fixed, usually on the initial syllable of a word. (The Germanic stress-shift is hard to date, probably because it was a gradual and sporadic process; it seems to have varied in its effects on the various Germanic dialects.)

The origins of this stress-shift are still a matter for scholarly debate; a recent plausible suggestion, which has caused some considerable excitement amongst historical linguists, is that it is a contact-phenomenon, the result of interaction between the Northern Indo-European languages (such as Celtic and Germanic) and what is known as Old European.

Old European was a non-Indo-European language which had existed in the northern half of Europe since the last Ice Age 10,000 years or so ago. It was swept aside by the usage of the advancing Indo-European peoples, leaving traces only in a few place-names (notably of rivers) and in a few isolated pockets, represented in the twentieth century by Basque. Old European seems to have had initial stress, and the implication is that Germanic developed a new stress-pattern through what is known as 'substratum influence'.

However it arose, the shift of stress away from inflectional endings made them vulnerable to what might be termed 'phonetic attrition'. It is therefore no surprise that inflectional syncretism results, as has been seen already in a comparison of the Old English and Old Saxon noun-paradigms with the older Gothic practice. And, at later stages in the history of English, the loss of inflections must have been encouraged through interaction with Norse, whose inflectional system was distinct.

2. Most prepositions in Present-Day English derive ultimately from adverbs, and something of this origin is seen in the element-order of Old English. Thus *H– cwæþ þ m mannum tM* and *He cwæþ tM þ m mannum* may both be translated into Present-Day English as 'He spoke to the men', but it is possible in Old English to parse *tM* as either an adverb or a preposition. The adverb *tM,* in Old English an 'extra', 'adjunct' element in the clause with a *lexical* function, has become in Present-Day English an essential *grammatical* word tied to a particular kind of phrase. The process is one of grammaticalisation, as defined on page 142 above. (For the derivation of prepositions from adverbs, see, for example *ODEE* sv. 'to'; the old adverbial use survives in fossil idiomatic expressions such as *to and fro*.)

By the time of recorded Old English, it is possible to establish a group of prepositions (which we will, arbitrarily, take to include the so-called postposition, as in *him tM* 'to him'); but it is still true to state that prepositions were not as essential to the meaning of the text as they are in Present-Day English. Important work by A. Dancev has shown three things:

- 'The more clear-cut a given pattern [in its formal distinctiveness], the higher the probability for the occurrence of prepositionless instances.' Thus, for instance, prepositions are less frequent with the dative plural *-um* than with the dative singular *-e*.
- There is a relation between the meaning of the noun and the presence or absence of a preposition. Words referring to parts of the body, such as *cn–ow, –age, tMð,* and *tunge,* supply the bulk of prepositionless constructions.
- There are 'recurrent collocations [i.e. formulae]', consisting of 'consciously archaic' and stereotypical constructions found in poetry and in the rhythmical prose writings of Archbishop Wulfstan, himself a poet.

There would seem therefore to be definite evidence, from the Old English written record, that prepositions retained the potential of being excluded in favour of more synthetic constructions. The point of pressure is indicated by Dancev's point (i), which suggests that a functional cause lay behind the selection of the prepositional rather than the prepositionless construction, while his points (ii) and (iii) indicate that prepositionless constructions were somewhat old-fashioned by the end of the Old English period.

Dancev's first point has a wider significance, since it suggests that the obscuration of inflections was the principal reason for the selection of prepositions; when the inflection remained distinct, then the preposition was less common. The older view, a strongly functionalist one, was that prepositional phrases had become formalised so that inflectional endings became redundant, and therefore disappeared. However, C. Clark points out that, in the language of the *Peterborough Chronicle* Continuations, Contrary to the view that it was the previous existence of analytic machinery which brought about loss of inflexion, inflexional loss here seems to be more advanced than the procedures needed to replace it. Noun-inflexions [in the Continuations] are virtually reduced to the Modern-English level, whereas the analytic procedures destined to supply their place-fixed word-order, prepositional constructions-are only partially developed.

The quotation from Clark's study leads us to the remaining grammatical development of relevance to the argument at this stage: the institution of a fixed word-order.

Although Old English word-order is certainly more flexible than that of Present-Day English, this is not to say that regular patterns had not emerged. The main element-order patterns in Old English may be roughly summarised as follows (where S=subject, P=predicator): SP appears typically in main clauses (i.e., 'verb-second'; as in Present-Day English, the predicator immediately follows the subject of the clause): for example *Sum swîþe gel red munuc côm sûþan ofer s*'A certain learned monk came from the south over (the) sea.'

S...P appears typically in subordinate clauses (i.e., 'verb-final'; as in Present-Day German, the predicator appears at the end of the clause): for example *þe hit r geseah* 'who had seen it' (*lit*. 'who it formerly saw'). PS appears typically in questions, and after initial adverbials, especially *Þâ* 'then' (i.e. 'verb-initial'; as in Present-Day German, the predicator precedes the subject): for example *Þâ wearð se cyning Ôswold swîðe œlmesgeorn* ' then King Oswald became very charitable'.

These patterns, however, are not strictly adhered to; rather, they are the unmarked patterns, deviation from which is a sign of stylistic salience ('foregrounding'). Thus a skilled writer of prose such as Ælfric was able to adopt unusual word-orders for the purposes of literary effect, for example: *Sço ylce rôd siððan...þ r stôd* 'That same cross stood there afterwards' (*lit*. 'That same cross afterwards...there stood') (main clause).

The traditional view is that Old English is at an intermediate stage where the S…P element-order, characteristic of all clause-types in more archaic Indo-European languages (cf. e.g. Latin), is being steadily replaced by SP element-order: This verb final unmarked order was inherited from proto-Indo-European. A second order, also inherited from proto-Indo-European-verb initial-was a marked order in these early Germanic dialects, used in commands, conjoined clauses, and dramatic sentences. These two orders were evidently supplemented by a third order-verb second-which came on as a strong innovation.

The older S...P ordering as 'unmarked' and available in main clauses appears in the Gothic Bible and in the oldest Germanic runic inscriptions, for instance the famous fourth-century Gallehus horn inscription, transcribed and transliterated. However, by the seventh century runic inscriptions cease to maintain this element-order; a good example from this date is the Early Old Northumbrian runic inscription on the Ruthwell Cross, traditionally interpreted as part of an early version of *The Dream of the Rood:* 'krist waes on rodi' 'Christ was on the cross'.

It would appear that the shift from S…P to SP was well under way by this time. Although Old English word-order, therefore, was still very flexible in comparison with Present-Day English, the key requirement for flexibility, the maintenance of an inflectional system to indicate the relationships between words, was, itself under pressure. As Clark puts it: Sentence structure might *a priori* be expected to become less flexible: for, with subject-noun, object-noun, and indirect-object-noun (and on occasion adverbial noun as well) formally indistinguishable, they may have to take up, as they do in Modern English, set positions with relation to the verb.

Of the three available unmarked Old English word-orders, S…P was unable to resolve this ambiguity when deviated **from** for stylistic effect. SP expressed a clear relationship between subject and verb, and it is undoubtedly for this reason that this structure was the one which succeeded. PS remained longer, but it had always been restricted to a particular set of environments and was not available as a general structural model.

The process, then, seems to have been a therapeutic one. Linguistic ambiguities appeared, and 'second-order' elements, such as emphatic prepositions and a fixed word-order based upon SP structure, took over. The final triggering was, presumably, the increased obscuration of inflectional distinctiveness which marks the shift from Old to Middle English and which was encouraged by the Scandinavian invasions. That ambiguities did exist is demonstrated once more by the *Peterborough Chronicle*. In the Final Continuation a number of ambiguities occur, where the old subordinate clause S…P ordering is retained, as a result of lack of clear inflectional marking, for example:

For œuric rice man his castles makede, ðat ani god hefden (?'for every powerful man, who had any property, made castles for himself').

As Clark puts it, 'the evidence suggests that loss of the dative case, for instance, takes place rather in spite of a lack of substitute procedures than because its functions had already been usurped by them'. Looking back over the three sets of changes described above, one important point might be made: each system produces variation, but the choice of one variable or another as ultimately 'successful' depends on the relationship between systems. To repeat a theme of this book: *tout se tient,* everything is connected to everything else.

The relationship between Old English and post-Old English developments in case and gender, prepositional usage and element-order is one of interactive reinforcement. Over time, a major set of changes in the grammatical structure of English has been brought about; but these changes are the result of a series of minor developments which have constantly interacted over a great number of linguistic states.

These minor developments are the result of variation, deriving both from within the language and as the result of contact with other languages. Case- and gender-endings become slightly obscured as a result of changes in stress-patterns; adverbs become grammaticalised as prepositions in 'marked' conditions and begin to be more commonly used to avoid ambiguities arising from the obscuration of vowels in unstressed syllables; marked word-order patterns are extended to resolve ambiguities; in turn these developments encourage the further loss of inflectional endings whereby case and gender are marked. These individual changes have interacted to produce a major shift in the expression of relationships between words.

With hindsight, it is possible to see why some innovations failed, such as the incipient restructuring of the noun-system to reflect the animate-inanimate distinction in AB-language, the incipient restructuring of the system of modifiers to express case without gender or the growth of the impersonal construction. These innovations were unsuccessful because they did not cohere with the other tendencies in the language towards inflectional obscuration. These innovations were highly sophisticated, but had no future possibilities of development given the 'ecology' of the system. This argument could be pursued further, because the 'success' of the synthetic-analytic shift had implications for other parts of the linguistic system, notably prosody.

A 'typical' Old English phrase is trochaic, consisting of a stressed lexical element and a less stressed inflection, whereas a 'typical' Present-Day English phrase is iambic, consisting of a less stressed modifying element (such as a determiner, a preposition or an auxiliary verb) and a stressed lexical element (such as a main verb or a noun). It is not surprising, therefore, that Old English poetry is based upon a trochaic metre with initial alliteration whereas later metres are ambic, with final rhyme. The interest of this example, of course, is that linguistic changes in one part of the system can have innumerable implications elsewhere in the system: *tout se tient.*

GRAMMATICAL APPEARANCES AND CREATIONS

NON-VERBAL

The grammatical forms and constructions appearing in the diversified literary texts of the 16th and earlier 17th centuries are themselves extremely diversified. Hence it is almost impossible to give a simple and unified description of them. The task would be relatively simple, to be sure, if we were to choose only those literary works composed specifically for an intellectual audience, for their authors were men trained in the forms and usages of classical grammar, and the English they wrote was shaped, almost unconsciously we may assume, towards patterns of correctness like those set down for the Latin language.

As they knew it from classical texts, that language had a very consistent and logical code of relations. Under its influence, questions of English inflection, grammatical agreement and sentence structure were handled more or less consistently by the more learned writers over a long period extending from the age of Humanism to the Commonwealth. The standards of correctness assumed by John Milton in his English prose writing will not be found to be very different from those assumed by Thomas More in his, although certain usages had of course been modified in the interval, and certain constructions of the 16th century had become archaic or had been completely dropped by the latter 17th.

Later the drives towards consistency increase while the structure became markedly simpler. When the survey of grammatical usages is extended to embrace all sorts of writing, from tragedies to comedies, from sermons to popular satire and *novelle*, the situation becomes more complicated. Pamphleteers set themselves the task of gathering and using the locutions of the less educated speakers of English, including derelict members of the underworld.

Writers of comedies strove to reproduce the colloquial language of popular, non-courtly elements in their audiences. On these informal levels of discourse there was a fairly wide range of choice in accidence and syntactic usage. A single author like Shakespeare or Ben Jonson will reveal variations in practice according to the type and level of the discourse. Therefore any description of usages in these matters ought properly to be accompanied by many qualifications.

In a short account we can only indicate in a general way the range of forms and constructions appearing in the typical literary compositions of the age. Some of the constructions would be inadmissible today, but although these are conspicuous, they are by no means in the majority. The simplest manner of presentation will be to call attention to those usages which differ from the modern.

Nouns show an inflectional scheme which is almost without exception identical with today's. An interesting variation appears in the treatment of abstract nouns, which in ModE normally have no plural, except by way of personification. Today an abstraction is regarded as indivisible; the plural of *information* is not *informations* but *pieces of information*. In Shakespeare's time, however, the plural was regularly used in a distributive sense: We'll make our *leisures* to attend on yours; your better *wisdoms*; break not your sleeps for that.

The genitive singular of nouns had developed regularly from the ME ending *-(e)s*. For masculine nouns however a periphrastic form appeared, at least in print, with an enclitic pronoun his functioning instead of -(e)s, for instance: *Mars his* armour for: the armour of *Mars*, or *Mars's* armour. The origin of this construction is in doubt. Although grammatical gender had disappeared, pronoun references sometimes indicate that a few regularly neuter nouns were endowed with a new masculine or feminine gender through a kind of personification, perhaps under the influence of Latin categories.

Hamlet says to Horatio:

Since my dear soul was mistress of her choice,
And could of men distinguish, *her* election
Hath seal'd thee for *herself*.

In *The Tempest Gonzalo* says to his companions: You would lift the moon out of her sphere, if she would continue in it... without changing. Here the Latin nouns *anima* and *luna* may have affected the pronoun references. The same is true of feminine references for the names of countries, as when Deloney writes: Englands valor [sic] was more than *her* wealth.

The pronoun forms were still not completely settled. Among those of the personal inflection, *hit* still appeared in the 16th century for the neuter gender, with genitive *his* and dative *him*. For the second person, the general form *you/ ye* in both singular and plural seems to have gained acceptance more rapidly in upper class groups (aristocracy and wealthy middle class) than elsewhere. The less formal writing of the time reveals the existence of unstressed forms for various pronouns: *'a* [Ù] is written for *he* by Shakespeare; *'em* appears for *them* 't for *it* in contractions like *'tis*, and so on. Dialect passages in the comedies testify to a survival of the old Southern form *ich* for I. It was familiar in contractions like cham for I am and chill for I *will*.

The construction of pronoun forms in the sentences of formal prose was relatively strict, following the patterns familiar in modern prescriptive grammars. But in the more elastic usage of the drama, many deviations may be found, as the following examples from Shakespeare will indicate:

'Tis better *thee* without than *he* within
Praise *him* that got thee, *she* that gave thee suck

...between my good man and *he*
But *she*, I can hook to me
you have seen Cassio and *she* together

Some of these deviations from strict usage arise when the pronoun is separated from the grammatical form (verb or preposition) controlling it. Such a separation permits the speaker to forget or modify the structure upon which he first embarked. Thus the example from *Othello* is understandable because the uninflected noun *Cassio* intervenes between the verb and the inflected pronoun object. If the order were reversed, *Othello* would hardly say: seen *she* and Cassio, even in the most informal conversation; nor would a phrase like: between he and my good man be likely even in a broad comedy like The Merry Wives.

Ellipsis and shifts in construction account for colloquialisms in construction like the one from the Winter's Tale, which is the equivalent of: As far as she is concerned, or: She is the sort who... In addition, it has been pointed out by Jespersen that factors of euphony may have dictated the choice of the oblique for the nominative case, or the reverse: the line cited from Macbeth gains force by its echo of identical vowel sounds in thee: he. Finally, the oblique case is still preferred to the nominative in certain absolute and fragmentary constructions where the pronoun is not joined to the verb, as in Cleopatra's question: Is she as tall as me?, or in contemporary exclamations like: What? Me dance?

A curious example of deviation from modern habits of speech appears in the employment of what we may call a generic singular pronoun of indefinite reference. A plural noun may be followed by a singular pronoun referring to it, when the former designates a group of people. In such cases the singular pronoun stands for a generic representative of the group. The usage is not unknown in ME:

For if there come to an abey to pore *men* or thre And aske of hem helpe par seinte charité, Unnethe wole any don *his* ernde other 'ong or old, But late *him* coure ther al day in hunger and in cold. Here the plural noun *men* is referred to later as *his* in the third line and *him* in the fourth. We find the same sort of substitution of a generic singular for an expected plural in popular literature dealing with types of persons in the nether world: tricksters, vagabonds and the like.

Descriptions of these types frequently begin with a plural noun and then shift to a singular pronoun in reference. An early example is to be found in Copland *Hye Way to the Spitall-House*:

They that dooth to other folkes good dede,
And hath themselfe of other folke more nede,
And quencheth the fyre of another place,
And leueth *his* owne, that is in wors cace,

Whan it is brent, and woteth not where to lye:
To the spyttell than must *he* nedes hye.

Here the shift from plural to singular may have been aided by the ambiguity of the verb form in *-eth*, which in the South might have been either singular or plural. But the same sort of shift is to be found elsewhere, quite frequently. Robert Greene, in the Second Part of Conny-Catching, speaks thus of thieves who use a long-handled hook in robbing: they let it out and hook or curb whatsoever is loose and within reach, and then *he* conueies it to the warp.

John Awdeley, describing the practices of sturdy vagabonds in the 16th century, habitually slips over from a plural noun to a generic singular pronoun: These kynde of deceyuing Vacabondes haue other practises... and when *he* hath agreed of the price, *he* sayeth. Similarly Thomas Harman writes: to one man that goeth abroad, there are at the least two women, which neuer make it straunge when they be called, although *she* neuer knew him before.

Sometimes on the other hand the shift is from singular to plural, as also exemplified in Harman: some yong Marchant man... whose friendes hath geuen them a stock of money... Finally, among the looser constructions of personal pronouns we find two pleonasms already sanctioned by tradition. These are: an anticipatory pronoun doubling for a following noun in the same construction, or a reprise construction. A shift of case construction may occur with either of these pronoun-noun pairs, especially in informal writing. Shakespeare has: my lord, *she and that friar*, I saw *them* at the prison; and: *He* that retires, I'll take *him* for a Volsce. Both of these show incongruity in case construction.

The repeated pleonastic pronoun was used colloquially to gain emphasis as in Ben Jonson's: I scorn it I, so I do, or: another, he cries souldier. Reprise constructions in formal discourse employed the appositional pronoun to recall a noun separated from its verb by a long series of interrupting modifiers. Thus Shakespeare's Ulysses speaks of Achilles as the *proud lord*, and then in the fifth line following returns to him by means of an appositional *he* with repeated auxiliary:

Shall the *proud lord*
That bastes his arrogance with his own seam,
And never suffers matter of the world
Enter his thoughts, save such as do resolve
And ruminate himself, shall he be worshipp'd
Of that we hold an idol more than he?

The anticipatory *it* in apposition with a noun clause or an infinitive was of course sanctioned in the most formal English: Is it not monstrous that this player here... Could force his soul....

The interrogative and relative pronoun forms were also, like the personal ones, handled with considerable freedom in stage dialogues. Of the former, it may be said that the oblique case could be either *who* or *whom*, almost indifferently, as in Hamlet's elliptical question: Between *who?*, and Orlando's complete one: *Who* ambles time withal?. As with the personal pronouns, a crossing of constructions, often due to a parenthetical remark, may lead to a confusion of cases, for instance in the lines: The mariners... *who*, with a charm join'd to their suffer'd labour, I have left asleep. Jonson was somewhat stricter than Shakespeare in his treatment of who / whom as disjunctive interrogative pronoun appearing in head position apart from the verb.

But he too permits who in head position when the governing word is a distant preposition: *Who* would you speak with?; I see *who* he laughed at. An uninflected relative pronoun, giving no overt clue to its construction, may lead to a shift in agreement, as in Shakespeare's lines: 'tis your graces /*That* from my mutest conscience to my tongue /*Charms* this report out. Not only *who* and *which* but also other relative pronouns were still loosely expressed with duplication of forms, as in the 15th century. Thus we find not only *the which* but *the which that*, for persons as well as things, and in the genitive case, *that his* as well as *whose*: A wight *that... his* every step hath left the stamp. Relative pronouns were frequently omitted as in ME and ModE, thus producing asyndetic contact clauses.

Reflexive, indefinite and emphatic pronouns were not as yet fixed in the schemes familiar today, but the differences were not striking. Among the forms then accepted which have since disappeared from the language were: an uninflected plural of *other* (e.g., those *other* came); the simple forms *who, what for whoever, whatever*; reflexive forms lacking the suffix -self (e. g., he clothed *him* hastily).

Though these deviations from modern usage give a special flavour to Tudor and early Stuart English, they do not signify any very important difference in structure. Adjectives and adverbs were in many cases less consistently distinguished than today. That is to say, the suffix *-ly* was less generally used as a sign of adverbial function. Adverbs originally distinguished from cognate adjectives by the suffix -e had long since been made identical with them. Shakespeare and his contemporaries quite freely used Romance as well as Germanic adverbs lacking the typical suffix, in phrases like: wondrous strange, seeming virtuous queen, *noble* spoken, and so on. The use of *more* and *most* in degrees of comparison was still (as previously) not yet fixed according to precise rules.

Periphrastic comparison may appear instead of a suffix with monosyllables (*most vile, most brave*), and polysyllables may employ the suffixes *-er* and *-est*. The choice between periphrasis and suffixation in verse was no doubt sometimes conditioned by rhythms.

The same factor (or else rhetorical emphasis) may have determined the choice of double comparatives and superlatives, which were still current: This was the *most unkindest* cut of all. Regularising of the usages was to occur in the latter 17th and the 18th centuries. The double negative still appears sporadically in the latter 16th century and lingers into the 17th: No king can govern, *nor no* god please.

Verbal Forms and Constructions

The verb forms and their sentence functions reveal some of the most striking deviations from our present standard usage. In discussing them it is particularly difficult to maintain the traditional separation of morphology or accidence from syntax. Concerning the principal parts of verbs and the general division of conjugations into strong and weak, it may be said briefly that the transfer of verbs from the former conjugation to the latter continued steadily. It has been estimated that about 30 verbs were lost to the strong conjugation in the 16th and 17th centuries. Among the surviving strong verbs, there was a perceptible tendency to level preterite and past participle forms into one, as in Shakespeare's: are *broke* and: have *spoke*; have *chose*. The -en ending of strong past participles was lost in some instances, but not universally. We find forms like: is *forgot*, is *writ*, but also: *(be)gotten*.

The *-ed* ending of weak verbs was still frequently syllabic, as versification shows, in formal if not informal speech. The same ending was sometimes omitted from the past participle of weak verbs derived from Latin ones with the suffix *-ate* (itself originally a sign of the past participle). The omission reflected a knowledge of Latin morphology.

In the third person singular of verbs in the present tense, the fluctuation between *-es* and *-eth* no longer has any dialectal significance. In the third person plural, however, the situation is more complicated. Here we find a zero ending in most cases, but also occasionally *-es* and *-eth* also. When one of the two latter appears, the reason may be: (1) that the form chosen was acceptable in general colloquial speech; (2) that it represented a restricted dialect (*-es* for the North and *-eth* for the South); or (3) that it simply resulted from a syntactic confusion on the part of the individual writer.

Shakespeare has: My old *bones aches* in a prose passage, and in verse the line: On chaliced *flowers that lies*, where the choice of an *-es* form may have been dictated in part by the needs of rime. Robert Greene, in the preface to his first tract on the sharp practices of the underworld, writes: my ripe *daies cals*; and later: the three knaues comes. Here the *-es* forms in the plural may be regarded as evidence of Northern dialect influence still affecting Southern English. On the other hand, when Greene and others have expressions like: how doth all our good friends, this verbal form may likewise be regarded as a survival of a Southern plural ending. At the same time Greene also writes: how *fare* all our friends, which is the more usual form (both examples in his pamphlet on *Cosenage*). We deduce that the Southern verbal inflection had a limited currency in London speech of the time.

In some cases the choice of forms may well have been due to a dislocation of the sentence, and the question becomes one of syntax. In a complex sentence probably not clearly thought through, Greene writes: the villanous *vipers*,...being outcasts from God, vipers of the world, and an excremental reuersion of sin, *doth* consent. Here the form *doth* may simply be a shift to the singular resulting from the intervention of modifiers and appositional expressions between subject and predicate. Similarly, ambiguous relative pronouns may cause a shift in agreement, as in Copland's line: These be *they that* dayly *walkes* and *jettes*, or: For all *estates* that thyder *was* comyng. But in the following lines from the Hye Waye, Copland's shift of person from second to third has no such justification, nor need we assume that the form *biddeth* was actually a generally acceptable alternate for the normal *biddest*:

> "Copland," quod he, "art thou a-thyrst, And byddeth me a-fore the to drynke?"

In some instances, particularly in the latter 16th century, unexpected or unusual forms are to be regarded as individual writers' slips and idiosyncrasies, rather than as testimony to a widespread habit of speech. Thus we may interpret the reading in *Julius Caesar*: The *posture* of your blows *is* yet unknown. The unorthodox agreement is natural in rapid dialogue, but would hardly occur in a learned text.

The system of verbal auxiliaries was also diversified and still unsettled as compared with today's. Within the period being discussed there was a marked expansion in the auxiliary use of the verb *to do*. It began to assume four main functions:

- To emphasise the message conveyed by the main or "notional" verb (to use Jespersen's term), as in Othello's lines: Perdition catch my soul But I *do love* thee!, and Orlando's: I do desire we may be better strangers. This appears to have been the first semantic area of expansion.
- To delay the notional verb to a later position in the sentence, especially in negative statements. Shakespeare has: I *do not like* her name, but also: I *like not* that, with the notional verb directly after the subject.
- To formulate questions. The forms of *do* thus permit inversion in word order and yet keep the subject in its normal position preceding the notional verb. Here too Shakespeare's usage in the prose dialogues of his comedies, probably typical of good colloquial speech of the time, may be seen to fluctuate. Rosalind's rapid interrogation of her cousin Celia includes such questions as: What *said he?* How *looked* he? Wherein *went he?* But also: *Did he ask* for me? *Doth he know* that I am in this forest?. When no interrogative word introduces a question, and when both subject and object are nouns, the function

of *do* becomes important in avoiding ambiguity between nominative and accusative constructions. For instance, the question: *Loves the king* the queen? is ambiguous, whereas *Does the king love* the queen? is not. With questions involving pronouns the problem of ambiguity doer not arises, but these too have been attracted into the *do*-pattern in ModE.

- To substitute for a notional verb previously introduced. This function was already familiar in Chaucer. An example from Shakespeare is the line spoken by Octavius to Brutus: Not that we love words better, as you do.

The choice of a construction with *do* or without it was of course sometimes dictated by the needs of verse rhythm. Even in prose — especially oratorical prose, but apparently elsewhere as well — the *do*-constructions may have been favoured at times to obtain a desired cadence of speech.

Other auxiliaries were extending or specialising their scope along with *do*. The verb *to be* began to be used to express an aspect of continuous action for the notional verb. The result was in the end the creation of an entire verbal inflection called the continuous or progressive conjugation in modern grammars. Shakespeare offers fairly numerous examples of this conjugational system: the same pulpit whereto *I am going*; we are still handling our ewes; our thane is coming,. While this function of *to be* was just beginning to expand, another one was contracting: namely the function of an auxiliary forming the perfect tenses with intransitive verbs of motion, analogous to the use of to *have* with transitive ones. Shakespeare still uses *to be* frequently in such locutions: *Is Banquo gone?*; I would the friends we miss *were* safe *arrived*.

While the auxiliary *have* was steadily taking over the perfective function everywhere in popular speech during the 17th and 18th century, formal religious prose remained strikingly conservative in this respect. The reason is that the Authorised Version of the Bible consistently preferred the more archaic treatment of intransitive verbs in the perfect tenses, and these in turn affected sermons and other types of solemn discourse. The auxiliaries *shall* and *will* were moving into the rather complex patterns of modern usage, but the formulation of rules and the strict observance of them belong to the latter 17th century.

Meanings of futurity and desire overlap in *will, would*; of futurity and obligation in *shall, should*; and there were other nuances of meaning as well. Probability and doubt are expressed in clauses like: this *should be* the place; though hell itself *should gape*. Habitual action is expressed by *will, would*: foul deeds *will rise*; and there are still other functions discharged by this pair of auxiliaries. The remaining auxiliaries like *may, can, ought*, which are widely employed in ModE, had a somewhat more restricted currency in the 16th and 17th centuries. This was because the subjunctive mood still functioned then to indicate a number of relations which the auxiliaries have since taken over. The subjunctive appeared in dependent clauses associated with verbs suggesting contingency, desire, command, concession, etc. Reported speech put into the subjunctive may suggest doubt; notice the contrast implied in Othello's statement: I think my *wife be* honest and I think she *is* not. Other illustrations are:

Note if your lady *strain* 'tis fit that Cassio *have* his place
'Tis a shrewd doubt, though it *be* but a dream
I'll cross; it, though it *blast* me
See whe'r Brutus *be* alive or dead

When *if*-clauses expressed a possibility, either indicative or subjunctive might appear: If thou *art* privy to thy country's; fate If thou *hast* nature in thee, bear it not If music *be* the food of love, play on if none *appear*

Conditions contrary to fact are regularly in the subjunctive: if my heart *were* in your hand; if a man *were* porter of hell-gate. Parts of speech were often unconventionally handled in Elizabethan English. A shifting back and forth from verbal use to nominal, from nominal to adjectival, and so on, reflects a stylistic freedom eschewed during the later classical period. Similar to it was the freedom manifested in word formation, whether by the creation of compounds, as in Shakespeare's *heaven-kissing* hill, or by the unconventional attaching of prefixes and suffixes, as in such words as *unpeople* for *depopulate*, and *enskied* for *exalted*.

The shifting of grammatical categories was facilitated, of course, by the loss of inflections in late ME. Rarely by now did any overt sign indicate the part of speech to which any word normally belonged. Shakespeare exemplifies more often than most the ready transfer of parts of speech; and what he was doing boldly, others also did with greater caution.

He uses a noun as a verb in expressions like: how might she *tongue* me, and: *he pageants* us; also an adjective as' a verb: the grief *violenteth*, or a noun as an adjective: my *salad* days / When I was green in judgment. Moreover, normally intransitive verbs may appear as transitive: [this] *dances* my rapt heart, and: he meant to *quail*...the orb. At the same time, Shakespeare was aware that such linguistic practices could easily become ridiculous. He burlesques them in the broken speech of Hugh Evans, a Welsh character in *The Merry Wives of Windsor*, whose imperfect diction is also made comically pretentious: I will *description* the matter to you; can you *affection* the 'oman?

The Beginnings of English Lexicography

The free treatment of parts of speech is but one symptom of an exploratory attitude to language and its techniques characteristic of the later Renaissance in England. The archaising school of poetry, represented by Edmund Spenser, stimulated curiosity about older words, and the influx of new terms from other languages called attention to the variety of the contemporary vocabulary. It is not surprising therefore that the systematic study of that vocabulary had its beginnings in the same period. Linguistic studies in the Middle Ages had not been aided by complete lexical registers for the tongues concerned, not even for Latin.

Only rare and difficult words were usually explained, or synonyms for them were given in the vernacular, in marginal or interlinear notes of individual manuscripts. Such jottings, called glosses, were sometimes listed separately as a kind of appendix to a difficult text. Complete interlinear translations also existed. These aids did not always follow the alphabetic order, however, and each was usually attached to a particular text. The first step towards more systematic presentation was the setting up of word-lists for students' aid, independent of specific texts. Such an aid for schoolboys was the Promptorium Parvulorum, a non-alphabetical English-Latin word-list written about 1440 and published by Caxton's successor Pynson in 1499. Caxton himself had previously published some French-English vocabularies and conversations to aid merchants and other travellers abroad. Wynkyn de Worde and Sir Thomas Elyot also did Latin-English lists. In the mid-16th century these works were superseded by others more closely resembling modern alphabetical dictionaries, but in all of them the purpose served was the mastery of some foreign language, not a better understanding of the native.

Such books included John Vernon trilingual Dictionarium in Latin, English and French; John Withal Short Dictionarie for Yonge Beginners in English and Latin, and Richard Huloet Abecedarium also in English and Latin. This last work contained about 26,000 English words in alphabetical order, followed by the Latin equivalents. Huloet appears to have used a French work by Stephanus, Dictionaire François-latin, besides earlier lists of synonyms and explanations, both Latin-Latin and Latin-English. He included illustrative phrases as well as definitions. The Abecedarium was revised by John Higgins in 1572 and published as Huloet Dictionarie. At the same time, vocabularies for students of Italian and Spanish appeared: Florio Firste Fruites and Stepney Spanish Schoolemaster.

The pioneer dictionary of English terms explained in English was Robert Cawdrey Table Alphabeticall (1604). This made no pretensions to completeness, however. It was limited to rare, difficult words and ones borrowed from foreign languages. Cawdrey, interestingly enough, did not have school-boys in mind as the public expected to benefit primarily from the information he offered.

Rather, he was addressing the newly educated women of the Renaissance, now eager for further knowledge. The alphabetical list was offered, he said, "with the interpretation thereof by plaine English words, gathered for the benefit & helpe of Ladies, Gentlewomen, or any other unskilfull persons." Cawdrey's debt to earlier bilingual dictionaries is apparent. John Bullokar, who is to be distinguished from the Bullokar mentioned, contributed *An English Expositor* which like Cawdrey's had the restricted aim of "teaching the interpretation of the hardest words used in our language." The same limitation appears in the work of Henry Cockeram.

His *English Dictionarie* divided its list of strange and difficult terms into several parts, each alphabetically arranged; the "vulgar" words were for instance separated from the more "refined and elegant" ones. The public he aimed at was apparently broader than Cawdrey's. Among the social groups mentioned are "as well Ladies and Gentlewomen, Schollers, Clarkes, Merchants, as also Strangers of any Nation" who might wish to perfect themselves "in reading, writing and speaking." The usefulness of Cockeram *Dictionarie* to such groups of people was increased by the inclusion of names from classical mythology, which played so large a part in the literary allusions of the time. Later writers in the 17th century built on the first pioneer works, while expanding them through the addition of new areas of terminology. Thomas Blount, the author of a *Glossographia* was a lawyer, and while he made use of various Latin and English dictionaries that had preceded his, he also expanded his material by drawing on a French legal glossary, Rastelle *Termes de la Ley*.

He gave etymologies, and also acknowledged his debt to his predecessors in many if not all instances. Two years later, John Milton's nephew Edward Phillips produced his *New World of Words*, with 11,000 entries. It was indebted to many predecessors, including learned Latin works of the 16th century which indexed geographical, historical, mythological and other terms. Phillips did not always acknowledge his debts nor use them intelligently.

Blount expressed his indignation at the mechanical lifting practised by Phillips, in a diatribe entitled *A World of Errors*. Nevertheless, Phillips *New World* went through a number of later editions. It was used as a foundation for the *English Dictionary* of Elisha Coles, a schoolmaster, who abbreviated what Phillips had given but also expanded it by including words in dialect and cant. A Latin work by StephenSkinner

Skinner, *Etymologicon Linguae Anglicanae*, stressed the origins of English words from various languages, including not only French and Latin but also Anglo-Saxon and what he called "Teutonic." That is to say, Skinner gave analogous forms in Dutch and other Germanic languages. His work was used in turn by an anonymous writer in *Gazophylacium Anglicanum*. Thus considerable foundation work was done in the 17th century, leading up to the lexicographers who were the immediate sources and models for Dr. Samuel Johnson in the 18th.In a less systematic way, meantime, certain writers were beginning to investigate the special jargons of the underworld created by mass unemployment in England. The dispossessed folk who had become sturdy beggars roaming the countryside, or thieves and tricksters inhabiting the nether parts of cities, had developed vocabularies of their own.

Their purpose was in part to evade understanding by the authorities of the law. Writers describing the life of the underworld introduced some of these special terms into their own work, sometimes in a haphazard way, sometimes in the form of short lists with explanations. Copland *Hye Waye to the Spiral-House* offered no glossary, though it included such curious words as:

Bewpere, 1. 497: accomplice, good companion. See *NED* s. v. *beau père*

Cove, 11. 1046 f.: man, person; from the Gypsy. See Partridge.

Feng, 1. 1049: to steal; an alternate form of *fang* in ME.

Frydge, 1. 394: to move restlessly about, to fidget, according to the *NED*, which suggests onomatopoetic origin. But the sense indicates: to beg, from OE *frycgean? Mychers*, 1. 141: "Those be *mychers* that lyue in trewandyse" (truancy).Cf. micher in 1 Henry IV, II, iv, and miching in Haml., III, ii. The *NED* relates *micher*, a secret or petty thief, to the verb *miche* derived from OFr *muchier, mucier*, meaning to hide, to skulk, to lurk.

Rogers, 11. 392 and 410: begging rogues who pretend to be poor scholars. Partridge, citing Copland as authority, relates this to the word *rogue*; but cf. also the name *Roger*. *Sapyent*, 1. 432: a quack who pretends to be a physician; from Latin *sapiens*.

Tomblyng cast, 1. 372, i. e., *tumbling cast; to make a t. c.*: a metaphor for the act of being hanged. It will be seen that these expressions come from many different sources. Some of them died out of currency, others like *cove* have persisted until the present. Here and there in his conny-catching pamphlets Robert Greene introduced short lists of underworld terms. They were grouped together according to the practices dealt with, not in the order of the alphabet. Here are a few examples, slightly revised (for Greene gives his definitions first, his terms last:

Bong, boung: a purse. The term *bung-nipper* for cutpurse persisted into the 18th century (Partridge).

Cuttle-boung: a knife used in cutting the strings of a purse.

Foin: pickpocket. Partridge cites Greene as sole authority for this.

Rutter: "he that maketh the fray," i. e., provokes a planned quarrel.

Shels: "the monie." Special use of the ordinary word *shell?* Partridge does not give this noun, but only the verb derived from the noun, in the sense of: to strip, to hand out, etc. *Smoaking*: "spying of him" (i. e., the victim). Partridge gives only later meanings of the 17th and 18th centuries: to ridicule or affront. The meaning of detection may not be connected with Standard English *to smoke* from OE *smoca*, but with a derivative of OE *smcian*, to flatter or seduce.

Verser: "he that plaieth the game; he that bringeth him [the victim] in."

A short list of names for various types of neglectful apprentices was appended by Awdeley to his *Fraternitye of Vacabondes*, but the elegance of the terms, often derived from Latin, makes them suspect as representatives of genuine underworld cant: *Cory fauell* is he, that wyl lye in his bed, and cory [i e., curry] the bed bordes on which he lyeth in steade of his horse. — Cf. *curry favel* in the *NED*. The expression comes ultimately from the French *Roman de*

Fauvel. *Greene Winchard* is he, that when his hose is broken and hange[s] out at his shoes, he will put them into his shooes againe with a stick, but he wyll not amend them. *Nunquam*, is he that when his Maister sendeth him on his errand he wil not haue done it in halfe an hour or lesse.

Harman also appended to his *Caueat* an alphabetical list of various types of rogues (but without definitions), and a non-alphabetical list of general terms in the "leud, lousey language of these lewtering Luskes and lasy Lorrels," with synonyms by way of explanation. Some typical examples are: *Autem*: a church; origin unknown. Partridge implausibly suggests: from *anthem*.

Bene: good; *benshyp*: very good.

Bowse: to drink. Cf. ModE *booze*, *bouse*, from Middle Dutch *busen*, *bousen*.

Cante: to speak. Probably an alternant form of *chant*, in Northern French dialect, ultimately from Latin *cantare*. *Dup the gyger*: to open the door. Partridge surmises that *dup* is derived from *do open* (not *do up*); *gyger*, the same as *jigger*, has no certain origin. *Gan*: a mouth; probably from Welsh *geneu*, *ganau*, says Partridge. But cf. also Icelandic *gana*, to gape.

Gentry cofes ken: a noble or gentleman's house.

Harmans: the stocks. Cf. *harman*, presumably derived from *hard man*.

Lightmans: the day. Cf. *darkmans*, the night.

Mort, morte: girl or woman; origin unknown (NED). Qualifying terms are used: e. g., *autem morte*, married woman, analogous to *autem cove*, married man. (In this combination, Partridge suggests that *autem* is derived from *altham*, a doubtful word meaning wife. But the derivation from *autem* meaning church seems to be easier and just as plausible.) *Rome*: in various compounds, with the sense of fine or superior. E. g.: *Rome bouse*: wine; *Rome morte*: the Queen; *Rome ville*: London. As may be seen, the etymologies of most of these words are fairly clear. They show very varied origins for the jargon of London's derelicts in the late 16th century. Writers like William Harrison in his *Description of England,* the author of the anonymous *Groundeworke of Conny-Catching*, and Thomas Dekker in his *Belman of London*, plagiarised Harman's terminology, together with his information. Their zeal in doing so testifies to an eager if not yet scientific interest in the language of the underworld of London.

2

Teaching Skills: Micro-Teaching

TEACHING SKILLS

The aim of all teaching activity is to facilitate and support student learning. Doing this in the best possible way is to show teaching skill.

TEACHING QUALIFICATIONS AND TEACHING SKILLS

Support for student learning can take many different forms. Some support activities can be directly perceived by the students. Other activities are less apparent, but still important since they help create good working conditions for teachers and students and thereby have an influence on student learning. Teaching (including supervision and examination), the preparation of study guides and learning material, the development of courses and new methods, efficient administration and good pedagogical leadership are examples of different types of pedagogical work. Of importance is also what the teacher has done to develop and maintain his or her pedagogical competence. The different pedagogical activities a teacher has performed are all part of his or her teaching qualifications. These teaching qualifications are what the teacher presents as a basis for an assessment of teaching skills. Teaching skills are related to the way in which the teacher has performed the activities. The assessment of teaching skills should focus on how the teacher works, not what the teacher has done.

DEVELOPMENT OF SPECIFIC TEACHING SKILLS

Teaching can be analysed in terms of teacher behaviour at least at three levels, namely, teaching skills, general teaching behaviours and specific teaching behaviours. At 'the first level, teaching can be analysed into component teaching skills. Following the analysis at this level, teaching can be defined as a set of component skills for the realisation of a specified set of instructional objectives. It means teaching itself is a complex skill comprising of a set of teaching skills. These teaching skills can be further analysed into sets of general teaching behaviours at the second level. Thus, teaching skills can be defined as a set of interrelated teaching behaviours for the realisation of specific instructional objectives. The set of instructional objectives to be realised by a particular skill will be limited in number as compared to the totality of instructional objectives. These teaching behaviours can be further analysed into specific teaching behaviours at the third level of analysis. These teaching behaviours of a skill, therefore, can be defined as a set of interrelated specific teaching behaviours contributing to the realisation of some aspects of the instructional objective to be realised by a particular teaching skill.

CONCEPT OF TEACHING SKILLS

"Teaching constitutes activities that are designed and performed to produce change in student behaviour." Komisar has pointed out that various specific activities included in teaching are introducing, demonstrating, citing, reporting, confirming, questioning, elaborating, etc., which may be considered as constituent skills of teaching. In simple words, teaching constitutes a number of verbal and non-verbal teaching acts like questioning, accepting student responses, rewarding, smiling, movements, gestures, etc. These acts in particular combinations facilitate the achievement of objectives in terms of student growth. A set of related teaching acts or behaviours performed with an intention to facilitate students' learning can be called a teaching skill. 'Teaching skills are specific instructional techniques and procedures that a teacher may use in the classroom'. The Asian Institute for Teacher Educators has defined teaching skills as 'specifically those activities of teaching that are especially effective in bringing about desired changes in students'. Mc Intyre and White have defined the term teaching skills as 'a set of related teaching behaviours which in specified types of classroom interaction situations tend to facilitate the achievement of specified types of educational objectives'.

Teaching Skills

You have already understood the concept of a teaching skill.

Introducing a Lesson

When one introduces a stranger to you, your reactions towards him/her or your responses during the conversation with him/her depend upon the introductory statements that are made about him/her. Similarly, when a teacher introduces a lesson or a unit, he/she gives a brief introduction about the lesson or the unit, in order to draw the students' attention to it. Generally, an introduction to a lesson includes what the teacher does with or without the help of the students upto the stage of stating the aim of the lesson. Teachers differ from each other in the way they introduce a lesson. Studies have shown that the students' learning of the new lesson or unit largely depends on the way the lesson is introduced. A teacher must possess the necessary skill to introduce a lesson or unit in an effective manner.

The components of the skill of introducing a lesson are:

- Desirable behaviours:
  - *Using previous knowledge*: The previous knowledge refers to knowledge already possessed by the students. If any new knowledge is to be added to the previous knowledge, there should be a logical continuity between them. New knowledge should also be relevant to previous knowledge of students. When we present new knowledge to the students, we have to bring their previous knowledge to their conscious level.
  - *Using appropriate devices*: Here, 'device' refers to the technique that a teacher uses while introdu-cing a lesson. Such devices can be:
  - Use of examples
  - Questioning
  - Lecturing describing narrating
  - Story telling
  - Dramatisation
  - Audio-visual aids and
  - Experimentation. The appropriateness of the use of each of these devices depends on its suitability to the maturity level, age level, grade level, interest, experience of the students and also on the lesson to be taught.
- Undesirable behaviours:
  - *Lacking in continuity*: Continuity refers to the sequence of ideas or information being presented. While introducing a lesson, continuity breaks when the statements made for questions asked by the teacher are not logically sequenced.
  - *Making irrelevant statements*: A statement or a question which a teacher makes while introducing a lesson, is said to be irrelevant when it is not related to the aim of the lesson. Such statements or questions do not contribute to the effectiveness of the skill in terms of establishing rapport with the students. Sometimes such statements also confuse the students.

Explaining

In our day to day life you find persons explaining some idea or phenomenon by going deep into the matter with appropriate examples, logically organising the ideas, using certain non-verbal gestures, etc. You also find persons who cannot explain clearly. They jumble up ideas. They not only confuse the audience but also get confused themselves. This is because they do not present ideas in a logical sequence. In classrooms right from grade I through higher grades, a teacher explains ideas and concepts. It is a most commonly used skill and is the essence of instruction. When a student does not clearly understand the ideas which his/her teacher tries to convey, he/she generally asks for an explanation.

A teacher is said to be explaining when he/she is describing 'how', 'why' and sometimes 'what' of a concept, phenomenon, event, action or condition. Explanation can also be defined as an activity to bring about an understanding in someone about a concept, principle, etc. Explanation involves filling up the gap in one's understanding of the new phenomenon by relating it to his/her past experience. Thus, explanation depends on the type of the past experience, the type of the new phenomenon and the type of relationships between them.In a classroom, an explanation is a set of interrelated statements made by the teacher related to a phenomenon or an idea, in order to bring about or increase understanding of the students about it. While giving explanation, we generally explain causes of the phenomenon, reasons for the action, various steps involved in arriving at the particular result, or various events that have occurred earlier resulting in the event being explained. All such causes, reasons, steps, events, etc., are called 'antecedents'. Such antecedents result in the phenomenon, event, result or action. Each of these is known as a consequent. Thus an explanation involves giving antecedents to a consequent, which can be diagrammatically presented as follows:

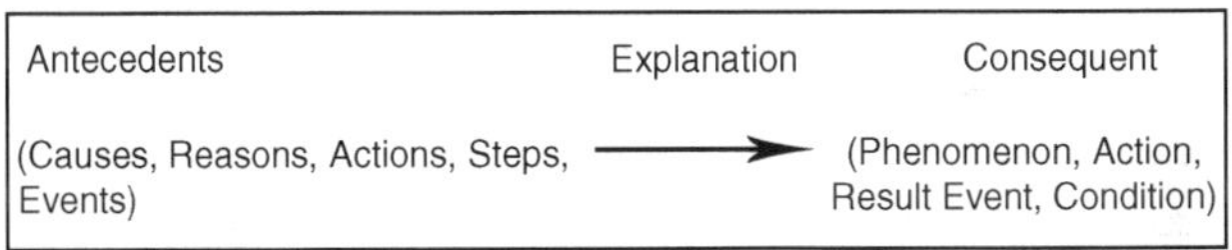

There are various techniques through which we can explain an idea, phenomenon, etc. They are question-answer technique, use of audio-visual aids or by making certain related statement concerning what we have to explain. Sometimes we use all the techniques simultaneously to make explanation more effective. To summarise, the desirable teacher behaviours for effective explanation should include, using only relevant statements, having continuity in statements, using vocabulary which the students know, being fluent in speech, avoiding vague words and phrases, using beginning and concluding statements and testing students' understanding by putting a few questions.

Questioning

Questioning is an important teaching skill that a teacher must learn. A teacher needs to put meaningful questions to the students during the teaching-learning process. You may be curious to know more about 'meaningful questions'.

CHARACTERISTICS OF EFFECTIVE TEACHING STRATEGY

For educational communication to be effective, a proper teaching strategy needs to be adopted. The selection of suitable teaching strategy depends upon the task, context and the teacher's discretion.

Nonetheless, a good strategy:

- Captures and maintain interests;
- Interprets the concepts clearly;
- Encourages critical thinking;
- Applies the learning in problem-solving; and
- Stimulates self-learning.

For this, it is important to select and organise the material taking into consideration learners' abilities, interests and psychological factors into mind. The sequencing of information, *i.e.*, moving from familiar to unfamiliar, simple to complex, general to specific and concerte to abstract needs to be done. Utilisation of illustrations, audio-visual aids, humour, questions use of exercises and assignments for continuous assessment increases the level of interest of students. Short, active responses during the course of the listening facilitate a greater degree of attentiveness and active participation by children.

Communication for Enhancing Children's Competencies

Communication enables development of listening and speaking skills for acquiring new concepts. While planning suitable tasks we need to bear in mind the age level and the interests of the children. The same activity can be varied for different age groups.

While planning suitable listening speaking and comprehension activities for learners, the following questions need to be raised:

- What type of listening activities actually go on in real life?
- What are the particular difficulties likely to be encountered by learners when coping with them?

We would like our children to go through activities which equip them to deal with real life situations effectively. In order to do this we have to create situations in the classroom which are as close to real life as possible.

To do this, we might need to look at:

- *Environment clues*: These include the facial expressions, posture, eye-direction, proximity, gesture and tone of voice of the speaker. In addition, related noises, visual materials such as illustrations, diagrams or maps may be deliberately introduced to make the listening experience as close to real life as possible.
- *Communication in real life*: Communication is interrupted by various stimulus such as person, action, visuals, happenings, etc., in the environment. In real life, stretches of heard speech are broken up by being spoken by different people from different directions. Even when there are long periods of seemingly uninterrupted discourse-talks, instructions, anecdotes, etc., these are often broken down into smaller units by the physical movement of the speaker - pauses, audience reaction, changing environmental clues. More formal stretches of

speech - lectures, broadcasts, reports are usually less interrupted.

- *Formal/Informal communication*: It is necessary to draw a distinction between formal and informal communi-cation used in most spontaneous conversations. You would have noticed a range of formality, stretching from the extremely formal (speeches, lectures), to the fairly formal (news reading), to the fairly informal (television interviews), to the very informal (gossip, conversations, phone chats). As teachers, you need to be aware of these aspects to identify the special characteristics of speech that go with the degree of formality for effective communication.

There is a distinct difference between the auditory effect of a piece of spoken prose and that of informal conversation. The former is characterised by a fairly even pace, volume and pitch. Spontaneous conversation, on the other hand, is jerky, has frequent pauses and overlaps, goes intermittently faster and slower, louder and softer, higher and lower. Hesitations, exclamations, emotional reactions of surprise, irritation or amusement are bound to cause uneven and constantly changing rhythm of speech. Informal speech also contains a lot of colloquial terms, which are often spontaneous. The listener needs to develop some skills to identify the characteristics of this kind of speech. The message of a piece of spontaneous talk is delivered much more slowly, with a lot of repetition and irrelevant talk, than that of a rehearsed or planned speech.

In addition to preparing the activities keeping real life aspects in view, you can use variety of occasions in classroom to impart the skills of listening for:

- Main ideas,
- Important details,
- Sequence of events.

In this context, let us discuss two types of problems that have been identified to be most resistant for instructions:

- *Overuse of preferred information*: Many pupils tend to ignore important information and rely excessively on the facts that appeal to them. Their attention has to be consciously drawn to other relevant facts.
- *Lack of comprehension monitoring*: Many pupils tend to understand narratives, descriptions and explanations one fact at a time, without being able to evaluate the facts or see inconsistencies in the facts. They need to be given several such tasks, initially as reading tasks, where their eyes can move back and forth to detect inconsistencies. Later similar tasks can be given as listening task. The stories they have heard, the places they have visited, the home environment, the programmes they have been listening to on television all provide the backdrop against which they able them to view and give meaning to the various sounds. You can specifically develop tasks which will help

children to improve some particular aspects of their listening. Efficient, active attentive listening needs to be taught at all grade levels.

Teacher-Pupils' Communication

Different types of communication serve different purposes. We can utilise these effectively to facilitate teacher-pupils' communication.

Interpersonal Communication

The teacher who values good rapport with children takes time to listen to children. This is where the student and the teacher have a real opportunity to grow and to change together. Generally, teachers say eighty per cent of the words in classroom. S/he may try to maximize informal interactions this would increase interaction amongst students. Endless repetition can be avoided by challenging children to listen carefully.

If additional clarification is required, the children should be encouraged to help each other. New topics, instructions and activities need to be planned carefully to correlate with the child's attention span. Variety adds interest, renewed enthusiasm and better listening opportunities in the classroom. They should not become tedious, boring or overwhelming. You also need to reward and commend good behaviour.

Sincere statements to the class at appropriate times might include:

- I appreciate your attention to what was taught.
- I can tell by your answers that you're listening carefully for main ideas.
- I see that you stopped what you were doing to be ready for these directions.

Individual statement of appreciation and observation are always prized by children. Honest, non-judgemental, positive feedback is a reward highly valued by students. These type of comments as quite different from empty praise. It specifically tells students what the teacher values in their task or behaviour. Children will often follow the teacher's example by commenting on good listening by their peers.

COMMUNICATION SKILLS

COMMUNICATION: THE CONCEPT

The word 'communication' is derived from Latin word, 'communis' meaning commonness of experiences. However, communication cannot be defined through a single definition. Different people perceive it in different ways in different contexts. Communication has heen described as "the transfer of conveying of meaning", "transmission of stimuli,' 'one mind affecting another'; 'the mechanism through which human relations exist and develop, or sharing of experience on the basis of commonness". Communication involves interchange of meaning among individuals. This occurs mainly through verbal and non-verbal symbols, such as language, gestures - a shrug of the shoulders, a nod, facial expressions and actions. Same cultural context makes communication easier because words essentially represent what members of a society decide it would stand for. The knowledge of these symbols, signs and meanings is essential for effective communication. For example, let us take a simple word like 'chair'. To some, it may be a thing to sit on, however, in certain other contexts, it can denote a desired position. Thus we realise that pattern system of communication are influenced by sociocultural- political and economic contexts. Depending on the environment or surroundings in which communication takes place, it can be defined as a process of sharing or exchange of ideas, informataion, knowledge attitudes or feeling among two or more persons to elicit the desired/intended response.

Elements of Communication

Communication is a dynamic process involving active interaction between sender and receiver and variety of inputs. Effective use of communication in a classroom situation between teacher-pupil or pupil-pupil can accelerate the pace of actions.

Following are the elements of communication:

- Source
- Message
- Channel
- Receiver
- Feedback

The Source

Source is the communicator. S/he encodes the purpose in the form of a message, to pass it on to receiver and also decides the medium-channel to use for communication.

The Message

Message may be an idea, information or attitude. It can be purposive or non-purposive. Messages drafted for achieving the specific behavioural objective are purposive. Messages with no intention to influence the behaviour are formed as non-purposive. For effective communication, the messages should be short, precise and in simple language. Clarity of message and style of presentation can enhance the effect of communication.

The Channel

The channel for communication is a medium, a carrier of information from the source to receiver and *vice-versa*. This may be verbal, non-verbal, written, printed, visual, etc. TV, Radio, newspaper, etc., are used as means for mass communication.

The Receiver

The receiver is recipient of the message. In the case of mass media, the readers, viewers and listeners are the receivers. In a classroom situation, the teacher is the source, the message is the instruction/lesson and pupils are the receivers.

The Feedback

Receiver's response to communicator's message and *vice-versa* is termed as the Feedback. Feedback is quick in face-to-face communication. This may be verbal or non-verbal. Receiver's feedback to the communicator becomes a stimulus for him/her. This provides an opportunity to gauge the effectiveness of communication and helps in improving the quality of further communication when needed.

Process of Communication

Communication is a necessary condition for growth and transmission of cultures, the continuity of societies and the effective functioning and control of social groups. The process of communication involves interaction between the communicating individuals. In education communication the response (feedback) evoked in the receiver (learner) becomes a stimulus for the communicator (teacher) to which s/he responds. Thus, in face-to-face communication, the source (teacher) and receiver (teacher-student) are at once both response and stimuli. This process continues between the players (source and receiver) in conversation game in which a number of intervening variables such as individual differences, levels of perception, motivation level, etc., are involved.

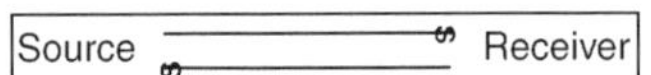

Another important feature of communication is that the recipient (teacher) infers from the behaviour of communicator (pupils), what idea or feeling the other person is trying to convey. S/he then reacts not to the behaviour but to the inferred idea or feeling. The other person then reacts to his/her response in terms of his/her inference of the idea/feeling and the meaning behind it. Communication accomplishes its purpose accurately if the message is interpreted in the same way by the communicator and by the recipient of the communication. Communication depends on the comprehension and communication skills of the individuals.

ENQUIRY TRAINING

Enquiry training model was developed by Richard Suchman to teach students a process for investigating and explaining unusual phenomena. The main objective underlying the model was that the scientific process skills are developed in the students to enable them to organise data, reason about cause and effect, and build and test theories. He modeled the model along the lines of the methods employed by creative researchers especially scientists. He identified the components of the enquiry process and built them into an instructional model which he called 'enquiry training'.

Suchman bases his enquiry training approach on four postulates. First, children are curious and eager to grow by nature. He emphasises that when children are faced with a puzzling situation they naturally get motivated to explore the data surrounding the discrepant event and think of arranging the data in a new way to find answers to the problem. The general goal of enquiry training is to help students develop the intellectual discipline and skills necessary to raise questions and search out answers stemming from their curiosity. Secondly, the process of enquiry can be taught to students. Suchman believe that students can become increasingly conscious of their process of enquiry, and that they can be taught scientific procedures directly. He emphasises that we can not analyse and improve our thinking unless we are conscious of it.

Thirdly, team approach is more useful than the individual approach to find solution to a problem.Suchman believes that the view point of a second person enriches our thinking; and that it is the cooperative enquiry that leads to the development of new knowledge. Fourthly, all knowledge is tentative. Suchman emphasises that the students should be made aware of the fact that all knowledge is tentative. Scholars constantly generate theories and explanations. After sometime, these theories are replaced by new ones, which conveys that there are no permanent answers to problems; new and sophisticated ways are investigated to' reach the solution of the problem, or new ways are detected to look at the problem itself.

Enquiry Training Process

In 'Enquiry training', the students are presented with a problem situation such as, an episode, experiment, story, etc., and are asked to enquire into it. In whatsoever form it is presented, it must essentially carry a discrepancy leading to a puzzle. Since the ultimate goal is to have students experience the creation of new knowledge, the confrontation should be based on discoverable ideas. After the presentation of a puzzling situation, the students are encouraged to ask questions. These questions have to be worded in the way that they are answered by a 'yes' or 'no'. The students are not to ask the teacher to explain the phenomenon to them, however, they can ask questions that are responded by the teacher only in a 'yes' or 'no'. Whenever a question can not be replied in a 'yes' or 'no' response, the teacher reminds them of the rules, and waits until they find a way of rephrasing the question in proper form. Comments such as, 'can you restate this question so that I can answer it with a 'yes' or a 'no' are common teacher responses when students slip out of the enquiry mode'.

Thus, at the first stage of the enquiry process, the students are taught to verify the facts of the situation, *i.e.*, the nature and identity of the objects, the events, and the conditions surrounding the puzzling event. As the students become aware of the facts, they form hypotheses, which guide them in their future enquiry. Using their knowledge about the behaviour of objects, students can turn their questions to the variables in the situation.

This they can do by conducting verbal or actual experiments to test these causal relationships, selecting new data, or organising the existing data in a new way to see what will happen if things are done differently. It may not be possible for the students to frame proper questions to test the causal relationships between variables unless they have sufficient information about the nature of the problem situation and its elements, and it is likely that they are to be overwhelmed by the many possible causal relationships. Finally, the students try to develop hypotheses that will fully explain what happened. In other words, it means that they reach the final explanation. However, they need to be cautioned that there can be many possible explanations, therefore, they should not be satisfied with the first explanation that appears to fit the fact. The main emphasis in this approach is on becoming aware of and mastering the enquiry process and not the content of any particular problem situation. The teacher also need not be too concerned with subject matter coverage or 'obtaining the right answer' for the reason that it would violate the real spirit of scientific enquiry, which emphasises team approach of searching together for more accurate and powerful explanations for every day phenomena.

Phases in Enquiry Training

There are five phases (steps) in the enquiry process. The first phase is the student's confrontation with the puzzling situation. The second and third phases concern with the data gathering mechanisms of verification and experimentation. In the fourth phase, students organise the data and try to explain the discrepancy. Finally, in the fifth phase, the students reflect on the problem solving strategies they use during the enquiry.

These phases are explained in some more details given below:

- *Phase-I*: *Encounter with the problem*: In this phase, the teacher is required to present the problem situation or puzzling event and explain the enquiry procedures to the students. The teacher is required to satisfy himself/herself that the students have understood the enquiry procedure (pattern of the yes-no question) and also the objectives fully. Then he/she can present problem situation to the students, which should essentially carry a discrepancy. The problem to be posed should be simple such as a puzzle, riddle, or magic trick that does not require much background knowledge. However, every puzzling situation can not be a discrepant event. It is, therefore, important to note that distinguishing feature of the discrepancy events is that it involves illogical phenomena that conflicts with the notions of reality. A problem may be puzzling simply because we do not know the answer, but simultaneously we do not need new concepts to understand it and therefore we do not need to conduct an enquiry. Thus, the problem to be taken for enquiry should essentially accompany a discrepancy but care needs to be taken that it matches with the cognitive level of the students.

- *Phase-II*: *Data gathering verification*: In this phase, students gather information about the problem in hand through observation or experience They are required to ask questions about objects, properties, conditions, and events in order to verify the information. Objects refer to determining the nature or identifying of objects. Properties refer to verifying the behaviour of objects and events are related to verifying the occurrence of an action. Wherever students deviate from verifying all the aspects of the problem, the teacher reminds them of the rules of the process and makes them aware of the type of information they are likely to seek and put them to work to change the questioning pattern.
- *Phase-III*: *Data gathering experimentation*: In this phase, students introduce new elements into the situation to see if the event happens differently. Exploration serves two functions, that is, exploration and direct testing. Exploration refers to changing things in order to see what will happen though it is not necessarily guided by a theory or hypothesis, but it may suggest ideas for a theory. Direct testing refers trying out a theory or hypothesis. The hypothesis determines the direction of data gathering. If the gathered data do not support a hypothesis, it is rejected and consequently alternate hypothesis is formulated and the process is repeated. Although verification and experimentation are described as separate phases of the enquiry training approach, yet the students' question usually alternate between these two phases of data gathering. The teacher does not need to be very rigid in following these two phases separately instead he/she should encourage students to generate questions that pertain to data gathering and consequently lead them to formulate the explanation.
- *Phase-IV*: *Formulating an explanation*: In this phase, the teacher calls on the students to formulate an explanation. It is possible that different students may put forward different explanations, however, some students may have difficulty in making the intellectual leap between the data they have gathered and a clear explanation. It is also possible

that they may give inadequate explanations omitting essential details. It has been experienced that sometimes several theories or explanations are possible based on the same information. In view of this, it is useful to ask all the students to state their explanations so that the range of differences is revealed. It is believed that the groups together can shape the explanation that fully responds to the problem situation.

- *Phase-V: Analysis of the enquiry process*: In this phase, the students are asked to analyse their pattern of enquiry. This would help them in finding out the questions that were most effective; the lines of questioning that were most productive and those that were not; or the type of information they needed but could not obtain. The teacher asks students to recall the question they have raised and to identify those questions that led them to explanation but not others. In this way, the teacher goes on repeating the whole process of enquiry so as to make students aware about the pattern of questions needed to be raised during the phases of verification and experimentation that have helped them to reach at final explanation and also making the enquiry process conscious one so that steps are systematically taken to improve it.

Enquiry training approach promotes active, autonomous learning as the students themselves formulate question and test ideas. It calls upon students to take courage to ask questions, and helps them to become more proficient in verbal expression as well as in listening to others and remembering what has been said. The chief learning outcomes of this approach are the involvement of varied processes such as observing, collecting and organising data, identifying and controlling variables, framing and testing hypotheses, formulating explanations and drawing inferences. The magnificent integration of these several process skills into a single, meaningful unit of experience is the chief characteristic of this approach.

This all depends when both the students and the teacher try for their balanced roles. The teacher selects the problem situation in accordance with the students' cognitive level; acts as a referee throughout the enquiry process; responds warmly to students' question; brings them back on the right track if they deviate; facilitate discussion and interaction among students; and finally helps them to arrive at explanations. The students on the other hand, actively participate in finding out the discrepancy from the problem; raising pinpointed questions; process data in a systematic sequence; tolerating ambiguity; and formulating explanations.

THE STATE OF LITERACY LEARNING

As Carroll figured out well over 100 years ago, and as readers of this volume will discover, time is of the essence. This is especially true when it comes to teaching all of America's children to be literate in the technological world of the 21st century, because all children, including those with disabilities, must now participate in the high-stakes assessment that states and school districts use to authenticate educational achievement. Standards-based educational reform efforts require that states and local school systems be held accountable for the learning of all children.

Federal legislation, including Goals 2000 of the Elementary and Secondary Education Act (ESEA) and the 1997 reauthorization of the Individuals with Disabilities Education Act. require that all students participate in large-scale state and local assessment programmes. The provision is that testing accommodations must be provided to those students with special needs who require such accommodations, including children with disabilities and those with limited English proficiency. For those children who are unable to take part in the general assessment, alternate assessments are proscribed. Further, the performance of students on state and district assessments who receive special education and related services must now be separated from the scores of other students and reported publicly, as are the scores of students in general education. At the end of 1999, preliminary data from 12 states indicated that the majority of students in special education required accommodations for reading, writing, and math assessments. Also, during the 1990s, in combination with federal and state requirement for large-scale assessments, substantial amounts of state and federal dollars were invested to raise the academic achievement of children chronically struggling with literacy.

In addition, the National Institutes of Health funded major research projects, as described in this volume, to achieve two purposes: One was directed to the identification of the cognitive and linguistic underpinnings of learning to read, and the other concerned in-depth study of evidence-based instructional practices that either prevented or ameliorated reading failure. As the new millenium begins, an important question is whether these efforts, grounded in standards-based educational reforms, resulted in positive changes in reading abilities across the diverse populations of American school children in general and special education.

Despite the concerted fiscal, research, and reform efforts of the 1990s, the 2000 National Assessment of Educational Progress (NAEP; National Centre for Education Statistics [NCES], 2001) continues to paint a distressing portrait for grade 4 reading achievement for the children who are the primary focus of this volume. For example:

- 37% of all grade 4 students are reading below the basic level when a proficient level of achievement is the expected standard. Reading below a basic level means that not even partial mastery had been attained of the knowledge and skills essential for comprehending narrative and informational texts. Importantly, proficiency in reading comprehension is defined as students' ability to "demonstrate an overall understanding of the text, providing inferential as well as literal information ... drawing conclusions, and making connections to their own experience".

- 71% of Caucasian students and 78% of Asian American students read at or above the basic level, whereas 35% and 46% of these two groups, respectively, read at the proficient level.
- The reading performance for 63% of African American students and 58% of Hispanic students in grade 4 fell below the basic level. Moreover, 60% of those from poverty level homes and 47% of children attending inner city schools were reading below the basic level.
- Finally, 39% of students who required accommodations to take the NAEP (e.g., one-on-one testing, small group testing, extended time, or the oral reading of directions) performed below the basic level. Only 30% demonstrated basic knowledge and skills for reading comprehension.

Two cautions are warranted in interpreting these data. First, population comparisons found to be statistically significant, such as the selected comparisons for race, ethnicity, or both, cannot be interpreted as statements about the absolute practical significance, or educational relevance, of the differences among these subgroups. Instead, the NCES urges that findings on subgroup differences should be used to inform and extend meaningful dialogue among the many members of the educational constituency, from policy makers to educators and the public, about the scope of the problem and its possible solutions.

Second, causal inferences cannot be made to how reading is taught in public schools because of the host of sociocultural and socioeconomic (SES) factors that are outside of teachers' control. These external factors also influence all aspects of learning to be literate. However, in regard to SES variables, recent longitudinal findings on home-school links between language and literacy development showed that excellent pre-school experiences in language and literacy learning can counteract home experiences that "offer well below average access to language and literacy support".

Given these two qualifications, the 2000 report card shows a widening of the gap in reading abilities. Good readers improved their scores, whereas poor readers fell further behind. But there are other gaps that contribute in significant ways to the failure to meet adequately the literacy needs of all children. Among these gaps are the disciplinary and professional schisms that continue to exist among researchers and professionals, who, by virtue of their diverse training and interests, hold different views on, or have different levels of understanding about, the central role of language in learning. One outcome is the translation of these divergent views into practices that are often incompatible with conceptual frameworks and evidence about relationships between the multiple dimensions of language and literacy learning. As Lewis Carroll voiced through the Walrus, the time has come to talk across disciplines and professions, as this volume seeks to do, about the overarching importance of language in the educational lives of children. The central thesis of this text is that human communication underlies the ability to benefit from spoken and written discourse.

ROLE OF LANGUAGE IN LITERACY LEARNING

Language is a tool for analyzing, synthesizing, and integrating what is heard or read in order to construct and express new interpretations. Early on, Halliday (1987) noted the absence of attention to spoken language processes in children's literacy:

Educational investigators of the fifties and early sixties were not concerned with the particular place of spoken language in the learning process. It was assumed that students learnt by listening, but the expository aspects of teacher's language were given little attention, while the notion that a student might be using his own talk as a means of learning was nowhere part of the picture.

Unlike the picture that Halliday painted of earlier decades, a significant number of disciplines are now engaged in the study of language. These disciplines include, among others, education, developmental psychology, the neurosciences, bilingual language learning, linguistics (including psycholinguistics), language science (specifically, speech—language pathology), and special education (particularly learning disabilities). Each discipline or specialty approaches the study of language from its own perspective, which makes for enlivening commentary and, occasionally, valuable new insights.

One of the critical insights that emerged from the research conducted during the late 1980s and the 1990s, is the crucial role of phonological sensitivity and phonological processing in children's ability to master the alphabetic principle and develop automatic and fluent word recognition and spelling skills. *Phonological sensitivity* generally refers to the ability to consider the units of phonological structure at increasingly deeper levels of analysis, from the syllable level to the segmental (phonemic) level. *Phonological processing* pertains to those information processing capacities that are recruited by various tasks and require some level of more explicit analysis, such as segmentation, blending, or sound deletion (phonological awareness), the repetition of nonwords (phonological memory), or rapid naming (phonological retrieval).

Letter name knowledge, knowledge of letter-sound names, and well-integrated phonemic awareness (sound-letter correspondences) are now well documented as the strongest kindergarten predictors of how adequately children will learn to read and spell in grade 1. Phonological retrieval, as assessed by rapid naming tasks, may contribute more to individual differences in reading fluency at grade 4 rather than index the speed of accessing the segmental level in earlier grades.

Contemporary models of reading disability from both the neuroscience and psychoeducational literature share the unitary view that a phonological core deficit is a primary cause of reading failure. This view has also been described as a causal chain model. Because the phonological route to recognize word meaning is not utilized efficiently, children do not have access to the meaning of print words, a situation that also affects their memory for spellings. Subsequent problems with text comprehension and related consequences, such as the development of more literate vocabulary and syntactic constructions that are facilitated through reading, are then attributed to breakdowns at the level of phonological processing. Because of the strength and stability of this scientific evidence, new avenues have opened for the early identification of risk factors and the prevention, or reduction in the severity, of reading failure. Moreover, the current cross-disciplinary consensus is that the phonological core deficit represents a language-related impairment.

In spite of this basic consensus, a significant disparity exists among disciplines and their associated professions in the scope and meaning of "language-related." This discrepancy has enormous significance for the conduct of research, as well as for the implementation of instructional programmes for struggling readers as a group, regardless of whether these readers receive general education, special education, or related services. Two perplexing questions are unresolved.

One concerns whether the spoken language basis of the "critical component skills" that comprise word recognition skills and that have been implicated in the failure to read and spell as the phonological core deficit is a first-order cause, or do other language subsystems make significant contributions to the picture of a phonological core deficit? The second question pertains to the "fuzzy boundary" issue. Are a language disability and a learning (reading) disability two sides of the same coin? Or do they represent separate and distinct conditions, which may co-occur, but are not identical? The fuzzy boundary issue is not trivial because the recognition of a boundary has been codified in IDEA for over 25 years.

Alanguage impairment and a learning disability are defined as two separate categories of disabilities. At the school level, this separation has resulted in the fragmentation of services for the very children who most need instructional and related services that are coherent, integrated, and coordinated. At the research level, dissimilar disciplinary interests in the domains that influence literacy development, such as "cognition, culture, socialization, instruction, and language", have motivated a diverse set of research questions on the causes and consequences of reading disabilities. An outcome of this extensive gap in research foci is a disconnection between what is known about aspects of spoken language development, including atypical language development, and how these same aspects may support or interfere with learning to read, write, and spell proficiently.

Bridging the Fuzzy Boundary Gap

On the surface, the notion that spoken and written language development and disabilities form a reciprocal relationship seems less a matter of speculation today than it was 10 years ago. To say that reading and writing are language-related skills or that early language disorders become school-age learning and reading disabilities, as Bashir and colleagues speculated earlier, is to express concepts that drive aspects of current thinking in speech—language pathology. However, although it may seem obvious in practice to state that children with language disabilities, reading disabilities, and learning disabilities may not be children from distinct populations, the evidence to date suggests caution in drawing this conclusion for two reasons.

First, apart from the extensive neuroscience and psychoeducational studies that have been conducted on phonological processing, other language-related abilities have not received sufficient empirical support for their contributions as primary risk factors in the failure to read and spell. However, a reason for equivocal findings on other language systems and processes may be due to the conceptual narrowness with which language is defined and assessed.

Language systems are typically defined in terms of structural forms, which usually refer to the phonological, morphological, and syntactic systems. Processes underlying spoken language comprehension, when addressed, are also evaluated narrowly, often with highly specific metalinguistic tasks that involve the existence of some level of syntactic awareness. Examples include measures of sentence grammaticality and sentence correction, both of which require mental comparisons of morphosyntactic structures. Performance on these kinds of judgment tasks may be highly influenced by at least five variables that seldom have been considered in phonological processing studies. These factors include: (a) the amount and nature of practice that children are given, (b) the manner of verifying that children understand task requirements, (c) the method of elicitation, (d) the materials used, and (e) the extent of sentence parsing complexity that children must engage in to make a correct judgment.

It should be pointed out that results from phonological processing studies do not deny the importance of these other language-related abilities in differentiating good readers from poor readers in kindergarten and grade 1. However, the predictive power of other measures, such as grammaticality judgments, is considerably less than is the predictive power of phonological processing skills, perhaps due to the lack of discriminative validity of the syntactic measures selected. Most of the neuroscience and psychoeducational studies that argue for the phonological core deficit model of reading disabilities have not included children with a full range of language abilities in proportion to the larger population of school-age children. A related methodological issue is that inclusion criteria for these studies often exclude children with reported histories of speech or language difficulties or exclude those children whose IQs are below a standard score of 80 to 85. Catts et al. pointed out that IQ tests are highly correlated with verbal abilities, which may eliminate those children whose more severe language impairments place them most at risk for reading disabilities. A possible result of this exclusion is to reduce the variability between good and poor readers in other language-related abilities. Thus, the important question is not whether IQ should be an inclusion factor for sample selection, but the extent to which IQ becomes a significant predictor variable following collection of the data.

More data are now available from cross-sectional and longitudinal studies in communication sciences and disorders that provide potential insights into the nature of the language differences that may exist between children who are primarily language learning impaired and those whose primary problem is a pure reading disability. These studies tend to share a distributed causality perspective, in contrast to the unitary concept underlying the phonological core deficit model.

In terms of more advanced vocabulary processes, derivational morphology appears to hold promise as an area that may potentially illuminate the fuzzy boundaries between aspects of a spoken language impairment and reading problems. Derivational morphology entails spelling—meaning relationships, rather than phoneme– meaning relationships, and is intimately tied to new vocabulary learning beginning in grade 3 when children are expected to use reading and writing as major vehicles to learn and express new information.

Knowledge of root and affix forms allows children to work through the meanings of less familiar words that they hear, read, or spell and requires the ability to analyze the nature of changes in either pronunciation (phonology, including stress patterns and vowels), spelling (orthography), or both pronunciation and spelling. Examples of these translations might be: (a) no change in pronunciation or spelling (warm to warmth), (b) spelling change (begin—beginner), (c) change in pronunciation (equal– equality) and (d) changes in both spelling and pronunciation (decide—decision).

In a study that refined Carlisle's framework, Windsor (2000) found that 10-to-12½-year-old children diagnosed with reading disabilities but who also scored below 1 standard deviation on a standardized measure of spoken language ability had significant problems with the accuracy of low-frequency derived forms presented orally. Specifically, decreased accuracy occurred when the derivation resulted from phonological changes. These children were significantly less accurate compared to same age peers, performing more similarly to children 2 years younger matched in terms of language age. Not surprisingly, performance on the oral derivation task also served as a predictor variable of both word recognition and passage comprehension.

Another promising avenue for investigating the overlap or distinctness of reading and language disabilities is the use of oral-writing contrasts within the same group of children. Two related studies, which are elaborated on in this volume, examined the morphosyntactic complexity of narrative and expository discourse in the spoken versus written samples of 10-to-12½-year-old children who met the previous criteria in Windsor (2000) for both learning and language disabilities.

Children were again matched with same-age and language-age peers. In the first study, 10 general language performance measures were compared for group, discourse genre, and modality. Only the frequency of morphosyntactic errors per Terminable unit (T unit), a unit based on the clause, for the written narrative and expository summaries differentiated the children with language learning disabilities from both their chronologically age-matched and language-matched peers.

In the second study, the most distinctive morphosyntactic violation that distinguished the group with language learning difficulties from the two other groups occurred only in the written discourse samples, particularly in the expository sample. This violation involved verb morphology, in this case selective omission of the regular past tense inflectional marker *-ed*, for example, "Paul and John walk (walk *ed*) home from school" and "He laugh (laugh *ed*) hard at the joke." In writing, but less so in speaking, the consistent pattern of the preadolescents with language learning disabilities was omission of this past tense marker, "rather than misapplication of *-ed* to present tense contexts", a pattern that distinctly differed from younger typically developing children.

This pattern suggests that, in preadolescence, the planning and organizational demands of writing, including the coordination of writing with spelling, may uncover persisting problems with clusters of less well-specified morphosyntactic representations that are not as evident as they are in the spoken language samples of younger children with specific language impairment. One important trend from longitudinal language research is that preschool language impairment, typically assessed in the semantic/syntactic and expressive phonology domains, remains associated with reading and spelling problems into at least late adolescence.

Another strand of longitudinal language research has provided more direct information on the relationship between language disabilities and reading problems. A well-drawn sample identified in kindergarten before reading difficulties emerged has been followed through grade 4. Findings indicate that the percentage of those with a pure reading disability remains small in comparison to those with language learning disabilities who also have reading problems. Those with a language learning disability evidence a broad spectrum of spoken language processing and production difficulties, not just problems with phonological processing.

There is increasing awareness across disciplines, which is particularly apparent in recent research on spelling, that it is necessary to acknowledge the multilayered, dynamic, and reciprocal nature of the relationship between spoken and written language development and disorders. One issue for unraveling the complexity of this relationship is that causes are difficult to distinguish from consequences. In both the unitary and distributed causality models, the consequences are similar. Children with reading, writing, and spelling problems encounter reduced access to meaningful learning, which then limits the extent to which they can benefit from literacy activities as a means for advancing their own language knowledge. As a consequence, they have less experience with literate forms and functions, from vocabulary to text structures to the many and varied types of inferencing that characterize proficient reading comprehension.

When children are continuously confronted with failure as competent learners and communicators, they have reduced motivation to learn, which then leads to further cycles of failure and reduced self-esteem. An outcome for too many, which can begin as early as grade 4, is emotional disengagement from schooling and formal dropping out in high school. In comparison, children who demonstrate achievement early in their school careers have the foundation to capitalize on their educational experiences because success promotes engagement and the motivation to learn.

A second issue pertains to the fuzzy boundary question. In the cross-sectional studies that found similar patterns of difficulty in older children with both language and learning disabilities, it becomes difficult to dissemble whether problems with derivations, which involve phonological change in the root form, or the omission of the past tense marker *-ed* in writing might stem from one of four possibilities. These include (a) less well-specified phonological representations, (b) broader information processing constraints, (c) variations in the quality of literacy instruction, or (d) a combination of all three variables that make unique contributions to profiles of difficulty in the spoken and print domains.

Furthermore, the cross-sectional studies included children already identified with word recognition and text comprehension problems; thus, the chronic effects of reading, writing, and spelling difficulties on other language domains becomes hard to untangle. Longitudinal research designs, such as Catts et al., offer the possibility to address more fully the fuzzy boundary question because children are identified with language learning problems prior to intensive reading instruction. Related to the resolution of the fuzzy boundary issue, Scarborough (2001) urges that future longitudinal research should also rethink how changes over time in the patterns of language and reading impairment are measured. Both the unitary and distributed causality models currently tend to approach change as linear or cumulative advances when real development change proceeds continuously as a spiral, in spurts followed by plateaus.

For example, the often observed phenomenon that some children with preschool language delays appear to "catch up" only to have new symptoms emerge during the elementary years, which are now identified as a learning disability, has been called illusory recovery. This deceptive recovery may be one of the main reasons for the boundaries that have been built between a language and a learning disability. Scarborough (2001) posits that illusory recovery can be explained by the *ascendency hypothesis.* In this model, growth is viewed as nonlinear. Developmental differences will be most apparent between individual children when typically developing children are reaching a post-spurt plateau in particular language or reading skills and slower developing children are just beginning a spurt ("a catch-up phase").

Milder language delays will be manifested as lags in a particular domain, such as vocabulary knowledge, reflected in a smaller quantitative gap in development between typically developing children and those with a vocabulary delay. More severe language problems, including reading problems, will be characterized by persisting problems across multiple domains with a larger developmental gap appearing. According to Scarborough (2001), over time, a single underlying language impairment will be expressed differently, not as subtypes, but in degrees of severity depending on the domain being assessed and the method of assessment.

The measurement challenge, therefore, is to employ tools of assessment capable of discerning individual differences when the skill of interest is ascending, not when it has plateaued (the "illusionary recovery" phase). Dynamic assessment methods, which are premised on concepts of scaffolded instruction, assess children's responsiveness to the construction of new understandings in a teaching situation and offer a means for determining children's potential to learn in a particular domain. If the "potential to learn with support" corresponds with the Scarborough (2001) notion of ascending skill, then dynamic assessment approaches may be valuable tools to employ in future longitudinal studies on the continuously evolving patterns of language development and reading disabilities.

Bridging the Research to Practice Gap

In the real world of schools, as the recent national assessment of grade 4 reading comprehension documents, the path toward literacy remains ill understood. For example, it is still unknown how decoding, or word recognition, skill specifically relates to reading comprehension. Because the path is not homogeneous for every child, a costly consequence is that services to both younger and older students from the preschool to postsecondary years tend to only partially address students' academic and social needs. An often-cited reason for this reduced enlightenment is the quality of professional preparation in the language basis of literacy for teachers and speech language pathologists.

In view of the strong empirical findings on connections between skills in phonological processing and mastery of the alphabetic principle, teacher education has been criticized on two grounds. One criticism is directed to the inadequate incorporation of these research findings into the undergraduate preparation of prospective teachers, as well as the in service knowledge of experienced teachers.

Lyon (1999) and Moats (1999) argued that translation of the scientific research into relevant classroom practices would prepare teachers to select assessment and instruction protocols that would identify and reduce the number of children at risk for failure as readers, writers, and spellers. Moreover, it appears that few teachers in either general or special education systematically and explicitly integrate text comprehension strategies into children's literacy experiences despite the positive scientific evidence for their use.

These include strategies for comprehension monitoring, organizing and connecting information, question answering, question generation, and summarization. Similar concerns have been expressed about the need to incorporate explicit strategy instruction into text composition, beginning in kindergarten.

A second criticism is the failure of the teacher education curriculum, including special education preparation, to include sufficient academic experience with the components of language structure (phonology, morphology, and syntax) and content (semantics). For example, Moats and Lyon (1996) cited the lack of a requirement for language study as a major factor responsible for the inadequate preparation of reading and learning disabilities specialists to teach reading, writing, and spelling. Scarborough et al. (1998) found that, in a sample of 46 well-educated adults enrolled in teacher education courses at two private colleges, only 28% could accurately map sound—letter correspondences. This low accuracy rate transpired despite the explicit instructions to "Determine which letter or letters correspond to sounds in the words". An outcome of insufficient professional preparation in language analysis is "insufficiently developed concepts about language and pervasive conceptual weaknesses in the very skills that are needed for direct, systematic, language-focused reading instruction, such as the ability to count phonemes and to identify phonic relationships".

An additional need is to support teachers in learning how to interpret errors in reading and spelling that indicate the level of analysis a particular child is using, such as the whole word, syllabic, onset-rime, or phonemic level. Moreover, for students to benefit appropriately from technology to support their literacy learning, such as computer-assisted instruction, teachers will need to understand the linkages among spoken language development, word recognition, and text comprehension.

Beyond these content knowledge needs for the more effective teaching of reading, a larger issue not yet resolved is how to restructure teacher education so that reading teachers are better prepared to manage the complexities and diversity of American classrooms.*Preparation of Speech-Language Pathologists in the Language Basis of Literacy.* As Moats and Lyon (1996) noted, the undergraduate and graduate level preparation of speech language pathologists requires study of the components of spoken language.

However, knowledge of the spoken language system does not readily translate into meaningful literacy assessment and intervention without equivalent knowledge of the language-based nature of the many forms of literacy. Two obstacles have contributed to less than full participation of speech language pathologists in literacy instruction.

One barrier for the development of more collaborative approaches to classroom-based services in language and literacy has been the long-standing confusion about the roles of speech-language pathologists in literacy instruction. The psychoeducational literature has seldom addressed this topic, but there is some acknowledgment that speech language pathologists have the professional qualifications for involvement in three areas, all of which are limited to the spoken language domain. These areas include:

- Administering diagnostic assessments of "reading-related language skills".
- Conducting language therapy for students with "language-based learning disorders" that targets oral language skills germane for reading success, such as phoneme awareness, vocabulary development, and inflectional and morphological markers.
- Coordinating services with the classroom teacher and parents of children with speech and language problems who, as grade level demands increase, are at continued risk for problems with reading fluency and text comprehension.

The position expressed is that, beyond these three areas, speech-language pathologists typically will not be responsible for basic reading instruction for children with either a language or a learning disability because this is the professional responsibility of the classroom teacher.

However, even when the service format in theory is one of collaborative teamwork, Giangreco, from the perspective of a special educator, cautions that the clinical competencies of speech language pathologists, or the educational competencies of teachers, are not sufficient to ensure positive educational and social outcomes for individual students. Instead, beyond professional credentials,

Giangreco makes the case that a clear team process for decision making must be in place. At a minimum, this process should include three components:

1. Developing a shared set of educational goals, which must incorporate the content areas of the general education curriculum in accord with the 1997 reauthorization of IDEA and be consistent with the educational standards and benchmarks established at the state and district levels.
2. Team members accepting that "in some cases, people from other disciplines might be more necessary in the implementation of services than people from their own discipline". This acceptance might include the speech-language pathologist embedding language-related literacy activities into typical instructional activities, which the classroom teacher then implements, or the use of small group co-teaching practices, which the teacher and speech-language pathologist jointly implement in the classroom.
3. Creating and maintaining a high level of involvement of family members and the general education teacher in order to problem solve the kind of specialist knowledge that might be most necessary at various points in time. As Giangreco pointed out, families and teachers have their own specialized knowledge about the children in their care, which, if utilized in meaningful ways, significantly contributes to the design of more appropriate classroom experiences and supports.

Ehren expressed a second barrier to the more intensive participation of speech language pathologists in literacy instruction. The concern is that, in assuming greater classroom responsibilities, their specific area of expertise in oral language will be lost. This attitude, if pervasive, may be a product of inadequate professional preparation in the language basis of literacy. The roles and responsibilities of speech-language pathologists in literacy learning for diverse groups of children, including those with language learning disabilities, has recently been delineated.

To some extent, this expanded position simultaneously agrees with and challenges prevailing views of other disciplines. Consistent with the theme of this volume, two premises motivate an expanded concept of involvement, both of which require more immersion in academic and clinical preparation for prospective, and practicing, speech-language pathologists. First, reciprocal relationships exist for the effects of instruction in spoken language domains and their outcomes for promoting growth in written language (reading, writing, and spelling). Second, instruction in written language domains also has reciprocal effects on further advancing spoken language development. Five sets of roles and responsibilities are outlined within a collaborative framework:

- Prevent literacy failure through fostering language acquisition and emergent literacy.

- Identify children at risk for reading and writing problems in relation to early identification, as well as identify older students with literacy problems.
- Assess reading and writing, particularly the language subsystems that relate to reading, writing, and spelling.
- Implement intervention protocols that meet individual student's needs and documenting outcomes for literacy problems.
- Assume other roles, such as assistance to general education teachers, parents, and students and advocate effective literacy practices.

A specific responsibility entails the provision of developmentally appropriate, comprehensive intervention programmes in authentic learning activities. Speech-language pathologists are urged to design programmes that centre on promoting literate language use through a balanced focus on fluent word decoding/spelling and language comprehension/composition skills.

Because the aim is to maintain children in the general education curriculum with appropriate supports, a strong position is taken. Evidence-based practices should be the core of intervention and "Important aspects cannot be omitted because an individual teacher may have an aversion to teaching certain elements or may particularly enjoy teaching another approach". In this era of standard-based reforms, successful achievement of these multiple aims will demand more collective responsibility for effects of instructional practices on children's learning, flexible teamwork, and the cooperative decision making structures that are essential ingredients of quality education.

In summary, it might be said that, at the intersection of the language, learning, and literacy crossroads, researchers and professionals from diverse backgrounds have found some common ground. Research, clinical, and educational practices of the past 15 years have moved the knowledge bases in language and literacy well beyond the 1980s. Many language-based intervention and instructional approaches for school-age children and adolescents now meet standards for evidence-based practices. In addition, there is a greater understanding and acceptance of the long-term and pervasive nature of language and learning disabilities. Now attention is being directed to the postsecondary educational needs of young adults with language learning problems who continue to struggle with academic and social success.

However, much of what is known about effective and balanced practices has yet to reach down into classrooms and intervention programmes, as testified to by the NCES (2001) "report card" on grade 4 reading achievement. The reasons for children's literacy failures are complex. Causes and their consequences are intertwined with (a) SES and sociocultural variations in home socialization practices; (b) the relative absence of teacher education in linguistics; (c) the relative dearth of knowledge about the language basis of literacy in the professional preparation of speech-language pathologists; (d) the fragmentation of services that defines a school culture in which collaborative teamwork, the integration of children's educational goals, and shared decision-making are not valued; and (e) the tendency to allow "methods," rather than strategic teaching, to drive instructional and clinical practices. Strategic teaching is metacognitively demanding. It presumes that reading, writing, and spelling are well understood as language processes and requires the skills to explicitly monitor students as they are engaged in these activities in order to know how to assist and encourage them in appropriate ways. By staying focused on the reciprocal nature of language—literacy relationships, researchers from different disciplines need to develop dialogues that will create more integrated research questions capable of addressing how underlying neurobiological mechanisms for spoken language affect literacy learning and how disrupted literacy learning may impact on subsequent language learning.

Other integrated research questions should concern the ways in which instructional variations, including the instructional patterns of classrooms, resource rooms, and clinical settings, affect children's motivation to learn, as well as what they learn, as readers, writers, and spellers.

Specialists from different professions concerned with language and literacy, as well as school administrators, must be encouraged to create more collaborative programmes that have clearly defined and coordinated decision-making processes in place. These problem-solving processes should empower teachers, reading specialists, speech-language pathologists, family members, and others to assume different roles and responsibilities in language and literacy teaching at different points in time, depending on a child's needs. Special education and related services should be directed to supporting children and teachers to the greatest possible extent within the general education curriculum. The intent of this book is to create a cross-disciplinary and cross-professional dialogue on the central role of language in all learning. Contributors represent multiple disciplines. Although their perspectives and focuses may differ, all share the understanding that language and literacy learning are inseparable. All are also committed to the belief, expressed by Lewis Carroll's *Walrus*, that time is now of the essence when it comes to talking about why so many children are locked out of the multiple linguistic worlds that only literacy has the power to create.

CURRICULUM THEORY AND PRACTICE

The idea of curriculum is hardly new-but the way we understand and theorize it has altered over the years-and there remains considerable dispute as to meaning. It has its origins in the running/chariot tracks of Greece. It was, literally, a course. In Latin curriculum was a racing chariot; *currere* was to run. A useful starting point for us here might be the definition offered by John Kerr and taken up by Vic Kelly in his standard work on the subject. Kerr defines curriculum as, 'All the learning which is planned and guided by the school, whether it is carried on in groups or individually, inside or outside the school.

This gives us some basis to move on-and for the moment all we need to do is highlight two of the key features:

1. *Learning is Planned and Guided:* We have to specify in advance what we are seeking to achieve and how we are to go about it.
2. *The Definition Refers to Schooling*: We should recognize that our current appreciation of curriculum theory and practice emerged in the school and in relation to other schooling ideas such as subject and lesson.

In what follows we are going to look at four ways of approaching curriculum theory and practice:

1. Curriculum as a body of knowledge to be transmitted.
2. Curriculum as an attempt to achieve certain ends in students-product.
3. Curriculum as process.
4. Curriculum as praxis.

It is helpful to consider these ways of approaching curriculum theory and practice in the light of Aristotle's influential categorization of knowledge into three disciplines:

1. The theoretical,
2. The productive and
3. The practical.

Here we can see some clear links-the body of knowledge to be transmitted in the first is that classically valued as 'the canon'; the process and praxis models come close to practical deliberation; and the technical concerns of the outcome or product model mirror elements of Aristotle's characterization of the productive. More this will be revealed as we examine the theory underpinning individual models.

CURRICULUM AS A SYLLABUS TO BE TRANSMITTED

Many people still equate a curriculum with a syllabus. Syllabus, naturally, originates from the Greek (although there was some confusion in its usage due to early misprints). Basically it means a concise statement or table of the heads of a discourse, the contents of a treatise, the subjects of a series of lectures. In the form that many of us will have been familiar with it is connected with courses leading to examinations-teachers talk of the syllabus associated with, say, the Cambridge Board French GSCE exam. What we can see in such documents is a series of headings with some additional notes which set out the areas that may be examined.

A syllabus will not generally indicate the relative importance of its topics or the order in which they are to be studied. In some cases as Curzon points out, those who compile a syllabus tend to follow the traditional textbook approach of an 'order of contents', or a pattern prescribed by a 'logical' approach to the subject, or-consciously or unconsciously-a the shape of a university course in which they may have participated.

Thus, an approach to curriculum theory and practice which focuses on syllabus is only really concerned with content. Curriculum is a body of knowledge-content and/or subjects. Education in this sense, is the process by which these are transmitted or 'delivered' to students by the most effective methods that can be devised. Where people still equate curriculum with a syllabus they are likely to limit their planning to a consideration of the content or the body of knowledge that they wish to transmit. 'It is also because this view of curriculum has been adopted that many teachers in primary schools', Kelly claims, 'have regarded issues of curriculum as of no concern to them, since they have not regarded their task as being to transmit bodies of knowledge in this manner'.

CURRICULUM AS PRODUCT

The dominant modes of describing and managing education are today couched in the productive form. Education is most often seen as a technical exercise. Objectives are set, a plan drawn up, then applied, and the outcomes measured. It is a way of thinking about education that has grown in influence in the United Kingdom since the late 1970s with the rise of vocationalism and the concern with competencies. Thus, in the late 1980s and the 1990s many of the debates about the National Curriculum for schools did not so much concern how the curriculum was thought about as to what its objectives and content might be. It is the work of two American writers Franklin Bobbitt and Ralph W. Tyler that dominate theory and practice within this tradition.

In The Curriculum Bobbitt writes as follows:

- The central theory [of curriculum] is simple. Human life, however varied, consists in the performance of specific activities. Education that prepares for life is one that prepares definitely and adequately for these specific activities. However numerous and diverse they may be for any social class they can be discovered. This requires only that one go out into the world of affairs and discover the particulars of which their affairs consist. These will show the abilities, attitudes, habits, appreciations and forms of knowledge that men need. These will be the objectives of the curriculum. They will be numerous, definite and particularized. The curriculum will then be that series of experiences which children and youth must have by way of obtaining those objectives.

This way of thinking about curriculum theory and practice was heavily influenced by the development of management thinking and practice. The rise of 'scientific management' is often associated with the name of its main advocate F. W. Taylor. Basically what he proposed was greater division of labour with jobs being simplified; an extension of managerial control over all elements of the workplace; and cost accounting based on systematic time-and-motion study.

All three elements were involved in this conception of curriculum theory and practice. For example, one of the attractions of this approach to curriculum theory was that it involved detailed attention to what people needed to know in order to work, live their lives and so on. A familiar, and more restricted, example of this approach can be found in many training programmes, where particular tasks or jobs have been analysed-broken down into their component elements-and lists of competencies drawn up. In other words, the curriculum was not to be the result of 'armchair speculation' but the product of systematic study.

Bobbitt's work and theory met with mixed responses. One telling criticism that was made, and can continue to be made, of such approaches is that there is no social vision or programme to guide the process of curriculum construction. As it stands it is a technical exercise. However, it wasn't criticisms such as this which initially limited the impact of such curriculum theory in the late 1920s and 1930s. Rather, the growing influence of 'progressive', child-centred approaches shifted the ground to more romantic notions of education. Bobbitt's long lists of objectives and his emphasis on order and structure hardly sat comfortably with such forms.

The Progressive movement lost much of its momentum in the late 1940s in the United States and from that period the work of Ralph W. Tyler, in particular, has made a lasting impression on curriculum theory and practice. He shared Bobbitt's emphasis on rationality and relative simplicity.

His theory was based on four fundamental questions:

1. What educational purposes should the school seek to attain?
2. What educational experiences can be provided that are likely to attain these purposes?
3. How can these educational experiences be effectively organized?
4. How can we determine whether these purposes are being attained?

Like Bobbitt he also placed an emphasis on the formulation of behavioural objectives:

- Since the real purpose of education is not to have the instructor perform certain activities but to bring about significant changes in the students' pattern of behaviour, it becomes important to recognize that any statements of objectives of the school should be a statement of changes to take place in the students.

We can see how these concerns translate into a nicely-ordered procedure, one that is very similar to the technical or productive thinking set out below:

- *Step 1:* Diagnosis of need
- *Step 2*: Formulation of objectives

- *Step 3*: Selection of content
- *Step 4*: Organization of content
- *Step 5:* Selection of learning experiences
- *Step 6:* Organization of learning experiences
- *Step 7:* Determination of what to evaluate and of the ways and means of doing it.

The attraction of this way of approaching curriculum theory and practice is that it is systematic and has considerable organizing power. Central to the approach is the formulation of behavioural objectives-providing a clear notion of outcome so that content and method may be organized and the results evaluated.

There are a number of issues with this approach to curriculum theory and practice. The first is that the plan or programme assumes great importance. For example, we might look at a more recent definition of curriculum as: 'A programme of activities designed so that pupils will attain so far as possible certain educational and other schooling ends or objectives.' The problem here is that such programmes inevitably exist prior to and outside the learning experiences. This takes much away from learners.

They can end up with little or no voice. They are told what they must learn and how they will do it. The success or failure of both the programme and the individual learners is judged on the basis of whether pre-specified changes occur in the behaviour and person of the learner (the meeting of behavioural objectives). If the plan is tightly adhered to, there can only be limited opportunity for educators to make use of the interactions that occur. It also can deskill educators in another way. For example, a number of curriculum programmes, particularly in the USA, have attempted to make the student experience 'teacher proof'. The logic of this approach is for the curriculum to be designed outside of the classroom or school, as is the case with the National Curriculum in the UK. Educators then apply programmes and are judged by the products of their actions. It turns educators into technicians.

Second, there are questions around the nature of objectives. This model is hot on measurability. It implies that behaviour can be objectively, mechanistically measured. There are obvious dangers here-there always has to be some uncertainty about what is being measured. We only have to reflect on questions of success in our work. It is often very difficult to judge what the impact of particular experiences has been.

Sometimes it is years after the event that we come to appreciate something of what has happened. For example, most informal educators who have been around a few years will have had the experience of an ex-participant telling them in great detail about how some forgotten event (forgotten to the worker that is) brought about some fundamental change. Yet there is something more. In order to measure, things have to be broken down into smaller and smaller units. The result, as many of you will have experienced, can be long lists of often trivial skills or competencies. This can lead to a focus in this approach to curriculum theory and practice on the parts rather than the whole; on the trivial, rather than the significant. It can lead to an approach to education and assessment which resembles a shopping list. When all the items are ticked, the person has passed the course or has learnt something. The role of overall judgment is somehow sidelined.

Third, there is a real problem when we come to examine what educators actually do in the classroom, for example. Much of the research concerning teacher thinking and classroom interaction, and curriculum innovation has pointed to the lack of impact on actual pedagogic practice of objectives. One way of viewing this is that teachers simply get it wrong-they ought to work with objectives. I think we need to take this problem very seriously and not dismiss it in this way. The difficulties that educators experience with objectives in the classroom may point to something inherently wrong with the approach-that it is not grounded in the study of educational exchanges. It is a model of curriculum theory and practice largely imported from technological and industrial settings. Fourth, there is the problem of unanticipated results. The focus on pre-specified goals may lead both educators and learners to overlook learning that is occurring as a result of their interactions, but which is not listed as an objective. The apparent simplicity and rationality of this approach to curriculum theory and practice, and the way in which it mimics industrial management have been powerful factors in its success.

A further appeal has been the ability of academics to use the model to attack teachers:

- I believe there is a tendency, recurrent enough to suggest that it may be endemic in the approach, for academics in education to use the objectives model as a stick with which to beat teachers. 'What are your objectives?' is more often asked in a tone of challenge than one of interested and helpful enquiry. The demand for objectives is a demand for justification rather than a description of ends. . . It is not about curriculum design, but rather an expression of irritation in the problems of accountability in education.

CURRICULUM AS PROCESS

We have seen that the curriculum as product model is heavily dependent on the setting of behavioural objectives. The curriculum, essentially, is a set of documents for implementation. Another way of looking at curriculum theory and practice is via process. In this sense curriculum is not a physical thing, but rather the interaction of teachers, students and knowledge. In other words, curriculum is what actually happens in the classroom and what people do to prepare and evaluate. What we have in this model is a number of elements in constant interaction. It is an active process and links with the practical form of reasoning set out by Aristotle.

Teachers enter particular schooling and situations with:

- An ability to think critically-in-action
- An understanding of their role and the expectations others have of them, and
- A proposal for action which sets out essential principles and features of the educational encounter.

Guided by these, they encourage:

- Conversations between, and with, people in the situation

Out of which may come:

- Thinking and action.

They:

- Continually evaluate the process and what they can see of outcomes.

Perhaps the two major things that set this apart from the model for informal education are first, the context in which the process occurs ('particular schooling situations'); and second, the fact that teachers enter the classroom or any other formal educational setting with a more fully worked-through idea of what is about to happen. Here I have described that as entering the situation with 'a proposal for action which sets out essential principles and features of the educational encounter'. This form of words echoes those of Lawrence Stenhouse who produced one of the best-known explorations of a process model of curriculum theory and practice. He defined curriculum tentatively: 'A curriculum is an attempt to communicate the essential principles and features of an educational proposal in such a form that it is open to critical scrutiny and capable of effective translation into practice'.

He suggests that a curriculum is rather like a recipe in cookery:

- It can be criticized on nutritional or gastronomic grounds-does it nourish the students and does it taste good?-and it can be criticized on the grounds of practicality-we can't get hold of six dozen larks' tongues and the grocer can't find any ground unicorn horn! A curriculum, like the recipe for a dish, is first imagined as a possibility, then the subject of experiment. The recipe offered publicly is in a sense a report on the experiment. Similarly, a curriculum should be grounded in practice. It is an attempt to describe the work observed in classrooms that it is adequately communicated to teachers and others. Finally, within limits, a recipe can varied just as to taste. So can a curriculum.

Stenhouse shifted the ground a little bit here. He was not saying that curriculum is the process, but rather the means by which the experience of attempting to put an educational proposal into practice is made available. The reason why he did this, I suspect, is that otherwise there is a danger of widening the meaning of the term so much that it embraces almost everything and hence means very little. For example, in a discussion of the so-called 'youth work curriculum', the following definition was taken as a starting point: 'those processes which enhance or, if they go wrong, inhibit a person's learning'.

This was then developed and a curriculum became:

- 'An organic process by which learning is offered, accepted and internalized'.

The problem with this sort of definition, as Robin Barrow points out, is that what this does is to widen the meaning of the term to such an extent that it just about becomes interchangeable with 'education' itself. More specifically, if curriculum is process then the word curriculum is redundant because process would do very nicely! The simple equation of curriculum with process is a very slap-happy basis on which to proceed. We also need to reflect on why curriculum theory and practice came into use by educators (as against policy-makers). It was essentially as a way of helping them to think about their work before, during and after interventions; as a means of enabling educators to make judgments about the direction their work was taking. This is what Stenhouse was picking up on.

STENHOUSE ON CURRICULUM

As a minimum, a curriculum should provide a basis for planning a course, studying it empirically and considering the grounds of its justification. It should offer:

In planning:

- Principle for the selection of content-what is to be learned and taught
- Principles for the development of a teaching strategy-how it is to be learned and taught.
- Principles for the making of decisions about sequence.
- Principles on which to diagnose the strengths and weaknesses of individual students and differentiate the general principles 1, 2 and 3 above, to meet individual cases.

In empirical study:

- Principles on which to study and evaluate the progress of students.
- Principles on which to study and evaluate the progress of teachers.
- Guidance as to the feasibility of implementing the curriculum in varying school contexts, pupil contexts, environments and peer-group situations.
- Information about the variability of effects in differing contexts and on different pupils and an understanding of the causes of the variation.

In relation to justification:

- A formulation of the intention or aim of the curriculum which is accessible to critical scrutiny.

There are a number of contrasts in this model of curriculum theory and practice as compared with the product model.

First, where the product model appeals to the workshop for a model, this process model looks to the world of experimentation:

- The idea is that of an educational science in which each classroom is a laboratory, each teacher a member of the scientific community...The crucial point is that the proposal is not to be regarded as an unqualified recommendation but rather as a provisional specifica-tion claiming no more than to be worth putting to the test of practice, Such proposals claim to be intelligent rather than correct.

Thus, in this sense, a curriculum is a particular form of specification about the practice of teaching. It is not a package of materials or a syllabus of ground to be covered. 'It is a way of translating any educational idea into a hypothesis testable in practice. It invites critical testing rather than acceptance'.

Second given the uniqueness of each classroom setting, it means that any proposal, even at school level, needs to be tested, and verified by each teacher in his/her classroom. It is not like a curriculum package which is designed to be delivered almost anywhere. Third, outcomes are no longer the central and defining feature. Rather than tightly specifying behavioural objectives and methods in advance, what happens in this model of curriculum theory and practice is that content and means develop as teachers and students work together.

Fourth, the learners in this model are not objects to be acted upon. They have a clear voice in the way that the sessions evolve. The focus is on interactions. This can mean that attention shifts from teaching to learning. The product model, by having a pre-specified plan or programme, tends to direct attention to teaching. For example, how can this information be got over? A process approach to curriculum theory and practice, it is argued by writers like Grundy, tends towards making the process of learning the central concern of the teacher. This is because this way of thinking emphasizes interpretation and meaning-making. As we have seen each classroom and each exchange is different and has to be made sense of.

However, when we come to think about this way of approaching curriculum in practice, a number of possible problems do arise. The first is a problem for those who want some greater degree of uniformity in what is taught. This approach to the theory of curriculum, because it places meaning-making and thinking at its core and treats learners as subjects rather than objects, can lead to very different means being employed in classrooms and a high degree of variety in content.

As Stenhouse comments, the process model is essentially a critical model, not a marking model:

- It can never be directed towards an examination as an objective

> without loss of quality, since the standards of the examination then override the standards immanent in the subject. This does not mean that students taught on the process model cannot be examined, but it does mean that the examinations must be taken in their stride as they pursue other aspirations. And if the examination is a by-product there is an implication that the quality the student shows in it must be an under-estimate of his real quality. It is hence rather difficult to get the weak student through an examination using a process model. Crammers cannot use it, since it depends upon a commitment to educational aims.

To some extent variation is limited by factors such as public examinations. The exchange between students and teachers does not float free of the context in which it arises. At the end of the day many students and their families place a high premium on exam or subject success and this inevitably enters into the classroom. This highlights a second problem with the model we have just outlined-that it may not pay enough attention to the context in which learning takes place.

Third, there is the 'problem' of teachers. The major weakness and, indeed, strength of the process model is that it rests upon the quality of teachers. If they are not up to much then there is no safety net in the form of prescribed curriculum materials. The approach is dependent upon the cultivation of wisdom and meaning-making in the classroom. If the teacher is not up to this, then there will be severe limitations on what can happen educationally.

There have been some attempts to overcome this problem by developing materials and curriculum packages which focus more closely on the 'process of discovery' or 'problem-solving', for example in science. But there is a danger in this approach. Processes become reduced to sets of skills-for example, how to light a bunsen burner. When students are able to demonstrate certain skills, they are deemed to have completed the process. As Grundy comments, the actions have become the ends; the processes have become the product. Whether or not students are able to apply the skills to make sense of the world around them is somehow overlooked.

Fourth, we need to look back at our process model of curriculum theory and practice and what we have subsequently discussed, and return to Aristotle and to Freire. The model we have looked at here does not fully reflect the process explored earlier. In particular, it does not make explicit the commitments associated with phronesis.

CURRICULUM AS PRAXIS

Curriculum as praxis is, in many respects, a development of the process model. While the process model is driven by general principles and places an emphasis on judgment and meaning making, it does not make explicit statements about the interests it serves. It may, for example, be used in such a way that does not make continual reference to collective human well-being and to the emancipation of the human spirit. The praxis model of curriculum theory and practice brings these to the centre of the process and makes an explicit commitment to emancipation. Thus action is not simply informed, it is also committed.

It is praxis:

- Critical pedagogy goes beyond situating the learning experience within the experience of the learner: it is a process which takes the experiences of both the learner and the teacher and, through dialogue and negotiation, recognizes them both as problematic...[It] allows, indeed encourages, students and teachers together to confront the real problems of their existence and relationships. . . When students confront the real problems of their existence they will soon also be faced with their own oppression.

We can amend our 'curriculum as process' model to take account of these concerns.

Teachers enter particular schooling and situations with:

- A personal, but shared idea of the good and a commitment to human emancipation,
- An ability to think critically, -in-action
- An understanding of their role and the expectations others have of them, and
- A proposal for action which sets out essential principles and features of the educational encounter.

Guided by these, they encourage:

- Conversations between, and with, people in the situation

Out of which may come:

- Informed and committed action.

They:

- Continually evaluate the process and what they can see of outcomes.

In this approach the curriculum itself develops through the dynamic interaction of action and reflection. 'That is, the curriculum is not simply a set of plans to be implemented, but rather is constituted through an active process in which planning, acting and evaluating are all reciprocally related and integrated into the process'. At its centre is *praxis*: informed, committed action.

How might we recognize this? First, I think we should be looking for practice which does not focus exclusively on individuals, but pays careful attention to collective understandings and practices and to structural questions. For example, in sessions which seek to explore the experiences of different cultural and racial groups in society, we could be looking to see whether the direction of the work took people beyond a focus on individual attitudes. Are participants confronting the material conditions through which those attitudes are constituted, for example?

Second, we could be looking for a commitment expressed in action to the exploration of educators' values and their practice. Are they, for example, able to say in a coherent way what they think makes for human well-being and link this with their practice? We could also be looking for certain values-especially an emphasis on human emancipation.

Third, we could expect practitioners committed to praxis to be exploring their practice with their peers. They would be able to say how their actions with respect to particular interventions reflected their ideas about what makes for the good, and to say what theories were involved.

CURRICULUM IN CONTEXT

To round off this discussion of curriculum we do need to pay further attention to the social context in which it is created. One criticism that has been made of the praxis model (especially as it is set out by Grundy) is that it does not place a strong enough emphasis upon context. This is a criticism that can also be laid at the door of the other approaches. In this respect the work of Catherine Cornbleth is of some use. She sees curriculum as a particular type of process.

Curriculum for her is what actually happens in classrooms, that is, 'an ongoing social process comprised of the interactions of students, teachers, knowledge and milieu'. In contrast, Stenhouse defines curriculum as the attempt to describe what happens in classrooms rather than what actually occurs. Cornbleth further contends that curriculum as practice cannot be understood adequately or changed substantially without attention to its setting or context. Curriculum is contextually shaped. While I may quibble about the simple equation of curriculum with process, what Cornbleth does by focusing on the interaction is to bring out the significance of context.

First, by introducing the notion of milieu into the discussion of curriculum she again draws attention to the impact of some factors that we have already noted. Of especial significance here are examinations and the social relationships of the school-the nature of the teacher-student relationship, the organization of classes, streaming and so on. These elements are what are sometimes known as the hidden curriculum.

This was a term credited to Philip W. Jackson but it had been present as an acknowledged element in education for some time before. For example, John Dewey in *Experience and Education* referred to the 'collateral learning' of attitudes that occur in schools, and that may well be of more long-range importance than the explicit school curriculum. A fairly standard definition of the 'hidden curriculum' is given by Vic Kelly. He argues it is those things which students learn, 'because of the way in which the work of the school is planned and organized but which are not in themselves overtly included in the planning or even in the consciousness of those responsible for the school arrangements.

The learning associated with the 'hidden curriculum' is most often treated in a negative way. It is learning that is smuggled in and serves the interests of the status quo. The emphasis on regimentation, on bells and time management, and on streaming are sometimes seen as preparing young people for the world of capitalist production. What we do need to recognize is that such 'hidden' learning is not all negative and can be potentially liberating.

'In so far as they enable students to develop socially valued knowledge and skills...or to form their own peer groups and subcultures, they may contribute to personal and collective autonomy and to possible critique and challenge of existing norms and institutions'. What we also need to recognize is that by treating curriculum as a contextualized social process, the notion of hidden curriculum becomes rather redundant. If we need to stay in touch with milieu as we build curriculum then it is not hidden but becomes a central part of our processes.

Second, by paying attention to milieu, we can begin to get a better grasp of the impact of structural and socio-cultural process on teachers and students. As Cornbleth argues, economic and gender relations, for example, do not simply bypass the systemic or structural context of curriculum and enter directly into classroom practice. They are mediated by intervening layers of the education system. Thus, the impact of these factors may be quite different to that expected.

Third, if curriculum theory and practice is inextricably linked to milieu then it becomes clear why there have been problems about introducing it into non-schooling contexts like youth work; and it is to this area which as suggested, now turn.

CURRICULUM AS THE BOUNDARY BETWEEN FORMAL AND INFORMAL EDUCATION

Jeffs and Smith have argued that the notion of curriculum provides a central dividing line between formal and informal education. They contend that curriculum theory and practice was formed within the schooling context and that there are major problems when it is introduced into informal forms of pedagogy.

The adoption of curriculum theory and practice by some informal educators appears to have arisen from a desire to be clear about content. Yet there are crucial difficulties with the notion of curriculum in this context.

These centre around the extent to which it is possible to have a clear idea, in advance (and even during the process), of the activities and topics that will be involved in a particular piece of work:

- At any one time, outcomes may not be marked by a high degree of specificity. In a similar way, the nature of the activities used often cannot be predicted. It may be that we can say something about how

> the informal educator will work. However, knowing in advance about broad processes and ethos isn't the same as having a knowledge of the programme. We must, thus, conclude that approaches to the curriculum which focus on objectives and detailed programmes appear to be incompatible with informal education.

In other words, they are arguing that a product model of curriculum is not compatible with the emphasis on process and praxis within informal education. However, process and praxis models of curriculum also present problems in the context of informal education. If you look back at at our models of process and compare them with the model of informal education presented above then it is clear that we can have a similar problem with pre-specification.

One of the key feature that differentiates the two is that the curriculum model has the teacher entering the situation with a proposal for action which sets out the essential principles and features of the educational encounter. Informal educators do not have, and do not need, this element. They do not enter with a clear proposal for action.

Rather, they have an idea of what makes for human well-being, and an appreciation of their overall role and strategy (strategy here being some idea about target group and broad method *e.g.* detached work). They then develop their aims and interventions in interaction. And what is this element we have been discussing? It is nothing more nor less than what Stenhouse considers to be a curriculum!

The other key difference is context. Even if we were to go the whole hog and define curriculum as process there remain substantive problems. As Cornbleth and Jeffs and Smith have argued, curriculum cannot be taken out of context, and the context in which it was formed was the school. Curriculum theory and practice only makes sense when considered alongside notions like class, teacher, course, lesson and so on. You only have to look at the language that has been used by our main proponents: Tyler, Stenhouse, Cornbleth and Grundy, to see this. It is not a concept that stands on its own. It developed in relation to teaching and within particular organizational relationships and expectations. Alter the context and the nature of the process alters. We then need different ways of describing what is going on. Thus, it is no surprise that when curriculum theory and practice are introduced into what are essentially informal forms of working such as youth work and community work, their main impact is to formalize significant aspects of the work. One of the main outcome of curriculum experiments within youth work has been work, for example in the field of health promotion, which involve pre-specified activities, visiting workers, regular meetings and so on. Within the language of youth work these are most often called programmes or projects. Within a school they would be called a course. What is being suggested here is that when informal educators take on the language of curriculum they are crossing the boundary between their chosen specialism and the domain of formal education. This they need to do from time to time. There will be formal interludes in their work, appropriate times for them to mount courses and to discuss content and method in curriculum terms. But we should not fall into the trap of thinking that to be educators we have to adopt curriculum theory and practice. The fact that so many have been misled into believing this demonstrates just how powerful the ideas of schooling are. Education is something more than schooling.

CURRICULUM DEVELOPMENT

CURRICULUM DEVELOPMENT SCHOOLS

Developing curriculum that meets the needs of middle school students is a complex process that rarely follows a prescribed pattern. Teachers may come up with ideas for projects, themes, and activities on the way to work, in the middle of class, during a conversation with a colleague, and even in the shower. Some teachers begin with a theme while others start with habits of mind they want their students to acquire. Some teachers use state frameworks and standards as a starting point to curriculum development. Still others build a unit from an idea for a project. The purpose of this guide is not to dictate how teachers should develop their curriculum, but rather to propose that certain basic principles underpin curriculum development. Middle school curriculum should respond to the unique educational and social needs of this age group; it should be based on content standards, habits of mind, and thinking skills; and promote collaborative teaching, learning, and assessment opportunities that enable all students to achieve high standards. In addition, the model calls for middle school teachers to develop curriculum organized around themes and essential questions.

Themes such as power, balance, relationships, and patterns are the big ideas that unify teaching and learning experiences. Essential questions are the two to three important questions about a theme that students and teachers consider throughout a unit in order to provide focus and stimulate enquiry. Finally, the approach to curriculum development integrates teaching and learning with a process of ongoing assessment. Ongoing assessments, both formal and informal, give teachers, administrators, and students an understanding of how well they are doing and what they need to do to continue to improve.

One of the main goals of the design is to raise the level of discourse among teachers by helping them exchange ideas about student learning, instructional methods, and curriculum development. Conversations with colleagues energize teachers and help them to learn from each other, often leading them to try new methods in the classroom. These conversations also draw teachers' attention to issues of equity as they focus on the diverse instructional needs of all students.

FIVE PRINCIPLES OF CURRICULUM DEVELOPMENT

- Curriculum should be grounded in an understanding of the middle school child. Curriculum development and teaching methods are based on an understanding of the middle school child as an intellectually capable, complex person who is responsive to challenge.
- Curriculum should be based on what we want students to know and be able to do. All curriculum development, teaching, and assessment are tied to a broader definition of standards than the typical state standards, which tend to be content-focused. The curriculum includes habits of mind, skills development, and in-depth study. Beyond state and local standards to define what students need to do to be thoughtful, caring, and valued members of the community.
- Students and teachers should be engaged in authentic, intellectual work. All student work should have significance beyond the classroom. This work should be purposeful and rigorous, and it should develop skills and knowledge that will prepare students for high school and beyond. As a result.
- Assessment should demonstrate that students can do important work. A crucial part of curriculum planning is developing formal and informal assessments to understand what students know and what they are learning in relation to the learning goals.
- A coherent curriculum should be developed across the entire school. Teachers and administrators use a process called "mapping" to build a well-articulated, coherent curriculum across the school.

CURRICULUM SHOULD BE GROUNDED IN AN UNDERSTANDING OF THE MIDDLE SCHOOL CHILD

Schools ensure their curriculum and teaching methods are based on an understanding of the middle school child as a complex person who is vulnerable as well as responsive to challenge. Students in this age group experience a wide range of physical, social, and intellectual development. While some students are approaching adult physical development and stature, others look as if they could still be in elementary school. Some students are able to sit still for long periods of time while others need to be more active.

Socially, it is during the middle school years that students begin to perceive the larger world around them and question their place in that world, often becoming self-conscious and unsure of themselves. Many are beginning to come to terms with their ethnic and gender identities. Intellectually, middle school students are gradually moving from concrete to formal operations. They are making a transition from thinking logically about their own real-life experiences to reasoning about abstract concepts and ideas. In response to the unique needs of their students, middle schools need to organize their instructional programmes and adopt teaching and learning methods that are most effective with this age group.

Middle school students:

- Are capable of critical and complex thinking and develop these skills by using them
- Are capable of responding with high achievement when challenged and engaged
- Show variability in themselves and need variety in their day and in what is asked of them
- Need increasing autonomy and responsibility as well opportunities to demonstrate that they can behave responsibly
- Have abundant energy and interest that should be tapped instead of squelched
- Are willing to take risks if they believe they are in a safe and trusting environment

Placing the needs and capabilities of middle school students at the center of curriculum planning, teaching, and assessment makes student learning more active, engaging, and profound. Improvements of this magnitude will occur only if teachers work collaboratively to create learning opportunities based on these beliefs. For example, to develop higher-order thinking skills, teachers ask students to grapple with open-ended questions based on meaningful work and to synthesize information so they can support their opinions with evidence.

Believing that young adolescents are capable of high achievement means teachers must raise their expectations for the quality of student work and build in the support necessary to help all students meet higher standards. In order to allow middle school students to demonstrate they can act responsibly, teachers must genuinely ask students to use good judgment by, for example, having them make public presentations and by giving them choices.

Giving students these opportunities may very well be a dramatic change for a middle school that has focused more on controlling the behaviour of students than on letting them make decisions for themselves. In the vignette that follows, Ms. Harrison organizes class time, paying close attention to the social and educational needs of young adolescents. This type of active and varied learning environment creates significantly deeper learning experiences for a greater number of students.

CURRICULUM IS BASED ON WHAT WE WANT STUDENTS TO KNOW AND BE ABLE TO DO

Curriculum standards are more broadly defined than the content standards that most state governments have developed in the recent past. A school uses state standards in discussions to define for itself what students need to learn in order to be thoughtful, caring, and valued members of the community. Instead of merely ensuring that students attain curriculum standards limited to content knowledge, schools also provide opportunities for students to develop the habits of mind and thinking skills that will prepare them for a thoughtful and successful future. As schools and districts create their own standards, they include three types of *learning goals* for students: habits of mind, skills, and content standards.

These goals are kept at the forefront of the school community for all to see and for students and staff to strive for. By focusing on more than just content standards, teachers aim to teach students to become compassionate and caring individuals who can think critically, access and synthesize information, clearly communicate their ideas, and develop deep understanding.

STUDENTS AND TEACHERS SHOULD BE ENGAGED IN AUTHENTIC, INTELLECTUAL WORK

A school to integrate curriculum development, teaching, and assessment. What the school has determined students should know and be able to do drives curriculum development, teaching, and assessment. In this way, the focus is on student learning and growth, not on how much material is "covered" in a year. Curriculum and instruction need to provide students with opportunities to engage in authentic, intellectual work that has significance beyond the classroom. This means moving beyond textbook-based instruction towards project-based curriculum that incorporates a wide variety of instructional materials and strategies and promotes challenging, intellectual work that connects to the real lives of students.

Project-based instruction provides increased opportunities for students to engage in authentic, intellectual work and creates a shift in the teacher's role. Sometimes the teacher may be the facilitator who guides students in a discussion about their science experiments, while at other times the teacher may set up a project for students that includes gathering oral histories of senior citizens.

In still another role, the teacher may model his or her own writing to begin teaching students how to write a poem. Teachers will use teaching techniques that ask students to participate actively in learning and in applying knowledge, skills, and habits of mind. For example, students would not only study outstanding published poetry, but they would also write their own poetry and publish it in magazines they create or in national periodicals for youth. In science, students will be expected to create their own hypotheses and test them through investigation and research.

Curriculum based on authentic, intellectual work:

- Is purposeful, rigorous, and related to the real world
- Focuses on developing complex and critical thinking skills
- Is project-based and active in nature, allowing students to use their energy and creativity to enhance their learning

- Balances depth and breadth of material
- Explores relationships and connections, and integrates information across disciplines
- Is based on a multiple-draft process where students receive feedback from teachers and others to improve their work
- Explicitly teaches literacy across all content areas
- Integrates themes, essential questions, and standards into the daily work of students
- Addresses the variety of student learning styles by using a wide range of methods
- Allows students and teachers to take on numerous roles
- Allows for reflection and self-assessment

ASSESSMENT DEMONSTRATES THAT STUDENTS CAN DO IMPORTANT WORK

A crucial part of planning engaging learning oppor-tunities for students is developing formal and informal assessments to understand what students know and what they are learning in relation to the unit's learning goals. Assessment asks students to demonstrate what they know and can do. Teachers gather this evidence throughout a unit of study or period of time, and also in a final, culminating project or performance.

Very early in the curriculum development process, teachers think about assessment and how students will demonstrate that they have achieved the learning goals. Instead of waiting until the end of a unit of study to create a test or assign a project, teachers create assessment activities at the beginning because the assessments help determine what students will be doing as the unit progresses. To accommodate the wide range of learners in their classrooms, teachers devise a variety of assessments that include projects, exhibitions, portfolios, and demonstrations. Such assessments ask students to explain, interpret, apply, analyse, synthesize, solve problems, and communicate information. Teachers also ask their students to demonstrate understanding of others and themselves as examples of how they have learned.

Making sure assessments are "transparent" gives students a clear understanding of what is expected of them in terms of the quality of their work and how their work will be evaluated. Teachers can use rubrics, develop assessment criteria with students, and display models of exemplary work to help students understand what is expected of them. Rather than just giving students a grade that tells them how they did in relation to each other or to an unidentified standard, teachers' use assessments that give students specific feedback which will help them improve. Assessment tasks based on learning goals help students know what is important to learn and assist teachers in understanding how effective their teaching is.

Characteristics of Assessment

In the model, assessment:

- Is transparent—students know the criteria, learning goals, and timing of assessment
- Drives curriculum planning and teaching—what students are asked to do depends on how they will be asked to demonstrate their learning
- Takes many forms including projects, exhibitions, portfolios, and demonstrations
- Helps students, teachers, and parents understand what a child
- knows and can do and allows them to understand what a child needs to do to improve
- Is ongoing, tied to the learning goals, and used to inform curriculum planning, teaching, and professional development

A COHERENT CURRICULUM SHOULD BE DEVELOPED ACROSS THE ENTIRE SCHOOL

As teachers develop curriculum based on learning goals and guided by themes and essential questions, they create learning experiences that are more thoughtfully organized. But it is not enough to have many thoughtfully designed experiences if they have no connection or relationship to each other. The school engages in a process called "mapping" that leads to a coherent curriculum within grade levels, between grade levels, and across the entire school.

If you follow middle school students around for a day, it's easy to see how fragmented and incoherent their learning experiences can be. There are redundancies and omissions in learning because one teacher rarely knows what other teachers are doing. This fragmentation is due in part to the way curriculum has been developed over the years. Topics might be included because teachers want to teach a particular topic, they might be held over from an earlier curriculum, or in response to perceived student deficits.

In order to build curriculum across a school, the teachers and administrators use mapping, a process that involves asking these four questions:

- What do we want our students to know and be able to do?
- What are we currently teaching?
- Where are the redundancies and the gaps between what we should be teaching and what we are teaching?
- What will we do about the redundancies and gaps?

CURRICULUM PLANNING

This section of the Curriculum Guide is designed to help teachers understand the components of planning curriculum in the model. It begins with a brief description of each component, followed by a more detailed explanation of the components, how teachers use them, and guidelines on what to consider when creating curriculum. This section also includes a Curriculum Planning Template that will aid teachers in planning units of study in the model. The template is designed to help teachers ask the questions that lead them to developing meaningful learning experiences for their students. Based on broad themes, these learning experiences use essential questions and a variety of instructional and assessment techniques to drive deep enquiry. This section closes with a completed template for a unit developed by a teacher. All the curriculum planning materials that follow are meant to be flexible tools. They may be used to help a single teacher develop a unit for one subject, or an academic team builds an interdisciplinary unit around a common theme. In our work with schools, teachers are first developing units just as to this model, they benefit from a structure that guides them through the planning process. As teachers become more familiar with each component, they will be able to begin planning with any component and build units that intertwine all components.

COMPONENTS OF CURRICULUM PLANNING

- *Theme*: The theme is the concept or big idea that the study is centered around. It should be a concept that is important to humanity and can be explored across disciplines, eras, and cultures. For example, power, force, patterns, and freedom are all appropriate themes.
- *Essential Questions*: These questions help focus students on the most important aspects of the theme. Teachers and students consider two or three substantive questions throughout the unit and look at them from multiple perspectives.
- *Learning Goals*: These goals describe what students should learn and be able to do as a result of the unit of study. Learning Goals are divided into three areas: habits of mind, skills, and content standards.
  - *Habits of Mind*: The ways of thinking and being that the school values
  - *Skills*: What students will be able to do by the end of the unit
  - *Content Standards*: The knowledge that students will acquire during the unit
- *Assessment*: Divided into Culminating Assessment, Ongoing Assessments, and Reflection, assessment is designed so that students and teachers know how they are doing and what they have to do to improve.
  - *Ongoing Assessments*: The work and assignments that show how students are doing as the unit progresses.
  - *Culminating Assessment*: A project or per-formance that asks students to apply the knowledge, skills, and habits of mind they

develop throughout the unit. All the work and learning of the unit build towards the creation of the culminating assessment.

  - *Reflection and Self-assessment*: Occurs throughout the unit as a part of ongoing assessment and at the end of the unit when students and teachers look back on the unit to see what worked well and what can be improved.

- *Selection and Sequence of Learning Experiences*: These are the ways in which students engage with the content, learn the skills, and develop the habits of mind that are the goals of the unit. The sequence of activities should be designed to move students towards achieving the learning goals and creating the culminating assessment.

Theme

A theme is not an individual topic that students study; it is a broad concept that is important to humanity and can be explored across disciplines, eras, cultures, and through many modes of experience. It serves as the organizing center of the unit, the concept that ties all work together. Themes focus a curriculum on the structures, relationships, and cycles that make up the world around us. When teachers organize a study around a theme, they create learning experiences that allow students to engage in the higher-order thinking skills that require them to access, analyse, synthesize, and communicate information.

Themes address a more complex definition of our world, one that studying discrete events or content does not allow. Students who study a curriculum based on a provocative theme begin to connect knowledge across time, discipline, and geography. Although themebased units do not have to be interdisciplinary, when connections between disciplines become more transparent, students begin to link what they are studying to what they already know.

When working in a theme-based study, students learn to develop a greater understanding of the world around them rather than learning in order to know more facts or do well on a test. The most important facet of a theme is its ability to bridge disciplines and allow students to study the connections. For example a seventh grade team doing a half-year study on the theme of *Change: Cycles and Transformation* could consider how change is reflected in each discipline.

In science, students could investigate adaptation, evolution, and the growth cycle. In social studies, students could study the political, economic, and sociological issues that drive the development of nations. In math, students might analyse data from the science or social studies classes to see how statistics and graphs can be manipulated to support or defeat change. In English, reading coming-of-age novels from around the world could lead students to write biographies of a diverse group of local community members.

Choosing a Theme

- Themes
- Support a wide-ranging study
- Engage students by being tied to their interests and concerns
- Are compelling enough to be explored in depth
- Can be explored from many disciplines
- Bridge time, geography, and cultures

Essential Questions

Essential questions are the overarching questions that help to focus a theme-based unit and prompt students to dig for deeper meaning. Growing out of the theme, essential questions deal with the concepts that are at the center of the field of study. They are not easily answered with facts and figures, but instead lead to other questions that will engage students and deepen their enquiry. Curriculum and assessment are centered on the content and skills students need to address the essential questions effectively.

In a unit on:

- *Change*: Cycles and Transformation, possible essential questions are:
  - What forces drive change?
  - What makes you change?
  - How has technology affected change in different societies?

To consider the essential question *How has technology affected change in different societies?* students need to understand the concepts of technology and development. They must have knowledge about a range of societies across time and how and why they developed. Students must be able to synthesize this information and communicate it in a form that demonstrates they can develop hypotheses and support them with evidence. Thus, the teacher, using essential questions, creates experiences to ensure that all students learn the necessary content and develop skills needed to address questions thoughtfully and thoroughly.

From the outset, essential questions should be shared or developed with students. Including students in framing or rewording essential questions will help them take ownership of their enquiry.

Characteristics of Essential Questions

Essential questions share certain characteristics that allow them to engage students and push them to think more deeply.

Essential questions:

- Are open-ended and may not have an obvious right or wrong answer
- Prompt students to make connections between ideas and/or disciplines
- Challenge students to see from and understand different perspectives, make discoveries, and analyse new evidence

- Are provocative and engaging
- Are asked again and again as students' understanding, knowledge, and skills develop and deepen
- Are modeled after the questions that practitioners in a field ask as they engage in their work
- Frame the information that students will explore during the unit of study

Learning Goals

The learning goals of a unit are based on a broad definition of standards that includes what students should know, how they should act, and how they should interact with each other.

When developing a unit of study, teachers select specific content standards, skills, and habits of mind that will serve as learning goals for that study:

- *Habits of Mind*: The ways of thinking and being that schools help all students acquire. They are lenses through which students see the world. Habits of mind help guide a person's thinking, actions, and interactions. For example, when looking at an historical event one habit of mind might be to use multiple perspectives and ask, *Whose viewpoint is represented here?* Another habit of mind could be to use evidence by asking, *What evidence do I need to support my position?* Habits of mind assist students in all content areas and help them become life-long learners. Habits of mind can be adopted school wide or created by teachers individually.
- *Skills*: What students will be able to do by the end of a unit or study.
- *Content Standards*: The knowledge that is important for students to learn during a unit of study.

Teachers' choices of learning goals are based on student needs and interest, teacher knowledge, and the theme or content being studied. Teachers should decide on a limited number of learning goals that develop a variety of learning styles and skills.

From the beginning, learning goals should be shared or even developed with students. If they know what they are striving for, students are better able to assess their own progress and achieve the learning goals. Teachers should choose activities and instructional methods based on how well they will move students towards successfully meeting the identified standards, skills, and habits of mind.

Characteristics of Learning Goals

Learning goals:

- Are linked to district and state standards
- Incorporate skills, content, standards, and habits of mind

- Are challenging but achievable
- Are explicit and understood by all students
- Are used by students while they are doing the work of the unit
- Are used by teachers while they are designing assessment tasks, projects, and the work of the unit
- Are connected to the everyday life of students

Table. Examples of Learning Goals

Content Standards what Students be Able to do	Skills what Students should being that a School	Habits of Mind the Ways of Thinking and Values	should Know
What a fraction is	Gather evidence by using different type of historical sources	*Persistence*: Using a variety of methods before finding a correct solution	
The properties of matter	Write an original story that demonstrates		
The major events leading up to and during the American information	understanding of plot, theme, point of view, and climax	The ability to use evidence to evaluate sources of Revolution	
Story elements including plot, theme, point of	Use computation of fractions to solve problems	The ability to view an event from multiple perspectives	
view, and climax specifying variables to	Devise an experiment be changed or controlled	*Ownership*: What is my role and responsibility?	

CURRICULUM DESIGN

A curriculum is a series of activities in which students engage with subject matter. Because everything cannot be studied at once, these activities must be orchestrated in some way. This arrangement is called curriculum design. Whether the subject is geometry, visual arts, or map skills, it is arranged in ways that emphasize some aspects and implications of the subject and neglect others.

In this way, curriculum design is among the most powerful tools educators can use to influence what students learn. Curriculum design can be viewed as an arrangement of materials prepared in advance and intended for instruction. Alternately, it can be considered as what emerges from interactions among teachers, students, and materials. In either case, however, a given design suggests conscious planning and brings with it a predisposition to what subject matter and instructional arrangements count as educationally significant.

No definitive taxonomy of curriculum designs exists. Several design types, which are among the best known, are considered here: school subjects, social, personal relevance, and intellectual development. Designing a school curriculum should always include the state or national standards that support them—or both. Think of standards as tree limbs, and the good curriculum that results as the buds and blossoms that grow out of them.

School curriculum is an outgrowth of sound standards, and students grow and learn from organized and engaging curriculum that aligns with important standards:

- Identify the social studies learning standards for the state you are constructing the curriculum for. Each state's Department of Education website has them. In addition, the national associations for core instructional areas have sets of common standards for all states, such as the National Council of Teachers of Mathematics, the National Council of Teachers of English, and National Council for the Social Studies, the National Science Association and the International Reading Association.
- Develop a set of differentiated benchmarks for students to reach that align with the state or association standards. For example, if a social studies standard states, "Students will know what tools were used for early human survival," a differentiated benchmark would say, "Students will research and create three early human survival tools, measure and compare their mass, and then graph out the results." Benchmarks help students to take learning to the next step through action.
- Develop a list of student objectives that set forth what students will know and be able to do. For example, an objective for social studies might say, "Students will be able to understand that life is influenced by culture and environment," or "Students will interact in a variety of environments to discover cultural influences." With strong objectives in place, students become involved in active learning.
- Includes lesson samples and activity ideas that include strategies and techniques with a lot of different "doing" activities. Pair up the activities with the standards they support. For example, "Students will be able to understand that life is influenced by culture and environment" could involve activities with students comparing and contrasting different cultures, researching other cultures and writing essays, reports and stories.
- Include a listing of supplemental resources and tools to be used with the activities and benchmarks. Include a range of resources, such as encyclopedias (online or text), magazines, newspapers, internet sites, guest speakers, authors, fiction and non-fiction trade books, alternative text written at various reading levels, maps and artifacts.

FACTORS THAT INFLUENCE CURRICULUM DESIGN

OBJECTIVES

- Child psychology

- Economic factors
- Environmental factors
- Political factors
- Social factors
- Technological factors

CONTENT

- Influence of politics on curriculum
- Influence of society on curriculum
- Influence of economy on curriculum
- Influence of technology on curriculum
- Influence of environment on curriculum
- Influence of child psychology on curriculum.

HOW POLITICAL FACTORS INFLUENCE CURRICULUM DESIGN

- From your experience as a student and teacher, you may have noticed how politics influence education. This is why education is regarded as a political activity.
- National ideology and philosophy have a tremendous influence on the education system because
- Politics determine and define the goals, content, learning experiences and evaluation strategies in education.
- Curricular materials and their interpretation are usually heavily influenced by political considerations.
- Political considerations may play a part in the hiring of personnel.
- Funding of education is greatly influenced by politics.
- Entry into educational institutions and the examination systems are heavily influenced by politics.

HOW SOCIAL FACTORS INFLUENCE CURRICULUM DESIGN

When you examine the curriculum being offered in your country, one question you may need to deal with is the extent to which social factors or social considerations influenced the design of the curriculum. Society has its own expectations about the aims and objectives that should be considered when designing the curriculum.

It also has a perception of what the product of the school system should look like. It is therefore necessary for curriculum designers to take into account these societal considerations. If this does not happen, the curriculum becomes irrelevant.

As you know, a number of religions co-exist in countries in the SADC region. Your own community may include Christians, Muslims, Hindus and adherents of other religions. Their views must be considered when designing a curriculum. In Zimbabwe, for example, subjects such as sex education and political economy have proved difficult to include in the curriculum because of the resistance from some religious groups. These groups feel that including these subjects in the curriculum will undermine their belief systems. The same groups of people would not tolerate a curriculum that does not include religious and moral education. The design of curricular materials and their presentation should accommodate the culture of the society that the curriculum is seeking to serve.

You should, however, be sensitive to the fact that the curriculum can be used to perpetuate inequities. You may have a curriculum that is gender biased against female children because it includes instructional materials that portray negative attitudes towards women and girls.

It is therefore possible for culture to have both positive and negative influences on the curriculum. Pause for a moment and consider the number of groupings in the society in which you live. These can be professional associations, cultural groups and religious organizations. The list is endless. These groups can bring their views to bear on curriculum design. This is so because any curriculum of value must result from the broad consultation of a wide range of stakeholders.

HOW ECONOMIC FACTORS INFLUENCE CURRICULUM DESIGN

One of the reasons why education is financed by governments is to improve the country's economy. Therefore, the national curriculum should concern itself with the requirements of the economy. Perhaps you are wondering how the economy of the country affects the curriculum. The children you teach will need to be employed. The skills needed by industry should be translated into the content and learning experiences of these children. The skills, knowledge base and attitudes required by industry should be developed in the classroom.

You might have noticed some advertisements for vacant posts in your local media. Employers have basic requirements. Educational institutions find themselves working to meet these basic requirements academically and professionally. As you are reading this unit, you might be thinking of acquiring a higher academic or professional qualification. This would enhance your upward social mobility. The market forces dictate what should be included in the national curriculum. It also subtly determines the quantity of learners at different levels.

As a teacher, you require classroom supplies such as:

- Textbooks,
- Charts,
- Equipment, and
- Chemicals for science experiments.

These materials are products of industry. Without these materials, learning is compromised. It is therefore crucial that serious consideration be given to economic demands when designing the curriculum.

HOW TECHNOLOGICAL FACTORS INFLUENCE CURRICULUM DESIGN

The computer is the latest technological innovation that will have a significant impact on education and society. If you are not computer literate, you may feel that you are not up-to-date. In your area, you may have noticed that a number of schools have introduced computing as one of the subjects.

The intention is to equip the learners with the requisite computer skills and knowledge. In addition to computers, other forms of electronic media are being used in teaching.

These have provided a variety of learning experiences and have facilitated individualized learning. Curriculum designers cannot afford to ignore technology and its influence on the curriculum.

HOW ENVIRONMENTAL FACTORS INFLUENCE CURRICULUM DESIGN

Over time, people have become insensitive to their surroundings and natural resources. This has affected the sky, the land and the sea. The end result is that humanity is being adversely affected by these in-considerations. Industrial wastes have polluted the world.

For example, the ozone layer in the atmosphere, which protects us from harmful radiation from the sun, is being depleted. People want this redressed. It is through education that remediation can be effected. Consideration for the environment must of necessity influence curriculum design to ensure the survival of future generations.

MODELS OF CURRICULUM DESIGN

Curriculum design is a complex but systematic process. A variety of models of curriculum design in order to make this complex activity understandable and manageable. It is important that as a teacher to understand how the curriculum is being used in schools was designed.

OBJECTIVES

- Discuss various models of curriculum design.
- Compare curriculum design models.
- Explain steps in curriculum design in relation to models of curriculum.

CONTENT

- The objectives model,
- The process model,
- Tyler's model,

- Wheeler's model, and
- Kerr's model.

THE OBJECTIVES MODEL

The objectives model of curriculum design contains content that is based on specific objectives. These objectives should specify expected learning outcomes in terms of specific measurable behaviours.

This model comprises some main steps:

- Agreeing on broad aims which are analysed into objectives,
- Constructing a curriculum to achieve these objectives,
- Refining the curriculum in practice by testing its capacity to achieve its objectives, and
- Communicating the curriculum to the teachers through the conceptual framework of the objectives, evaluation is done at each stage of the curriculum design.
- Content, materials and methodology are derived from the objectives.

THE PROCESS MODEL

Unlike the objectives model, this model does not consider objectives to be important.

Using this model presupposes that:

- Content has its own value. Therefore, it should not be selected on the basis of the achievement of objectives.
- Content involves procedures, concepts and criteria that can be used to appraise the curriculum.
- Translating content into objectives may result in knowledge being distorted.
- Learning activities have their own value and can be measured in terms of their own standard. For this reason, learning activities can stand on their own. It is important to note that in the process model
- Content and methodology are derived from the goals. Each of them has outcomes that can be evaluated.
- The evaluation results from the outcome are fed into the goals, which will later influence the content and methodologies. Unlike the objectives model, there is no direct evaluation of the content and methodologies.

TYLER'S MODEL

Tyler's model for curriculum designing is based on the following questions:

- What educational purposes should the school seek to attain? What educational experiences can be provided that are likely to attain these purposes?

- How can these educational experiences be effectively organized?
- How can we determine whether these purposes are being attained?

Objectives of Curriculum Studies

The model is linear in nature, starting from objectives and ending with evaluation. In this model, evaluation is terminal.

It is important to note that:

- Objectives form the basis for the selection and organi-zation of learning experiences.
- Objectives form the basis for assessing the curriculum.
- Objectives are derived from the learner, contemporary life and subject specialist.

To Tyler, evaluation is a process by which one matches the initial expectation with the outcomes.

WHEELER'S MODEL

Wheeler's model for curriculum design is an improvement upon Tyler's model. Instead of a linear model, Wheeler developed a cyclical model. Evaluation in Wheeler's model is not terminal.

Findings from the evaluation are fed back into the objectives and the goals, which influence other stages Wheeler contends that:

- Aims should be discussed as behaviours referring to the end product of learning which yields the ultimate goals. One can think of these ultimate goals as outcomes.
- Aims are formulated from the general to the specific in curriculum planning. This results in the formulation of objectives at both an enabling and a terminal level.
- Content is distinguished from the learning experiences which determine that content.

KERR'S MODEL

Most of the features in Kerr's model resemble those in Wheeler's and Tyler's models.

However, Kerr divided the domains into six areas:

- Objectives,
- Knowledge,
- Evaluation
- School learning experiences. What you should note about the model is that:
- The four domains are interrelated directly or indirectly, and
- Objectives are derived from school learning experiences and knowledge.

In Kerr's model, objectives are divided into three groups:

1. Affective
2. Cognitive
3. Psychomotor.

The model further indicates that knowledge should be:

- Organized,
- Integrated,
- Sequenced, and
- Reinforced.

Evaluation in Kerr's model is the collection of information for use in making decisions about the curriculum. School learning experiences are influenced by societal opportunities, the school community, pupil and teacher relationships, individual differences, teaching methods, content and the maturity of the learners. These experiences are evaluated through tests, interviews, assessments and other reasonable methods. In his model, Kerr asserts that everything influences everything else and that it is possible to start an analysis at any point.

In designing a curriculum, you need to:

- Establish or obtain general goals of education.
- Reduce the general goals to specific instructional objectives, including objectives that cover different domains and levels.
- Assess prior student knowledge and/or abilities.
- Break learning into small, sequential steps.
- Identify teacher behaviour.
- Identify student behaviour.
- Write a description of the lesson.
- Evaluate to see if the intended outcomes have been achieved.

If you complete these eight stages, you would have conducted what is generally referred to as the task analysis process.

ADVANTAGES OF THE CENTRALIZED PATTERN OF CURRICULUM DESIGN

Some of the advantages of a centralised pattern of curriculum design are listed below:

- It makes it easy to achieve national goals, since all schools use the same documents.
- Learners can transfer from one school to another without being disadvantaged.
- Entry requirements for universities and colleges can be centrally determined and parity can be ensured
- Communication to schools regarding academic requirements is easy, since the Ministry of Education is directly involved.

- Learning materials can be mass-produced, making them less expensive for both producers and consumers.
- Institutions can be well staffed and richly serviced because they draw from a national pool of expertise and resources.

DISADVANTAGES OF THE CENTRALISED PATTERN OF CURRICULUM DESIGN

Some of the disadvantages of centralising the development of the curriculum are listed below:

- The process takes a long time before the final document is produced.
- The design is insensitive to the needs of some groups within the country.
- There are coordination and communication problems when para-statals are involved in curriculum design.
- There is limited participation by various members of the community, resulting in little commitment during the implementation stage.
- It stifles creativity and initiative on the part of the teacher and other community members.
- Generally, the centralised pattern stresses content, mainly knowledge, at the expense of the development of attitudes and skills. There is a scramble for certificates, with little regard for the development and demonstration of productive skills.

DECENTRALIZED PATTERN OF CURRICULUM DESIGN

The decentralized pattern of curriculum design occurs when the local authorities or individual states draft their own curriculum. This type of designing is common in developed countries. However, some developing countries with large populations and states, such as Nigeria, use the decentralized pattern of curriculum design.

This pattern of curriculum designing has the following characteristics:

- Local communities initiate the changes to suit their local needs.
- Teachers work with the parents to determine the content. The learning experiences are based on what is available.
- Subjects in schools could be the same, but the content will vary from school to school, state to state, or district to district.
- Each school, state or district has its own syllabus that is produced locally.
- Generally, the textbooks may not have been centrally approved.
- Each school, state or district has its own form of evaluation.
- Very few people are involved in curriculum designing.

You can now look at some of the institutions that are involved in designing the curriculum.

STATE OR DISTRICT BASED CURRICULUM DESIGNING

In principle, these have the same structure as the centralised structure that was discussed earlier in this section. The only difference is that each district or state will have the final approval on content. However, each curriculum produced should meet the national goals. In general, the same types of people involved in the centralised pattern are also involved at the state or district level.

LOCAL AUTHORITIES

Institutions and responsible authorities such as town boards and churches may be involved in curriculum development. Normally, they would depend on the teachers, heads of schools, subject specialists, industry representatives, researchers and consultants to draft the curriculum. Consultants and teachers usually outline the content and learning experiences. Assessment and evaluation are conducted by a board of the local authority's choice. Continuous assessment is generally the norm in schools with a decentralized pattern of curriculum designing. Like the centralised pattern, the decentralized pattern of curriculum designing has some advantages and disadvantages.

ADVANTAGES OF THE DECENTRALIZED PATTERN

The following are some advantages of the decentralized pattern of curriculum designing, to which you can add more.

The curriculum addresses local needs:

- The local community is directly involved and is committed to its implementation.
- The system encourages creativity and initiative on the part of the teacher.
- It takes less time to produce the curriculum than it would take when a centralised pattern is used.
- Students learn what is relevant to the local community.

DISADVANTAGES OF THE DECENTRALIZED PATTERN

The following are some of the disadvantages:

- There is no guarantee that national goals will be achieved.
- Learners cannot easily transfer from one school to another when their families move.
- There is generally a problem in developing or accessing teaching materials which, if available, are expensive to produce.
- There may not be adequate expertise in the local community to develop part of the curriculum

CURRICULUM IMPLEMENTATION

General curriculum *research* is nowadays in German speaking countries a fringe activity. After a boom in interest in the 1970s to which IPN has made trend-setting contributions we see very little recent publication activity in general curriculum research. Consequently, there is also very little specific investigation of curriculum implementation activities. It seems that the study of the processes of curriculum implementation has virtually dissolved to become one element of the more general field of innovation research and theory. And it surfaces from time to time when researchers venture to become practical with their innovative concepts, such as constructivist learning environments or quality evaluation in schools and find out that there are many obstacles placed on the path from concept to reality under practical circumstances.

Let me start with some *conceptual clarifications*. I understand innovation to be a social activity which aims at changes in four dimensions: *social practices*, the *beliefs and understandings* underpinning these social practices, its *material aspects*, and the *social and organizational structures* in which these practices are embedded and which themselves are associated with systems of resources, power and sanction/gratification.

An innovation is usually characterized through some materialized plan which describes the intended practices, and the aspired ways of changing them, and argues the theories which justify the rationale. It uses some material, other resources and specific social structures to make people act in another way. Its real test lies in being put into practice. Thus, innovation is a practice to change practices.

Consequently, a new curriculum may be described as an attempt to change teaching and learning practices which will also include the transformation of some of the beliefs and understandings hitherto existent in the setting to be changed. It is usually strong on the material side by providing a written curriculum, text books, recommendations for teaching strategies, working material for students, and probably also new artifacts for learning. It is usually less explicit on the organizational side but may also advocate the use of changed time tabling and new social structures, such as peer group interaction, decision making in the subject group, etc.

To distinguish these dimensions of innovation has two purposes: firstly, it describes innovation as a *multidimensional phenomenon*, and thereby, offers some categories for analysis and construction. Secondly, it draws attention to the empirical finding that concentration on some dimensions and neglect of other ones usually leads to deficient results.

There are scores of examples of curriculum reform which concentrated on the material side and the theoretical justification of their approach and assumed that changes in teaching practice and in the beliefs and understandings of practitioners would follow from their material input-which frequently turned out to be incorrect. In summary, those innovations are expected to be more successful which explicitly stimulate development on all four dimensions and do not assume that changes in one dimension will automatically follow from changes on other dimensions. Let me turn to the term *implementation.* Its history begins with becoming aware that it does not take place. It is not unfair to say that usually most of the attention and energy of early curriculum developers was focussed on the production side of their enterprise, on the materialized "plan" or "product". The idea was: If the product is good and if it is widely enough disseminated, it will be *adopted* by the realm of practice.

However, history showed that many–some say: most– curriculum projects of the 60s and 70s have not been put into practice in a way curriculum developers had hoped.

And that practitioners were not even always aware that they violated the developers' intentions. For innovating classroom practice, attention must obviously not only be given to the *production phase* of a curriculum, but also to what happens after the production. What processes happen under what circumstances if practitioners are supposed to "adopt" a curriculum?

Thus, the term implementation in a broad sense conceptualizes the process through which a proposed concept, model, topic, theory etc. is taken up by some practice. Fullan and Stiegelbauer distinguished three sub-processes in which an innovation is made work in order to produce outcomes. The processes that eventually lead up to and end with the decision to take up a specific innovation proposal have been called *initiation phase*.

In the *implementation phase* participants attempt to use the innovation proposal in order to change their practice. Frequently, extra support for translating the innovatory ideas into reality is offered on a project basis. Thus, while the initiation phase is concerned with the *nominal use* of a curriculum, the implementation phase focuses on the *actual* use. The study of implementation processes is concerned "with the nature and extent of actual change, as well as the factors and processes that influence how and what changes are achieved." Thereby, it aims to find out what type of extra support in the 'project phase' is appropriate to promote actual use of the innovation. In the *continuation phase* the innovation is built into the routine organization, and extra support is withdrawn. Thus, while implementation is concerned with initial use of the innovation under project conditions, continuation deals with mature use under standard conditions.

GENERAL STRATEGIES OF IMPLEMENTATION

How to deal with the "implementation problem", *i.e.* the problem that so many curricula have not been implemented, or positively: of stimulating a process in which a target group is changing their practices in a way which is considered as improvement?

The programmed approach aims to solve the implementation problem by concentrating on flaws in the specification of the "product", e.g:

- Gaps in the existing specification of innovations practices;
- Failure to articulate the innovation's implication for teachers behaviour, and
- Theoretical inadequacies with respect to identified means for achieving the intended outcomes of an innovation. .

In other words, the specification of the curriculum and of the implementation process is the problem; had they been clearer, problems of implementation would be fewer.

A contrasting conceptualization of the implementation problem is provided by the *adaptive-evolutionary approach* which accepts that the innovation as it has been devised will be modified in the course of its implementation. This is not only seen as just a feature of mundane circumstances wise and realistic persons have to accept but as an essential characteristic of implementation. This resonates a central finding of the Rand Change Agent Study: "The primary feature of effective implementation could be called 'mutual adaptation' in which the project is adapted to its institutional context *and* organizational patterns are adapted to meet the demands of the project."

Particularly with complex innovations, this approach claims that it is conceptually unsound, socially unacceptable, and empirically impossible to solve the implementation problem by programming the persons concerned with putting the innovation into reality through detailed elaborations of the desired practice and step by step specifications for the process of implementation.

Rather, innovators to provide their innovation, *e.g.* a new curriculum, to their audience as "intelligent hypotheses", but invite practitioners to rethink it and further develop it for the specific circumstances they are working in. They expect, even invite negotiation and transaction. They aim to stimulate practitioners to use their practical situational knowledge for implementation and for modifying the original models just as to the demands and resources of the specific locality.

EXCURSUS: STENHOUSE'S IMAGE OF THE ROLE OF TEACHERS IN CURRICULUM DEVELOPMENT

Let me elaborate the arguments which underpin an adaptive-evolutionary approach by reference to Stenhouse's Humanities Curriculum Project which was considered by Goodlad as one of "only a few instances of well-developed curricula that provided students experiential encounters with the problems and issues of their world".

Stenhouse argued against the idea to achieve quality changes of educational practice by "programming" teacher behaviour. To by-pass collaboration of teachers means to by-pass their rationality and their ingenuity, and this would not solve the implementation problem, but, on the contrary, make it worse. It is the practitioners who must bring a curriculum idea to life in their concrete interaction with specific students under local circumstances. For Stenhouse, curricula are attempts to communicate-hopefully intelligent–specifications of educational ideas and practices to teachers in order to stimulate their discussion, experimentation and critique.

A curriculum is a hypothesis, a starting point for reflection and development done by responsible professionals. *"A curriculum is an attempt to communicate the essential principles and features of an educational proposal in such a form that it is open to critical scrutiny and capable of effective translation into practice".*

Teachers are sometimes sceptical of the innovative products of researchers and curriculum developers. This maybe unpleasant for the developers, however, as Stenhouse argues, teachers' "pragmatic scepticism" should be taken as an impulse of questioning, of wanting to know better, of wanting to develop–in short: as an impulse to research.

If one aims "quality practice" one cannot wish that practitioners take a curriculum proposal literally, that they work towards a one-to-one translation of the curriculum proposal into practice, that they "apply" it the local practice as true as possible to the original intentions, since it is–as knowledge in general–preliminary, hypothetical, incomplete, more or less de-contextualized and worth of being scrutinized and developed.

Rather, one must wish that teachers take the specific circumstances of their locality and of their constituencies into account in order to produce and evaluate a local version of the curriculum which is adapted to what is productive and feasible under these specific circumstances.

- *"The mistake is to see the classroom as a place to apply laboratory findings rather than as a place to refute or confirm them. Curriculum workers need to share the psychologists' curiosity about the process of learning rather than to be dominated by their conclusions."*

Thus, the main actors of implementation are the practitioners themselves, because they are responsible for the educational process and they cannot pass on this responsibility to external agencies. External agencies and persons, such as researchers, curriculum developers, in-service trainers may support and stimulate the development of practice; decisions about initiating development and the control over its direction are the realm of practitioners' professional judgment. For Stenhouse, quality curriculum implementation necessitates curriculum research and evaluation as well as teacher development in the process of implementation and under practitioners' participation. Implementation must attend to specific local conditions and to process experiences of the persons involved in the process of implementation.

Curriculum development is not just the production of written goals and materials *before* classroom practice but, at the end, concrete interaction *in* the classroom between learners and teachers aiming to develop situations with high learning potential.

END OF EXCURSUS

To sum up this comparison of approaches to implemen-tation: While for the programmed approach *curriculum development* takes exclusively place *before* implementation, and implementation is application of pre-specified models, for the adaptive-evolutionary approach the curriculum is also made *during and through* implementation. In the programmed approach an implementation is *evaluated* through the correspondence between the actual use of the innovation and the developers' intentions.

An adaptive-evolutionary approach cannot just test the effects of an innovation against a set of pre-specified objectives, since responsibility for practice will ask for evaluating the overall effects, *i.e.* including side-effects. Thus, an evaluation must "provide a comprehensive understanding of the complex reality surrounding the programme" in order to "illuminate" the state of the innovation and the options for its further development for the different constituencies involved.

- *The Programmed Approach has Certain Strengths*: It takes care to communicate its intentions and ways of implementation as clear as possible and, thus, its evaluation criteria are unambiguous. However, it has also some weaknesses, the most important of which are, first, it is only suitable for such innovations which are actually programmable. Many researchers claim that curricula for more complex educational goals are not easily programmable because our knowledge about the conditions of application is not sufficient. Secondly, needs and characteristics of persons and organizations in different regions may vary so much that some leeway is desirable in order to cope with situational implementation problems.

The *adaptive-evolutionary approach* is strong in adapting an innovation to situational characteristics. It also claims that complex changes necessitate relearning and, thus, invites participants to participate actively in the process of implementation which is seen as a prime opportunity for internalizing the main characteristics of the innovation.

Its main weaknesses are:

- First, problems may arise because of ambiguous objectives, variation of ways of implementation, and shifting evaluation criteria.
- Secondly, evaluation of success is difficult and may vary between different persons and constituencies because no common criteria are available from the outset.

Similarly, Berman has argued that both approaches have their merits and that the implementation approach should be chosen just as to its fit to the specific implementation situation.

Thus, the programmed approach is appropriate if the amount of change intended is small or orchestrated in a gradual manner, if the curriculum may be specified just as to tested and widely known teaching methods, if the persons concerned by the implementation agree to objectives and methods, if the school is comparatively integrated and its environment comparatively stable. Where these conditions are not met, an adaptive strategy may be more appropriate.

Table. Indication for Curriculum Approaches

Programmed	Adaptive-evolutionary	Approach
Amount of change	small, step by step	big
Curriculum technology known methods	fixed, tested and methods	adaptive, open
Attitude of participants	agreement	conflict
Integration/Organization	high integration	diversity
Stability of environment	stable	unstable

In practice, any practical implementation project will be situated somewhere between the extremes of the dichotomy just introduced. However in my view, it makes sense for curriculum developers to ask themselves what type of solution of the implementation problem they-implicitly or explicitly–favour through their organization of the implementation process, and if this fits to the messages their curriculum implies and to the localities it has to work in.

FACILITATING AND LIMITING FACTORS FOR IMPLEMENTATION

Whatever the general strategy of implementation might be, it makes sense to know more about factors affecting implementation. Although there are a lot of individual and often contradictory research results in different implementation localities, there is, nevertheless, some convergence of research findings about key factors.

CHARACTERISTICS OF THE INNOVATION ITSELF

Characteristics of the innovation itself, in our case of the curriculum, affect the process of implementation. It is not surprising that the higher a *need* for the solutions the innovation proposes is, the better the chances for implementation are. Usually, a general feeling of need or the expression of need by some political body or by academia is not enough, rather this need must be perceived by the constituencies directly involved in the implementation. It follows that "careful examination of whether or not address priority needs" lays important groundwork before and during the production phase of a curriculum; and that frequent communication and open discussion of the curriculum's merit for coping with felt need must maintain and develop an awareness of this topic during the implementation process.

However, there are three complications with straight forwardly addressing needs: First, there is a need for the solutions offered by a curriculum must not just be 'one among many others'. Among the "overloaded improvement agendas" of today's schools there is often competition between various innovation proposals which leads not too rarely to vague development agendas within which no critical mass of improvement energy can be accumulated behind any of the projects. "Developing a vision" could be used as an instrument to prioritize among a set of desirables. Secondly and especially in the case of complex changes, both precise needs and solutions offered by the curriculum are not clear from the beginning. Thirdly, need interacts with other factors.

Another crucial factor is the innovation's *clarity*. Curriculum research unearthed examples of educational innovations where practitioners were not clear about what they were expected to do differently–what change meant for them in practice. At least in initial implementation phases teachers relish concreteness and tangibility. They expect that teaching strategies are clearly described and material is well-thought of. The proposal should be clear about ways of doing, but not too linear and restricting in the sense that just one way of doing is advocated and no alternatives are possible.

This need for clarity has been interpreted as expression of a feeling of role ambiguity in a situation of uncertainty produced by the new challenges of the innovation on one side and by the partly lacking competencies on the teachers' part. It was also found that a more flexible approach may be appropriate in later phases of implementation when teachers have strengthened their feeling of competence with respect to the innovation.

What does this finding mean for an adaptive-evolutionary approach? Wasn't it saying to be not too clear about ways of teaching to allow teachers' experimentation? In my view "no". Stenhouse advocated the curriculum as an 'intelligent proposal' and he certainly meant by this to be as clear as possible about what the proposal is. But at the same time, he thought, teachers should be encouraged and supported by resources and structure to evaluate this proposal under specific circumstances and to develop it further.

A third factor is *complexity* which reflects the amount of new skills, altered beliefs und different materials etc. required by an innovation. "... simple changes may be easier to carry out, but they may not make much of a difference. Complex changes promise to accomplish more, but they also demand more effort, and failure takes a greater toll. The answer seems to be to break complex changes into components and implement them in a divisible and/or incremental manner.". A fourth factor lies in the *quality and practicality* of the innovation proposal. Again, it is not the quality a panel of curriculum developers would attribute to the curriculum proposal, but the quality as it is perceived by the relevant actors supposed to implement the curriculum. One might distinguish several aspects of quality in this respect. Firstly, there is *conceptual quality* flowing from plausibility and coherence of the conceptual elements employed.

There is *formal or communicative quality* coming from the language, graphical and social design of the presentation of the innovation before and during the implementation process. And there is *practical or logistic quality* stemming from the availability of materials and other resources, such as, for example, time for development work or the consultation of external experts. As most innovation address 'urgent and ambitious needs', it happens that "decisions are frequently made without the follow-up or preparation time necessary to generate adequate materials". It must be stressed that "quality" with respect to implemen-tation points to the perceptions of the different stakeholders: Thus, an essential feature of quality is *contextual suitability:* It has been frequently demonstrated that imported programmes rarely work equally well in all contexts. Innovation proposals must fit to available funds, specific student characteristics, the communities' language patterns, teachers' abilities, parents' expectations, cultural values and much more.

"Quality" also means that a curriculum can pass the test of *the 'practicality ethic of teachers':* Teachers appreciate these ideas, proposals or teaching methods which have proven to "work" in practice or which promise by their appearance of practicality to do so. Those proposals are considered as 'practical' which "address salient needs, that fit well with the teacher's situation, that are focused and that include concrete how-to-do-possibilities. 'Practical' does not necessarily mean 'easy' but it does mean the presence of next steps."

LOCAL CHARACTERISTICS

A second set of factors focuses on local decision processes and local characteristics of the implementation, there is the *regional administration* and the attitude of regional administrators, inspectors and the like towards the local implementation process is essential if change is meant to be serious. Without support of regional administrators change may happen with individual teachers or single schools but it will most likely remain isolated in some innovative pockets without affecting the broader system. Just 'moral support'-in the sense of being given good words without any concrete implementation follow-through-will no be enough. "Teachers and others know enough not to take change seriously unless local administrators demonstrate *through actions* that they should."

There have been too many educational innovations without *adequate follow-through*. In some regions there is a *history of negative experiences* with previous implementation attempts which in itself is an unfavourable condition for change since system members may have built up a cynic or apathetic attitude towards change. Local administrators must show specific forms of *active support* including enduring support for school management and teachers, through realistic time plans and resourcing, and through an adequate information system about the innovation and its implementation. And they must demonstrate *active knowledge and understanding* both of the attempted change and the processes of putting it into reality in order to provide conducive conditions for the implementation.

Another factor are *community characteristics*. Even where communities are "not directly involved in implementation...they can become activated against certain innovations" if the planning and implementation process does not attend to the political undercurrents in the school's surrounding community. On the other hand, the inclusion of non-professional, such as parents and the public–at least in settings where community members are used to influence educational practice-can uncover objections and helps to accommodate to specific circumstances. Then, parents may be "one of the most powerful leverages to better implementation" if they are actively included in the implementation strategy through an adequate information system or realistic offers to participate in key phases of development and implementation. Finally, *contextual stability* makes a difference. It is much easier to successfully advance an implementation within a stable environment. "Marked social change usually disrupts reform projects that are already on the way."

ORGANIZATIONAL CHARACTERISTICS

Actors

Another crucial factor for implementation is the characteristics of the organization which is the venue for implementation, and, in particular, the role of the *management, i.e.* in the case of a school: the principal and the school management team. There is broad research evidence that principals, headpersons and school management teams cannot change schools just on their own, but that they are the single most influential group of persons to make change processes fail.

"The principal is the most likely person to be in a position to shape the organizational conditions necessary for success such as the development of shared goals, collaborative work structures and climates, and procedures for monitoring results." Change processes are in need of the management's active support and participation–not necessarily as curriculum experts, but as initiators, as 'change leaders'. Thus, the school leaders' *level of commitment* is a crucial feature: "The degree to which people are committed to a reform is reflected in the time and energy they devote to its implementation and in the extent to which they remain faithful to their role in the face of opposition and operational difficulties." Commitment is important at all levels of an educational hierarchy but particularly among the personnel at the top, so *e.g.* among school principals or top administrators of districts or ministers of education. They are in the position to give resources and impose both rewards and penalties, and they provide well-observed images for how seriously the innovation is to be taken.

Firestone and Corbett have identified four leadership functions which facilitate educational change:

1. Obtaining resources

2. Shielding the project from outside interference
3. Encouraging staff members and furnishing recognition from peers, experts and supervisors
4. Adapting standard operating procedures to the needs of the project at an early stage in the reform process and, as Huberman and Miles suggested, stabilise and codify the new practices in school house operating rules, revised curricula, training programmes, evaluation procedures and routine funding. In other words, the earlier–even in the 'project phase' of implementation–the curriculum is partially built into the routine operations of the school, the better.

In reality, headpersons frequently do not play an active role in implementation–not always because they do not like the innovation itself–but sometimes because they find it difficult to transform their traditional, more passive role into a new and more active role as 'facilitator of change'. Thus, some implementation programmes provide specific offers for principals and school management, *e.g.* specific workshops or optional coaching. These are to help them transform and maintain a conducive role among implementation processes which frequently do not pass without some conflict and pressure on the leader's role.

Teachers, their commitment and attitudes, competences, and interaction patterns make up another crucial group of factors for implementation. Both individual and collegial aspects are important. Teachers are a constant factor in the education system and thus have a key role for classroom innovation. If they are not motivated to engage with an innovation, then nothing will happen. In the German discussion, Havelock's position has been criticised in binding curriculum development to the "weakest element of the chain".

However, this involves, in my view, overstating Havelock's argument in the way that teachers have to accept *fully* the innovation at any time of the implementation process. Certainly, this cannot be expected. Certainly, every real innovation will involve some aspects which are new for teachers and which will encounter some sceptical reaction. Such discrepancies between claims of the innovation and acceptance of teachers may be important starting points for further development.

However, the relationship between "irritation" and "acceptance" must be in such a balance that participants are prepared to embark and continue with the implementation process. Curriculum research shows that it is possible to deal constructively with such discrepancies in implementation processes, but it also shows that it is easier in situations of face-to-face-contact and that, again, it is much more difficult to generalise results of those face-to-face negotiations to a broader group of users.

- *Participation in Decision-making:* Traditionally educational innovation has tended to follow a top-down pattern. However, it was frequently

> shown that including local personnel fosters more effective implementation. "Early participation increases teachers' willingness to continue new practices after the initial incentives have been withdrawn. Engaging teachers in their planning process also helps to equip them with skills required by the innovation and enhances the likelihood that the reform will be adapted to local circumstances." Thus, one of the mottoes of organisational development has been taken up also by implementation projects, *i.e.* to make persons affected by change to persons involved in change.

Certainly, the *individual teacher's* competencies and attitudes towards change itself and towards the specific innovation intended are important factors contributing to the quality and direction of the change process. Some *schools*, however, have more change-oriented teachers on their staff than others. This is not only due to recruitment but also–as school quality research has shown–an effect of specific school cultures.

Change involves the development of new practices and beliefs, *i.e.* it involves *learning*. Where these new practices and beliefs are not trivial we must assume that these processes *extend over time* and that they are *fraught with feelings* of being de-skilled, not knowing what to do, lacking instruments, competencies, and resources, etc.

Since it is an innovation the learning process will refer to practices already established, *i.e.* it will involve *re-learning.* Thus, the process of taking up an innovation may also be described in terms of a learning process of individuals, groups, and organizations, and actually implementation projects only can profit from what Mandl has explained as a constructivist view of learning.

Teachers seem to have *changing interests during different phases of implementation*. Initially, concrete proposal and non-paternalistic support seem to be important in order to counteract the feelings of being de-skilled and of time pressure which are connected with the innovation challenge. Later, a more comprehensive view on the substantive and methodical implications of the innovation proposal becomes possible. No wonder if the implementations process is seen as a "dynamic process of appropriating curricular concepts".

Individual teachers' learning is socially situated in a network of co-teachers, managers, administrators, and other relevant participants. It will be easier if it is situated in a such *network which is both sympathetic and competent* with respect to the changes aspired since it will be possible to collegially fill in individual's gaps of motivation and qualification.

"New meanings, behaviours, skills, and beliefs depend significantly on whether teachers are working as isolated individuals or are exchanging ideas, support, and positive feelings about their work. The quality of working relationships among teachers is strongly related to implementation.

Collegiality, open communication, trust, support, and help, learning on the job, getting results, and job satisfaction and morale are closely interrelated." Thus, some researchers equal successful implementation with succeeding in building up a *'community of learners'* with respect to the innovation, Such a 'community' invests in different occasions and instruments of collaborating, sharing, and synthesizing individual knowledge and research in order to make full use of the expertise which is 'distributed' within the relevant community and outside of it. Lave and Wenger have insisted that learning-by virtue of its social situatedness-also involves developing a specific *identity* in and *vis a vis* the respective 'community'. Similarly, to implement an innovation means for the practitioners involved in a long-term commitment to practice the innovation and to give it some centrality in their image of the profession and the organization.

Thus, implementation will be connected with some pressure to *transform professional identity*, and it will only be considered successful if this transformation is not just an individual one but is accompanied by other individuals' likewise transformation, or to put it in other words: some by some transformation of the respective community of practice.

Certainly, innovations necessitate also other non-professional participants' learning. In the case of curricular innovations it is obvious that *students' relevant competencies and attitudes* are an important factor in implementation. If the innovative proposal is unclear, against their perceived needs,. over-or under-demanding etc. it may lose students' active participation. Also janitors, clerical staff and *other participants* may be affected by the innovation, and in a position to actively support or block implementation.

Organizational Characteristics

Compatibility of the goals of the innovation and its implementation with the strategic long-term goals of the organization into which the innovation is to be implemented is crucial, too.

The same holds true for situational characteristics:

- *Organizational structures, instruments and processes* are important factors for implementation. An innovation usually aims at directly transforming some organizational structures and processes and in the process of doing so, also indirectly puts pressure on other organizational structures and processes.

The *system of incentives and the career patterns* valid in the organization to be changed must be re-thought in order to be in consonance with the innovation. For curricular innovations the structure of the *existing curriculum and assessment procedures* are particularly relevant: Attempting to change teaching and learning styles while syllabus and assessments remain unaltered will most likely run into difficulties.

Thus, implementation must work towards a fit between the *culture of the organization and both the culture of the innovation proposal and its implementation process.* Intensive collaboration, collegial reflection and sharing of individual knowledge are features which to some extent, run counter to the *culture of traditional schools* which may *e.g.* characterized by a frame of mind called "autonomy-parity-pattern" by Lortie.

This pattern is characterized by two rules which are considered crucial for smooth interaction between teachers:

- First, no grown-up person should interfere in a teacher's classroom.
- Secondly, all teachers are to be treated equally, regardless of their actual competencies, energy invested, and qualities displayed.

It has been shown that new challenges, such as school development or quality evaluation, tend to interfere with these rules since they usually opt for more coordination and sharpening profiles of the organization. And they are in need of delegation and differential taking up of development roles, and of evaluation which is necessary for rationally steering more autonomous organizations. In a recent study in vocational upper secondary schools we found that the relative weight of teachers who discard "autonomy" and "parity" as guiding principles for collegial life in schools is decisive for successful engagement in school development. The *culture of learning* valid in an organisation is particularly important because it does not only refer–in the case of curriculum implementation-to central content aspects of the innovation, but also to conditions of learning during the process of implementation. Using Weinert's definition, we see the organizational culture of learning as the totality of forms of learning and styles of teaching which are typical for an organisation at a given time including the anthropological, psychological, societal and educational orientation on which they are based.

It is considered conducive for implementation:

- If learning is awarded a high profile in the goals, vision, resources, and instruments of an organization
- If there are forums for learning and information exchange in the regular operation of the organisation
- If there are conducive images of learning continuously represented in the organisation by management and other participants; *i.e.* that the competent learner is valued, not just the full expert who is right in any case.

It follows that innovation also involves or necessitates an innovation of school as an organization, *i.e.* a process of system change or *organizational learning*. Organizational learning is–as has been frequently described–not a straight forward process because it deals with transforming structures which have been and are continuously partially self-produced and reinforced by the actors in the organization to be changed. Consequently, as suggested, expect some 'resistance' in the course of the implementation process and adverse reaction to innovation does not always aim at the characteristics of the innovation itself but sometimes at the pressure to transform one's way of working and relating to colleagues in schools.

GOVERNMENT AND OTHER AGENCIES

Priorities for education which arise from political forces, lobbying of interest groups and public concerns channel resources and gratification, "put pressure on local districts and also provide various incentives for changing in the desired direction." Its instruments are legislation, regional guidelines, incentives, sponsored projects etc. Fullan is critical of government agencies which all too often "have been preoccupied with policy and programme adoption, and have vastly underestimated the problems and processes of implementation. The policy maker and the local practitioner inhabit different worlds, each side ignorant of the subjective world of the other."

In fact, the *quality of relationships between central and local actors* is a key issue of implementation. However, all too often it has come "in the form of episodic events rather than processes: for example, submission of requests for money, intermittent progress reports on what is being done, external evaluations, all amounting to paper work, rather than people work." Through *resource support and training* external agencies can promote curriculum implementation. "...through resource support, standardization, and closer monitoring, state departments of education have sometimes directly influenced implementation of specific objectives, especially when local conditions were favourable. Mostly, however, lack of role clarity, ambiguity about expectations, absence of regular interpersonal communication, ambivalence between authority and support roles of external agencies, and solutions that do not work have combined to frustrate implementation."

PROCESS CHARACTERISTICS OF SUCCESSFUL IMPLEMENTATION

A more holistic and dynamic conceptualization is provided by a formulation of key process characteristics in successful improvement efforts. There is a small number of powerful themes which-in combination-make a difference." What are these themes?

PREPARATION, INITIATION AND PARTICIPATION

Reform needs some impetus to gets started. Some *preparatory collection and analysis of data* about the state of the system to be innovated will help to focus energy. A *'project architecture'* will have to be built up which includes formal and informal power centers and assigns specific roles to different constituencies involved and which is organizing social places and instruments for participation. Although *'participation and empowerment'* are key themes of the whole implementation process, that does not mean that widespread involvement at initial stages is "either feasible or effective". To introduce an innovation at the same time to the whole target group may not be the wisest strategy. "It is more likely the case that small groups of people begin and, if successful, build momentum. Active initiation, starting small and thinking big, bias for action, and learning by doing are all aspects of making change more manageable, by getting the process under way in a desirable direction."

VISION BUILDING

If an organization or a project has a vision, it permeates the organization with value and purpose which give direction and driving power for development. Louis and Miles vision has two aspects, an image of the organization to be changed, what it could or should look like, and an image of the change process, for the strategy for getting there. "While virtually everyone agrees that vision is crucial, the practice of vision building is not well understood." Most literature talks about what should or could be, however, there are only a few more thorough empirical studies of actual processes of vision building in education.

EVOLUTIONARY DEVELOPMENT

"For major change, highly specified planning is unwise. 'Have a plan, but learn by doing'". Successful schools, *e.g.* in the Louis and Miles study, "adapted their plans as they went along to improve the fit between the change and conditions in the school to take advantage of unexpected developments and opportunities." The art of implementation lies in blending top-down initiatives and bottom-up participation. Obviously, some pragmatic flexibility is needed "that permits a reform programme to accommodate unexpected, uncontrollable events while still attempting to preserve the main trust of the plan."

INITIATIVE-TAKING AND EMPOWERMENT

In Louis and Miles' study, "leaders in successful schools supported and stimulated initiative-taking by others; set up cross-hierarchical steering groups consisting of teachers, administrators, and sometimes parents and students; and delegated authority and resources to the steering group, while maintaining active involvement with the groups."

For organizational leaders it is obviously essential to get people to act and interact in purposeful directions, and if they do so, also to support them, to give them resources and to delegate power-without themselves fully pulling out of the process. Collaborative work cultures which may develop out of these networks of interaction provide support for the individuals, but also continuous motivation and pressure to go ahead.

PRESSURE AND SUPPORT

Innovation research teaches us that it is not as simply as 'pressure' equals bad and 'support' is good. The reason is that in organizations there are "many forces maintaining the status quo. When change occurs it is because some pressure has built up that leads to action."

'Pressure' is not to be equated with brute power and oppression, and in fact, such type of 'pressure' would rarely work effectively. Various arrangements of interaction between the implementers, such as meetings, collaborative working groups, presentation meetings etc., serve "to integrate both pressure and support. One of the reasons that peer coaching works so effectively is that it combines pressure and support in a seamless way."

- *As I said*: 'Pressure' is not simply bad and 'support' is good. Rather it seems that one without the other is bad for implementation. "Pressure without support leads to resistance and alienation; support without pressure leads to drift or waste of resources." An elaboration of this idea has been proposed by Strittmatter. He argues that in order to sustain change processes in schools there must be both motives of ability, necessity and volition. They are in a multiplicative relationship: If one of these three motivational areas is nil, the sum will be nil, *i.e.* the overall motivational energy will not be sufficient to sustain an extended change process.

STAFF DEVELOPMENT AND RESOURCE ASSISTANCE

Innovation necessitates new expertise. Educational establishments would rarely attempt to acquire this expertise by hiring additional personnel. Thus, innovation involves a process of relearning competencies and attitudes for the existing personnel. Many formats for training staff have been developed, such as *e.g.* written directions, periodicals, teachers' guidebooks, live or videotaped lectures and demonstrations, in-service workshops, on-site supervision. However, whenever relearning is to mean not only acquisition of new verbal power but of new and stabilised skills and action patterns, then relearning must be based on action and interaction over an extended time span.

Many attempts at change fail because they underestimate the individual and social energy that is necessary for re-learning. Staff development is too often designed as a one-off initiative at too early a stage of the change process. Pre-implementation training may be helpful for orienting people towards new aims and practices, however, support is most crucial when participants actually try to implement new approaches, *i.e. during* implementation, and in particular, during early stages of implementation.

"Learning by doing, concrete role models, meetings with resource consultants and other implementers, practice of the behaviour, the fits and starts of cumulative, ambivalent, gradual self-confidence are all crucial. Training approaches to implementation are successful when they combine concrete teacher-specific training activities, ongoing continuous assistance and support during the process of implementation, and regular meetings with peers and others."

MONITORING, EVALUATION AND PROBLEM-COPING

All serious improvement programmes will encounter problems. However, it makes a difference whether innovators are prepared to identify them quickly and develop coping measures or whether they avoid to face them.

Thus, self-reflection, self-evaluation and monitoring both the outcomes and the process of change is an essential element of every effective implementation strategy. Monitoring does not just fulfil a 'critical function' in identifying problems and failure. It has also a 'constructive' function in multiple respects: Certainly, it is meant to orient adaptation measures.

Organized effectively, it may provide some emotional support when implementation problems arise and when participants are in danger of falling into the "implementation dip", into the feeling that situational control is lost among changing circumstances and 'everything is getting worse'. Further, it may give access to good practical ideas which in traditional school cultures too often remain unknown and isolated as individual teachers' knowledge. Thus, monitoring may fuel exchange of implementation experience and collaborative planning of next steps by users and curriculum makers. Although most innovation researchers would agree to the importance of evaluation and monitoring of progress, it is "probably one of the most difficult and complex strategies for change 'to get right'. ...Accountability and improvement can be effectively interwoven, but it requires great sophistication." Evaluation is very often planned too late. People in initial phases of an innovation are pre-occupied with the "more practical" issues of making the innovation work.

As they feel that not everything is working as smoothly as they had hoped, they become more wary of evaluation because they fear that mistakes will become visible. Evaluation also threatens the long-standing culture of autonomy and parity in traditional schools by intruding into the privacy of the classroom and producing information which allows to differentiate between teachers. However, innovative schools do not only monitor progress, they also act upon the information collected in order to redirect their change process. Louis and Miles found that "unsuccessful sites used shallow coping strategies such as avoidance, denial, procrastination, people-shuffling, while successful sites engaged in deep problem-solving such as redesign, creating new roles, providing additional assistance and time and the like."

RESTRUCTURING

"Structure" is meant to "include organizational arrange-ments, roles, finance, governance, and formal policies which explicitly build on working conditions that support improvement.

" Our definition emphasized that innovation is always restructuring to some extent. In practice, the need *e.g.* for revised time tabling, shuffling resources, time for individual and team planning, time for visiting other colleagues or joint teaching, staff development policies and practices, new roles such as mentors and coaches etc. may surface during implementation. Where this task of restructuring is taken up explicitly and pro-actively in the course of the implementation, the chance of producing sustainable results will be higher.

INTENSIVE COMMUNICATION AND RELATIONSHIPS TO EXTERNALAGENCIES

In the perspective of systems theory organizations are special social systems which are made up of a special form of communication, of decisions. Organizational innovations aims at changing the decisions which are characteristic of the organization. In order to achieve this, phases of innovation must intensify the richness and variety of communication in an organization.

Practically, a pro-active in-house information policy is meant to feed in communication with relevant information, and the establishment of forums of information exchange and collaboration are supposed to intensify innovation-relevant communication. Also cross-departmental communication and exchange with external experts are supported in order to enhance the chance of seeing alternative solutions.

But also clear and pro-active information and communication with the organization's environment and the interested public is important in order to avoid adverse reactions, to make the innovative changes understood, and, at times, to invite alternative perspectives.

CONCLUSION

We have presented descriptions of implementation from three different angles, from the view of two broad 'philosophies' of implementation, from an analytic view on important factors contributing to successful implementation which have identified by innovation research, from the perspective of organizational developers formulating critical themes or process characteristics.

Out of the overlaps between these perspectives an image of implementation is emerging which may be characterized by the following elements:

- *Implementation Involves Changes in Behaviours and Beliefs and, thus, Involves Processes of Learning*: If these new practices and beliefs are not trivial, these processes will *extend over time* and will be *fraught with feelings* of being de-skilled, not knowing what to do, lacking instruments, competencies, and resources, etc.
- *Innovation Requires both Changes in Action and Attitude*: Contrary to the usual assumption, "it seems that most people do not discover new understandings until they have delved into something. In many cases, changes in behaviour precede rather than follow changes in belief." It follows first, that concrete instructions, materials, examples

and coaching or peer interaction which help to develop and modify practices are essential for implementation. Secondly however, changes in belief are not futile. Rather, they are essential to make sense of the new practices, organize them and hold them together in a system of meaning which is a precondition for extended practice and flexible adaptation to varying circumstances.

- *Implementation Involves Development and Evaluation:* To implement these new practices into a fairly complex new environment will not be done by just copying a master-plan or a model from some other place, but will involve some process of selection, construction, problem-solving, interpretation, and (re-)invention which 'situates' and changes the original model. This feature necessitates that the implemen-tation process and its products is monitored as it proceeds, and that the information produced thereby is used for fine-tuning or re-directing the implemen-tation process.
- *Implementation is Obviously Complex*: "Even if the need and the idea is right, the sheer complexity of the process of implementation, has, as it were, a sociological mind of its own, which frequently defies management even when all parties have the best of intentions."
- *Implementation is an Extended and Dynamic Process*: Learning extends over time and will change the situation in which it is to be learned. "Deeper meaning and solid change must be borne *over time*. With particular changes, especially complex ones, one must struggle through ambivalence before being sure that the new vision it workable and right ..."
- *Factors Affecting Successful Implementation are in a Systemic Relationship*: Set of factors "form a system of variables that interact to determine success of failure" "Single-factor theories of change are doomed to failure. ...Effective implementation depends on the combination of all the factors..."
- *More than that, Implementation will Involve Systemic Change and, thus, Necessitate Some Organization Development:* It follows that implementation will involve *learning processes on different levels*: Individual learning processes will be complemented by group learning and organizational learning which aims for changing relevant structures, processes, and cultures in a way which resonates with the main thrust of the innovation.
- *Implementation Involves Participation, Ownership and Development of Professional Identities:* Innovators will want to stimulate persons involved to more comprehensive participation. This is seen as a necessary precondition for successful innovation which asks for practitioners' commitment and "ownership". Ownership in the sense

of clarity, skill and commitment is not acquired easily; it is a progressive process which must be supported by the arrangements of the implementation process.

- As social and cultural learning theories stress learning new practices is interwoven with other actors' learning processes in a social setting, and is connected with processes of identity formation. Thus, implementation will always involve some *transformation of the professional identities* of the persons involved.
- *Implementation of Complex Innovations does not Lend itself to a Strict Separation of Phases of Research, Development and Implementation:* On one hand, issues of implementation must be anticipated in early phases of conceiving an innovation. On the other hand, implementation itself must be seen as a process of further developing the innovation proposal and of researching its effects and transformations under specific local conditions. In this perspective, implementation is understood as an element of a circular process of conceiving implementing reflecting, and re-conceiving innovations proposals, or of theory building, theory application, and testing of theories. If this argument makes sense, then research in implementation processes would hold more theoretical relevance than usually is attributed to it.
- *To Tighten the Relationship between Development, Iimplementation, and Research:* This is the shared message of Stenhouse's 'teacher as researcher'-model and the idea of 'modus 2-research' which is advocated by Reinmann-Rothmeier and Mandl as a complement to traditional research. They argue that knowledge should increasingly be developed in the context of its use; processes of problem formulation and solving should be based on heterarchic teams of persons from different disciplinary and professional backgrounds in a complex application-oriented environment. Modus 2-research opts against a strict separation between basic and application-oriented research: "Research becomes a cyclical process, in which theories and practical recommendations will be continuously analysed, tested in practice and revised, when necessary"

The complexity of the implementation process makes predictions of success risky. However, it makes it very profitable for curriculum makers to actively engage in this elusive process of supporting implementation. And it also makes it very *"profitable to monitor implementation* with care at each stage of the process, so that remedies may be applied periodically towards coping with unanticipated difficulties."

3

Text Selection Strategy

TEXT SELECTION STRATEGY

If you teach a ninth-grade science class, a strong possibility exists that half of your students will not be able to comprehend the textbook, even if the book has a ninthgrade readability level. This important chapter focuses on the readability of textbooks. First, you will learn several methods for computing or otherwise determining the reading difficulty of the textbooks you use. Second, you will be shown strategies for predicting how well your students will be able to comprehend their textbooks. Finally, you will see results from surveys and research studies that indicate how well people have to read to survive in school, to function well on the job, and to engage in pleasure reading.

Teachers make a single textbook appropriate to the range of individual differences in a class by using the single-text strategies, in two ways: (1) they use directed reading activities (DRA), reading and learning from-text guides, and the SQ3R method to adapt the text to individual differences among students; and (2) they teach students to use strategies for reading and learning from text on their own.

Another way the teacher makes the single text fit the needs of all students is to use some procedure for determining the *readability* of the text for a group of students. If the teacher can select a textbook that is about average in difficulty for the class, the text will be easier to adapt to the entire range of abilities in the class than a text that is closer to the low or high achievers.

If textbook selection is made during the summer when students are not present, the teacher has to rely only upon the characteristics of the text itself and personal judgment to determine whether the text would be appropriate for the class. For this purpose, the teacher can use either a *readability formula* or a technique for estimating readability. The formulas that we explain in some detail in this chapter are the Flesch Reading Ease Formula and the Fry Readability Graph. The technique for estimating readability is the SEER technique. However, if the students are available, then the teacher does not have to use a formula that *predicts* reading difficulty or a procedure for *estimating* readability. Instead, the teacher can actually try the material out with the students and find out how difficult *in fact* the text is for them. The "try out" types of readability testing are the cloze technique and the personal or informal reading inventories. These ways of determining readability require considerable student and teacher time but provide the best way of determining readability for a particular group of students.

DETERMINING READABILITY LEVEL TECHNIQUES

Determination of readability and reading difficulty fits into two categories: (a) computational and (b) noncomputational techniques. We first briefly describe each of these techniques and then explain in greater detail how to use or construct them.

Readability formulas of the computational type have been available for the past 40 years. All of them use some variation of sentence complexity and word difficulty. Three of the standard formulas in wide use are appropriate for somewhat different segments of the grade-level continuum. The Spache formula was designed for Grades 1-3, the Dale-Chall for Grades 4-8, and the Flesch formula for Grades 4 to college graduation. Although readability formulas have helped determine what makes reading easy or difficult, much is still unknown about reading difficulty.

The computational formulas are time-consuming and tedious to use. They require the user to count syllables, words, or sentences. Consequently, some researchers have developed procedures for reducing the time and tedium in computing readability levels of materials.

A noncomputational procedure has achieved the greatest reduction in time for estimating readability level. This procedure consists of matching unknown material to a standard scale. Although this third approach to determining readability level is somewhat subjective, it is nevertheless as accurate as some computational procedures.

The *cloze technique* uses a totally different way of determining reading difficulty level. To employ this technique in the original way, as defined by its inventor, Taylor, simply delete or omit every fifth word from a passage of approximately 250 words. Leave a sentence before and after each passage intact. A total of 50 words will be deleted from the passage. The reader's task is to infer from the remaining context what the missing words are, retrieve the exact words from vocabulary stored in his or her memory, and insert them into the passage.

When you score only the exact original word as correct, you prevent disputes from arising on whether a word is a synonym for the missing word or not. The cloze technique places a premium upon the reader's ability to infer the missing words from the semantics and syntax of the remaining words in the passage and upon the reader's vocabulary repertoire and ability to retrieve words from storage in memory. Since the reader also has to identify printed words in order to infer the missing words, the reader performing on the cloze test has to use semantics, syntax, graphophonemics, graphomorphemics, and reasoning processes. Look at this sentence: *After locating his flock, the shepherd gathered the sh*_____.The *semantics*, or accumulated meanings of the sentence, suggest what the shepherd gathered. The *syntax*, or the order in which words in English must occur, signals the type of word that should be coming next or at least soon in a sentence. In the sentence above, the noun determiner *the* indicates a noun belongs in the next slot in the sentence, the slot for the missing word.

Graphophonemics is the ability to give sounds to individual letters or to letter groups which function as single units, such as *sh*. *Graphomorphemics* is a two-part process. In one process, the student recognizes boundaries between meaningful units in words, such as *shepherd*.

Knowledge of words and word structures in English enables the reader to recognize and correctly segment words at their structural boundaries. Then the reader can apply graphophonemics to relate the units of print to sounds. The reader also has to use *reasoning processes*, such as inference, to try to determine the word that has been deleted. Hence the cloze technique is a way of assessing all of these systems and their operation in the process of reading. Of course, other factors also enter into replacing missing words, such as knowledge of an author's style.

A fourth way of estimating readability of content area materials is through a reading inventory based upon graded material drawn from a specific content area. In this procedure, an individual reads and answers questions on successively more difficult, graded paragraphs.

As the reader progresses through the paragraphs, more errors in answering comprehension questions occur, provided the questions that the teacher constructs are relevant and appropriately difficult for the grade level of the paragraphs. Later in this chapter we present information on how to construct these questions. The resulting score determines the reader's fluency, instructional, and frustration levels.

These levels use arbitrary criteria that teachers find useful. The *fluency level* is the grade level of a passage at which the reader can correctly answer 90% or more of the comprehension questions. The *instructional level* is the grade level of a passage at which the reader attains 70% to 90% comprehension. The *frustration level* is the grade level of a passage at which the reader's comprehension drops below 70%.

How readers respond to their difficulties in reading is also dependent on other factors, especially their interest in the material and their desire to read it. Now that we have had an overview of the various ways of determining readability and reading difficulty, we go into each way in greater detail.

The Flesch Reading Ease Formula

The Flesch Reading Ease Formula for computing readability level uses two criteria: number of syllables per hundred words and average number of words per sentence in a 100-word sample. The number of syllables in a word is an index of the difficulty of the word because longer words are usually more difficult. The words per sentence are an index of sentence complexity. Usually longer sentences are syntactically more complex and hence more difficult.

To use the Reading Ease Formula you will need to make two computations: (a) count the syllables in a passage that has approximately 100 words. Remember that a word has as many syllables as it has vowels or vowel-like sounds. Simply say each word and count the number of vowel sounds you hear. For words per sentence, count the number of words in the passage and then divide by the number of sentences in the passage.

The scales allow you to determine the Reading Ease Score. Just locate the words per sentence on the left scale and syllables per hundred words on the right scale. Then connect the points on the two scales with a ruler. The point where the ruler intersects the middle scale indicates the Reading Ease Score of the Passage.

Example:
Words per sentence = 15
Syllables per 100 words = 160
Intersection point = 57.
The score of 57 is the Reading Ease Score for the passage.

The Fry Readability Graph

This figure also contains directions on how to compute readability with an example. In the Fry technique, you find the average number of syllables and the number of sentences in three samples of 100 words. The large number between the lines on the graph which is closest to the point of intersection indicates the approximate grade level of the passage.

To use the graph to determine readability level, locate 141 on the top of the graph and put the finger of your right hand at this point. Then locate 6.3 on the left side of the graph and put a finger on your left hand on this number. Now move your right finger down and your left finger across the graph. Where they intersect you'll find a dot between two lines. The number between these two lines stands for Grade 7. Since the dot is close to, but not on line 7, you then estimate the readability of the passage is about grade level 6.9.

A procedure that does not compute readability, but simply judges it by comparison with a standard, is the SEER technique. Unlike the Flesch and Fry formulas, the cloze technique requires that a sample of the printed material must be *tried out* on the individual or group of students who are actually going to read the material. Thus, the cloze technique determines the difficulty of the material relative to the reading ability of the students who are actually going to read the material.

The Cloze Technique

In the cloze technique every 5th word from a 250-word passage is deleted, but the sentence before and after the passage is left intact. A modification calls for the deletion of every 10th word from a 500-word passage. The technique implicitly requires the reader to rely upon the syntax and semantics of the passage plus such aspects as writing style to infer what the missing words are and then to retrieve these words from his or her vocabulary repertoire. In scoring, only the the pretest are low and those on the posttest are high, a teacher can reasonably infer that students have learned the content during the course.

A limitation of the cloze technique is that it tends to work best only when the passages are near the reader's difficulty level. If the passages are too easy for students, the students are likely to insert many synonyms. These synonyms are then scored as errors. Consequently, easy passages lead to an underestimation of students' actual reading levels. At the other extreme, if the passages selected are too difficult, readers also obtain a low score for different reasons: they do not have the missing word in their vocabulary, cannot retrieve it from their memory, cannot use syntax or semantics from which to infer the missing word, lack motivation to search for it, or some combination of these reasons.

Hence, the cloze technique should be used cautiously. If reader's scores are low, get higher, and then become lower as they progress through graded passages, the passages which yielded the higher scores should be used for obtaining students' readability levels. Counting only exact words correct simplifies the task of scoring the cloze test because it eliminates pondering over what is a synonym and what is not. If you do decide to accept synonyms in scoring, allow students to judge which synonyms are acceptable; this will save you a classroom hassle. However, the meanings of the scores given in Box 10.3 are not appropriate when synonyms are accepted. Indeed, researchers have not devised any scoring method applicable to the use of synonyms. The cloze technique has advantages over other readability techniques because teachers can construct test passages easily and do not have to write comprehension questions, as they do when using the personal or informal reading inventory technique that is discussed next.

The Seer Technique for Estimating Readability Level

SEER is an acronym for "Singer Eyeball Estimate of Readability". It is a judgmental technique that involves taking a passage, usually a paragraph of about 100 words from materials of unknown readability level, and matching it to a paragraph in a set of scaled paragraphs whose reading levels have been computed and are indicated next to the paragraphs. The directions for using the SEER Scale tell the teacher to take a paragraph whose readability is to be estimated, move the paragraph up and down the scaled paragraphs until a judgment is made that the unknown paragraph is about equal in difficulty to a paragraph on the scale.

In making a judgment, the teacher is likely to use such criteria as sentence length, word difficulty, writing style, and concept level. Then the teacher notes the readability level of the paragraph on the scale that matches the paragraph whose readability level is being judged. If the difficulty of the unknown paragraph lies between two of the scaled paragraphs, assign the grade-level readability between the two paragraphs. The SEER technique is more accurate when the textual material for matching and the scaled paragraphs are in the same content area. The estimated reading level of a matching paragraph will be accurate, plus or minus one grade level, in two out of three cases. This technique of estimating readability is easier than the Fry technique's tedious and

Time-consuming computations. If the content of the scaled paragraphs and the paragraphs for matching do differ, the reading level estimation is likely to be off by about plus or minus 1.5 grade levels for two out of three comparisons. That means that the readability of a passage estimated to be at a Grade 10 level of difficulty might be somewhere between Grades 8.5 and 11.5. This measurement variability applies to all computational formulas. However, this degree of accuracy is still useful for practical purposes. To select passages for constructing a set of scaled paragraphs in a particular content area, such as history, biology, mathematics, literature, use the school library catalogs. Note that only the elementary school catalogs provide readability grade levels. Readability grade levels of 7-9 are implied by listing books in the junior high catalog, and readability grade levels of 10-12 are implicit in books listed in the high school catalog. If a book is not listed in the catalogs, the teacher can use the SEER technique. Another estimation formula determines the probable range of reading ability of a heterogeneous group of students. Although we have already presented this formula, we simply repeat it here: Expected range of reading level = T! × average chronological age of the group. Thus, a 10th grade class with an average age of 15 will have a 10-year reading range, from grade equivalent 5 to grade equivalent 15. The Flesch Reading Ease Formula and the Fry Readability Graph compute and predict the grade level of reading material from characteristics of the printed material alone. The SEER technique *estimates* grade-level difficulty.

Critique of Reading Difficulty Formulas

The reading difficulty of a text can be determined apart from any particular reader, as the Fry and Flesch formulas do. In addition to the criteria these formulas use for arriving at readability levels, we may also consider other features of the text. For example, a text may be relatively difficult because it has a high density of ideas and a high degree of interrelatedness or coherence among the ideas. But, whether these characteristics of a text are difficult or not also depend upon the reader's prior knowledge, vocabulary ability, reasoning processes, purposes, and goals in reading the text.

For example, if a text is densely packed with ideas but the reader's purpose is only to get the general idea of the text, the reader is likely to find the text easier than if his or her purpose was to comprehend the text fully. Hence, we recognize that the difficulty level of a text as computed by the Fry and Flesch formulas and as estimated by the SEER technique is only the *average* or *general* level of difficulty of a text.

To determine the difficulty of a text for a particular reader, for example, a student who was having difficulty in reading and learning from a text, we would examine factors not only within that text but also within the reader. In short, reading difficulty for a particular individual depends upon an interaction between the text and the individual.

Applications of Knowledge about Readability

Although teachers do not usually have time to modify teaching materials or write them, they sometimes find themselves working on summer projects to prepare materials for teaching. Sometimes a school district may even provide time for preparation of materials. Occasionally teachers take a course or participate in a workshop where they write materials for teaching. Then they can use their knowledge of readability criteria to modify or construct reading materials so as to make them easier or more difficult. Two variables that can be manipulated for this purpose are sentence length and word difficulty. Longer sentences are usually more syntactically complex and may have one or more embedded sentences, or subordinate clauses. Hence, combining sentences, especially where subordination results, is likely to increase the difficulty of the sentence, but not always.

Although it may at first appear more difficult, the longer sentence in 2, below, is easier than the three shorter ones in 1 because the reader does not have to infer the intersentence relationships: In the lab, Kimber mixed oxygen and hydrogen. He got water. (He also got an explosion.)

In the lab, Kimber mixed oxygen and hydrogen to get water (plus an explosion). Researchers have not discovered much about intersentence syntax and intersentence difficulties or about syntactic difficulties in different types of sentences and paragraphs. However, they have found out that students are more likely to comprehend written passages in which the syntax is the same as the syntax they use in their own oral language). Word difficulty is another variable to use for manipulating the difficulty of reading material. You can substitute synonyms of higher frequency to make the material easier and, conversely, synonyms of lower frequency to make the material more difficult. Armed with a Thesaurus and Carroll, Davies and Richman word frequency book, a teacher or writer can modify the difficulty level of textual materials.

But the teacher has to exercise judgment because word frequency counts do not encompass all indices of word difficulty. They do not account for difficulty of word identification in context or for the difficulty of the contextual meaning of words. Students might understand *run* as a verb form but have more difficulty in comprehending it as a noun form, or as part of an idiom (a *run* on a bank or a *run* in a stocking).

Although materials that the teacher has simplified may enable more students to comprehend the content of the materials, such simplification represents downward adaptation of the curriculum. Another tack to take is to *stimulate* the development of students by teaching them to comprehend more complex material.

For example, teach students to analyze complex sentences and make them simpler. Also teach them to comprehend the meaning of affixes (prefixes and suffixes) and roots so that they can analyze the meanings of complex words by breaking them into their constituent parts. Wolfe has reported considerable success in improving high school students' reading by having them learn affixes and roots and then using them in analyzing content area technical terms.

To help students develop toward greater maturity in reading and learning from text, follow a sequence like this: simplify material at first; then teach students to comprehend more complex words and syntactical relationships within and between sentences. For this sequential instruction, use textbooks you have selected from school catalogs that are graded in difficulty.

Obtaining Information

How well do students have to read? To answer this question, we would have to respond rhetorically by asking another question: how well do students have to read *for what purpose*? How well do students have to be able to do recreational reading at various levels of difficulty, or to do the practical reading required in everyday life (newspapers, job applications, receipts, recipes, directions, and so forth), or to comprehend job-required reading materials, or to learn from texts in various content areas? Researchers have used reading difficulty formulas to determine reading levels in each of these areas.

TYPES OF READING

Recreational Reading Levels

Flesch applied his Reading Ease Formula to various types of *recreational reading material*. A fifth-grade level of reading ability is necessary for comprehending print in comic books. *Time* magazine has an 8thto 9th-grade level of reading difficulty and *Atlantic* magazine a 10th- to 12thgrade level of reading difficulty.

Functional Reading

The army coined the term *functional reading* in World War II. Then, the term meant "the ability to understand written instructions for carrying out basic military tasks." A serviceman was functionally literate if he could read at least at the fifth-grade level.

Today, a higher reading level would probably be necessary for the attainment of functional literacy. However, neither university researchers nor public school officials have reached any agreement on a definition of functional literacy. Perhaps we can define functional literacy only in relation to a person's purpose, the requirements of the situation (reading government forms, textbooks, and so forth), and the school's expectation for successful accomplishment in reading and learning from text. For a cook in the army it would be one level; for a college student, another level; and so on. Hence, we could not state that functional literacy is at a fifth-grade, ninth-grade, or any specific grade level.

One way to determine *functional reading level* is to determine what adults actually read and how much time they spend on reading. Sharon conducted a cross-sectional survey of a national sample of 5,067 adults. The results indicated that the average adult reads for about 2 hours on a typical day, frequently while pursuing such daily activities as working, shopping, attending school or church or theater, traveling or commuting, as well as during free time. The survey indicated that adults read the materials listed below.

Newspapers: 70% of adults read newspapers for an average of 35 minutes a day.

Mail: 53% read mail for 5 minutes a day, but 96% receive mail every day.

Magazines: 40% read magazines for 35 minutes a day.

Books: 33% read books about 47 minutes a day.

When do adults do their reading? According to the survey, the higher an individual's socioeconomic status, the more reading he or she did. But 5% of all adults interviewed were unable to read (define as unable to read newspaper headlines) including 2.3% who were visually handicapped, 1.6% who were foreign language readers, and 1.1% who were illiterates (those adults who never learned to read in any language and did not have visual difficulties). The members of this nonreading group were also members of an extremely low socioeconomic group. They had to depend on others to read to them.

The National Reading Council, appointed by President Nixon, commissioned Louis Harris and Associates (1970) to measure the literacy rate in the nation, using a representative sample of 1,685 persons, ages 16 and up.

The study measured the "survival" literacy rate for functional, or practical, reading skills. These reading skills consist of the ability to read such application forms as required for obtaining a Social Security number, a personal bank loan, public assistance, medicaid, and a driver's license. Those who answered three questions incorrectly (30% of the items on the forms) were considered illiterate. The percentage ranged from 3% (public assistance form) to 34% (medicaid form). On the average, 1 out of 8 adults (or, at that time, 18.5 million Americans) would have had difficulty in obtaining government assistance because they could not read well enough to fill out the application forms.

The lowest age group in the Harris survey (age 16-24) had the lowest illiteracy rate (range 1% to 9%). The lowest illiteracy rate in the nation was found in the West and the highest was in the South. The remedy for inability to read application forms and other functional reading tasks is twofold: (a) simplify the language used in the forms, use larger print accompanied by pictured directions, and provide cassette tapes for auditory explanations; (b) seek to improve literacy, starting with high school students still in the functionally illiterate category, and reducing the relatively low rate of this group even further; then go on to older illiterates.

Textbook Difficulty

The two researchers then gave a general reading test to students enrolled in these courses. They found that the average reading ability of students was *below* the average difficulty of the texts they used—about 0.6 of a year below in food services, 1.0 years below in auto mechanics, 1.7 years below in building trades, 3.5 years below in welding, and 4.0 years below in radio and TV repair! The instructors of these courses corroborated the findings. They reported that over half the students in their courses could not comprehend their texts without the instructor's help.

What are Job-Related Reading Requirements?

Sticht and McFann used a specially constructed set of tasks based on actual reading done in various army occupations. As a criterion they used the percentage in comprehension scored by enlisted men with various levels of reading ability. Cooks, mechanics, and supply clerks whose general reading level was about 6.5 scored only 50% in comprehension, and students reading at grade level 12.8 got 90%. With a 70% comprehension score as the criterion, the reading level required to be a successful cook would be the 7th-grade level, for mechanics the 9th-grade level, and for supply clerks the 10-grade level. Additional data on reading, listening, and arithmetic requirements of military occupations that have civilian counterparts can be found in Sticht, Caylor, and Kern. "Literacy in the workplace" has become the title for a new field of research. Mickulecky and Strange report on several studies that indicate work-type reading differs considerably from school text reading. Middle-level workers and professionals spend an equal amount of their reading time in reading for application, assessment, and acquisition of new information. Workers' reading includes directions, diagrams, manuals, forms, flyers, computer print-outs and textbooks. The difficulty levels of these materials average 11th-grade level, but range from 9th grade to college level. They read to make applications, solve problems, relate information in the text to known information and form judgments.

They compare textual information against the actual equipment described. The reading often occurs in the context of a group, and workmen ask each other questions about their reading more than twice as often as high school students do. They average about 2 hours per days in reading, usually in short blocks of about 5 minutes per reading episode, whereas high school students spend about 98 minutes per day in reading. Since 95% of high school reading is from textbooks, mostly to learn factual information, Mickulecky and Strange conclude "there is little in the school experience to prepare new workers for the range of literacy strategies called for in the workplace."

In general, workers tend to read better than high school students. Blue-collar workers average between 10th and 11th grades in reading ability. Only 5% of blue-collar workers but 16% of high school juniors experienced extreme difficulty with a 9th-grade newspaper passage. Mickulecky and Strange think that "many individuals with low literacy abilities are not being allowed to enter or remain in the work force."

Even those with relatively high literacy abilities, but still below the expectations attained by those of equal intelligence and backgrounds, are not as likely to qualify for professional occupations that emphasize scientific knowledge. They are more likely to go into sales jobs where nonacademic skills are more important. In short, the required literacy level is relative to the reading demands of the occupation. In other words, inadequate literacy levels are not only likely to affect the job opportunities of blue-collar workers but also whitecollar professionals.

The assumption that training in general literacy would transfer to the specific reading demands of the workplace does not appear to be warranted. However, high schools cannot go the other extreme to train students for all the specific types of reading in the workplace. What they can do is teach students general reading ability, how to read some specific job-related materials, probably in conjunction with occupational courses for the purposes and in the way workers read on the job, perhaps enable them to learn how to learn job-related materials, and develop in students the expectation that they will have to learn how to read the specific materials in each particular job they enter. Employers will also have to learn that they will have to provide reading instruction on the job in specific job-related materials to high school graduates, whether they are blue- or white-collar workers. They will have to emphasize the specific types of reading, technical vocabulary, information, and procedures required for the job. The army has already accepted this requirement. Instead of general literacy training, the army provides for specific job literacy training in each of its 120 major military jobs.

Reading Demands of Texts in Academic Courses

High school texts vary considerably in difficulty level even in the same content areas. Belden and Lee found that four of five biology texts had average readability levels higher than the average reading levels of students in six Oklahoma high schools; only one text had a readability level suitable for 50% of the students who used it.

Mallinson, Sturm, and Mallinson, using the Flesch formula, found that 11 of 16 high school physics texts had 9th-grade readability levels; these texts were suitable for all students enrolled in physics classes. Three texts scored between 9th- and 10th-grade reading levels; they were appropriate only for average and better physics students. But, two texts were too difficult even for superior students!

These studies indicate that the teacher of content area classes should be aware that there is a range of texts from which to choose for content area instruction. If limited to one text, the teacher can probably select a text that is appropriate for at least half the class. But if more than one text is available, knowledge of the readability levels of texts and reading abilities of students would enable the teacher to select texts appropriate to the entire class.

To give the reader a concrete idea of the difficulty level of content area reading materials, we selected some texts used in some high schools in southern California. We took samples from them and computed their Flesch Reading Ease scores.

Of course, the passages in these texts do not represent the range of difficulty within each text. More difficult and easier passages could be found in each text. That is why an average based on at least three samples from three different parts of a text is necessary in establishing the reading level of the text.

Readability formulas have other limitations. They do not take into account the conceptual level nor the information density of the material. The algebra sample is equal in difficulty to the English sample, but the algebra vocabulary appears to be much more difficult than the English vocabulary. Hence, in addition to using a formula for assessing readability, teachers should analyze the content of a text to determine its semantic difficulty, information density, conceptual level, and style of writing. Unfortunately, scales for assessing semantic difficulty, or for conceptual levels, or for density of concepts or information, or for relating writing styles to difficulty of reading are not available. Consequently, teachers can make only subjective appraisals of these aspects of reading difficulty. At the college level (as well as at any other level) the question has to be: how well should a student have to read what kind of material and for what degree of comprehension? As Sticht and McFann (1975) pointed out, above, readers can have varying degrees of comprehension. Furthermore, required reading materials in college (as in other levels of education) vary in readability level; and the average and range of readability ability of college students also vary. The University of California, which has nine campuses, by law can accept only the top 12.5% of high school graduates who have taken a particular programme of academic courses. Hence, freshman clases consist of students from the upper 12.5% of their high school classes. To complete effectively in this freshman environment, a student should have reading comprehension abilities at least equal to those of the top 12.5% of high school seniors.

However, the California State University and College System, which is a separate system from the University of California, can accept the top one third of high school graduates. Students with reading abilities at least within the range of the 67th to the 99th percentile of high school seniors are likely to be able to compete with varying degrees of success in the State University and College System. The community colleges in California can accept any high school graduate. Consequently, a wider range of reading abilities occurs among the junior college population. Similar variation exists among institutions of higher education throughout the country.

Since teachers tend to normalize instruction, that is, teach toward the average student, the reading demands and criteria for successful academic accomplishment are likely to reflect the capacities and skills of the average student. In short, to decide what level of reading achievement a student needs to be successful at the college level, teachers have to know (a) a student's capacities (particularly the skills of reading and learning from text) and aspirations for achievement as well as (b) the demands of the institution and the average level of ability of students in the institution. sSpeed of reading, a factor that is important at any level, becomes increasingly significant as students progress through the grades and becomes crucial at the college level because of the heavy load of reading.

To determine why speed of reading is crucial at the college level, let's look at the reading requirements at college and compute the time required to do the assigned reading and complete the texts. D. W. Gilbert estimates that a college student at the University of California has 16,000 pages of reference reading to do each semester. The average college freshman reads relatively easy (sixth-grade level) material at a rate of 250 words per minute. Van Wagenen determined this speed in his rate-of-comprehension test. Computation gives, 32,000 minutes or 533 hours—about 13.5 forty-hour weeks! Since a semester is usually 18 weeks long, the students who reads at this average rate has to spend most of the semester reading assigned material in order to survive academically. Hence, students have to learn to be extremely efficient in reading and to develop effective strategies for reading and learning from text.

Instead of waiting until students reach high school or college, we need to start at earlier levels to teach them efficient and effective strategies they can acquire cumulatively as they progress through school. Prior to this chapter, we provided knowledge, strategies, techniques, and tools for teaching students with a wide range of individual differences to read and learn from a *single* text. We are now ready to explain ways of handling individual differences through strategies for reading and learning from multiple texts.

4

Communication in Audio-Visual Aids

AUDIO-VISUAL AIDS

By audio-visual aids, we usually mean the most modern or the most recently used of these methods. This is a summary identification of very old methods and very modern instruments, and one should react against it. Visual aids are far older. They correspond to a profound tendency among the immense majority of men: to materialise their thoughts in the form of graphic or sonorous images or to give their thoughts a concrete frame of reference.

Plato himself took care to set the scenery of his dialogues, and he used concrete words and concrete comparisons as foundations for his most abstract ideas. In France, the Très riches heures du duc de Berry bring out the importance which 'illustration' can take in a work which would have otherwise sunk into oblivion. Xylographic images preceded the printing press by three-quarters of a century and the first illustrated book by nearly a century.

The tremendous success of the 'images of Epinal' in books peddled from door to door in France was only a manifestation of popular taste in a society where illiterates continued to be in a majority and where images went with oral literature. Films, radio and television, considered as educational instruments, have merely developed – at a rapid rate – alongside older means whose importance remains considerable. Their common denominator lies in their function as aids.

This is not a theoretical conclusion, for it is confirmed by the very attitude of the educator. The educator basically must contribute to the training of the individual with a view to his integration into a given society and teach new ideas, facts and techniques to a specific public. It is thus relatively easy to define the goals at which the educator aims. Achieving these goals is another task which brings him face to face every day with the basic problem of pedagogy – that of transmitting or communicating ideas or information. To solve this problem, the educator resorts to infinitely varied means, among them audiovisual aids. If our purpose, therefore, is to aid the educator, we must then offer him as complete an arsenal as possible of these means. But it is the educator and the educator alone who chooses the means which is best adapted to his subject, his audience and his circumstances. It is thus clear that audio-visual aids cannot be separated from educational materials in general.

This tendency towards the use of concrete examples has developed through a complex process. At first, graphic representation was probably only a way to enable man to capture fleeting thoughts and the sole way of transmitting thoughts, compared to oral transmission which was subject to rapid distortion.

The invention of writing, a perfect example of a visual aid at its origin, proceeded from the same necessity. It would be interesting to study, for example, in the light of Mayan writing – of the Codex Troano – how man progressed from the talking image to the letter. We can therefore conclude that 'illustrations' were looked upon at first, at least by the most educated persons, as a minor complement to thought. The entire history of publishing until the end of the eighteenth century confirms this. But, in the twentieth century, powerful means of reproduction, associated with radio, cinema and television, have changed the aspect of the problem. Sound and visual 'illustrations' are no longer mere minor complements to thought but they directly influence the thoughts and the very conduct of millions of individuals.

It was therefore inevitable that a desire should spring up to master such a powerful instrument, to discipline it for better or for worse. But this coveted mastery is still rather crude: it is often reduced to the creating of a few conditioned reflexes, satisfying the merchant but not the educator. Certain of these audio-visual aids are both means of education and media for information and propaganda, and it is not always easy to draw the line between what belongs to the educator and what is within the province of information or propaganda.

It is also probable that the child is more affected by the violence of street posters and by the shock techniques of radio and television at home than by the visual aids used in school. Should we conclude then that these means are harmful and should we condemn them? This negative attitude would be most unrealistic. The only possible conclusion is to accept the need for basic research in these fields. It should bear essentially upon psychology and upon the social sciences. We educators have already ventured forth, but timidly, onto this terrain. Systematic establishment of contacts with research workers and specialised institutes is the duty of all those who are responsible at the national level for audio-visual services.

It can be reasonably hoped that this basic research will lead to a better use of audio-visual aids and to more scientific pedagogy based upon them. It is not difficult to observe that their use is continuing and developing outside the pale of any research. As a result, a pragmatic pedagogy is taking shape and not necessarily in contradiction to the results of the most scholarly research. Establishing or stimulating closer collaboration between research workers and educators, stimulating the writing of theses or documents containing the fruits of the work of both, and publishing and distributing the results of this work should also be the common task of pedagogical and audio-visual services. Until now, the problem of the use of audio-visual aids has been examined from an intellectual angle.

It also includes important practical and technical aspects. To tell the truth, techniques cannot and should not be separated from pedagogy. We have seen that audio-visual aids cannot be separated from educational materials as a whole, this conclusion being thrust upon us by the attitude of the user when confronted by these materials. Now this same user – whether a teacher, a professor or an adult educator – does not act any differently when pedagogy and techniques are involved. He can never be purely a pedagogue or purely a technician.

It is clear, therefore, that the pedagogy of audio-visual aids cannot be separated arbitrarily from audio-visual techniques. No one can hope to achieve good results unless he is a sensitive pedagogue and a skilled technician. The problem must be solved globally. Unfortunately, this initiation into techniques is not always carried out in the institutions where future educators are trained. In underdeveloped countries, the lack of qualified personnel is the most frequent obstacle to such an initiation.

But it is not the only one because similar shortcomings are often found in more favoured countries. Routine, lack of initiative and administrative delays are the main factors responsible for educational sluggishness. There is no doubt that audio-visual aids produce their best results when they are used in connexion with active teaching methods. Here, the task of educators is to draw the attention of their governments to these methods and to the recommendations of previous seminars concerned with the introduction of an initiation into film and radio techniques into normal schools and similar institutions. Finally, there are other questions which should be taken up in thorough and specific studies. They are related to the use of radio and television in the teaching of reading and writing and of languages. A great deal has been said about the 'singular, specific and irreplaceable services' which can be rendered, for example, by 'teaching by radio'.

A great many hopes were stirred as a result of statements repeated with such warm conviction that one could have believed them to be dictated by experience. First of all, we should note the ambiguity of the term 'teaching'. In the context of the statements to which we refer, this term covers both the teaching of subjects such as science and history as well as the teaching of reading and writing. One of the greatest problems which remains to be solved is the liquidation of illiteracy. Following hasty conclusions, a belief has grown that, thanks to radio, illiteracy can be liquidated quickly, easily and cheaply. But what do we know about it objectively? Until now, the number of experiments has been limited. Some of them were frankly admitted failures. Fortunately, as suggested, soon be in possession of an exhaustive report of the results obtained during the best known of these experiments, the one at Colombia. One of our experts has made a global study of these results from which we think that as suggested, be able to derive valuable lessons, if not definitive conclusions.

A few complimentary remarks should be made here. The first concerns the basic difference between teaching notions of history, geography, science, etc., by radio and the teaching of reading and writing. We say teaching by radio because the problem of teaching reading and writing by television is infinitely simpler and the results already acquired are sufficiently convincing. At any rate, it can never be said too often that the global use of audio-visual aids always gives the best results.

Opposing radio to television or both to films is a typical example of a false problem. In an educational campaign organised and carried out at a national level, all complementary means must be used if possible. It is also virtually certain that results are proportionate to the means employed in a geometrical, not an arithmetical, progression. In other words, overly strict economy does not pay. There lies a source of misunderstanding. Too often, it has been believed that making an expert and $10,000 worth of equipment available to a government was enough to solve the problem of audio-visual aids in a given Member State.

Audio-visual aids do not have this magic quality. They require serious study and, first of all, serious thought about the place which they should occupy in a budget. Pedagogical problems always end up by leading into budgetary problems – that is, in the long run, economic, social and political problems. The educator must play his pedagogical role. The tool which is offered to him – and this is the case of audio-visual tools – can multiply the activity of the educator in large proportion.

Therefore, the political authorities must be convinced of the necessity of a financial effort which is often considerably large. That is a point of view which often escapes the educator: he must also educate administrators and political authorities. Many mistakes begin here.

So far, we have talked about audio-visual 'aids' and 'means'. Educators obviously consider them from this angle in the best of cases. But will this tremendous development of mass information media which we continue to allow itself to be domesticated? Let us go to the heart of the matter: must we continue to consider these information media as blind forces whose unleashing – and, as far as the educator is concerned, the unleashing begins where his own control ends – would be an educational and cultural catastrophe? Or, to put things in a less impressive but equally embarrassing way, cannot audio-visual 'means' be allowed to play their role without the help or simply the intervention of the educator? Before issuing a condemnation without any possibility of appeal, perhaps it might be wise to remember that films, radio and television can only be arbitrarily separated from the social, economic and cultural context which gives them their means of existence. No doubt, the study of these problems takes us a long way from modest film strips, flannelgraphs, and even traditional black-boards which are still a luxury for thousands of schools. Let there be no misunderstanding. We know the importance of pedagogy in the use of audio-visual aids. We know that the training of good educators – in this case, good users of these didactic means – is a long and difficult matter. We know that we must think about the desperate problem of training teachers. But pedagogy itself is only a means whose end is education. And education, in the long run, is only a contribution – naturally, of capital importance – to the integration of the individual into a given society. It is in this perspective – from their production to their final use – that we must look at audio-visual aids and the various questions which they raise.

TEACHING AIDS

PRACTICAL EXAMPLES: CONNECTING THEORY WITH APPLICATIONS

Students have expressed concern regarding the need for more industrial and practical examples to reinforce theory in the classroom. The use of practical examples can help you connect engineering theory with practical applications for more effective teaching and learning. The introduction of practical examples does not imply an elimination of theory, but rather an enhancement of the theory taught in the classroom. It is important to simultaneously develop a theoretical and a practical base since neither is useful without the other.

The use of practical examples in the classroom is targeted at the following two main goals:

1. Help illustrate and explain new material making the theoretical basis of the material more accessible to the students. Practical examples help students understand the new concepts being introduced.
2. Teach students how to apply their knowledge of course material to new situations that are not directly covered in class. The goal here is to show the students not only that what they are learning has practical applications, but more importantly, how to apply their understanding of the basic principles to real engineering problems.

Scope

Practical examples can be included at all levels of the engineering curriculum. When determining examples to be used for instruction it is important to make the examples as clear and straight forward as possible. The key is to make the examples as simple as possible, and to make sure that they isolate the desired principle. Whenever possible, the examples should be designed so that the students' physical senses are brought into play. Examples that are likely to be enjoyed by the students include those that require them to use their sense of sight, feeling, hearing or smell.

The following guidelines should be remembered when implementing practical examples:

- Understand the example given and be able to explain it. If you cannot provide a clear explanation to the example, the example will confuse the students more than help them.
- Before giving a demonstration or take home assignment, carry out the assignment yourself. This will ensure that you know exactly what the students will "see". It will also help you to anticipate your students' questions. Giving an assignment or demonstration that doesn't work is frustrating to the students and is bad for your credibility.
- Choose examples that are relevant to the students. Examples that the students can observe first hand as opposed to those in a film or on TV are better. Try and find examples that the students can observe on campus or at home. Pull examples from current events like, for instance, explaining the cause for a design failure of a collapsed bridge recently in the news. Explain the basic principles behind a new or commonly used product like the fluid mechanics aspects of a Bernoulli disk drive in a computer.
- Allow ample time in class to discuss the example.
- Consider having the students prepare a written report to document what they have learned. Have them include a list of the basic principles involved.

CATEGORIES AND TYPES OF PRACTICAL EXAMPLES

Practical examples can be grouped into two broad categories: A) those that help in the Explanation of Theory and New Concepts, and B) those that illustrate the Application of Basic Principles. In addition, practical examples can also be broken down into different types based on the format in which they are used.

For example, one can design practical examples that are based on:

- Analogies,
- Observations,
- Demonstrations (experimental or mathematical),
- Sensing phenomena, and
- Observing secondary effects.

Explanation of Practical Example Types

Analogy

The analogy is a very helpful tool for explaining new concepts. Here, the instructor links the new concept to an idea which the students can easily picture in their minds. An example of an analogy would be to explain the concept of the conservation of energy in terms of money in a bank. One can imagine the money in a checking account as being analogous to kinetic energy. Similarly, money in the savings and money market accounts can be thought of as being analogous to pressure and potential energies, respectively. Just as money can be transferred between the three different accounts, so can energy between the three different forms. The concept of frictional energy losses can now be easily related to the debiting of money from the accounts.

Observations

Observations that the student can make outside of class can help demonstrate basic principles being currently studied in class. The example can be carried out as a take home assignment where the students are required to go and observe a phenomena that they can readily see, feel, hear and smell, and later summarise their observations. The students bring their observations to class and the instructor leads a discussion of what the students observed and what those observations mean. This type of exercise not only helps with the understanding of a new concept or basic principle but teaches the students how to observe a phenomena before trying to analyse it.

Demonstrations: (Experimental or Mathematical)

The demonstration example can be done either as an experimental exercise carried out in class with small experimental models, or as a mathematical exercise carried out on the "chalkboard" to explain a physical phenomena. This can be particularly instructive when the students are aware of the phenomena but are not able to explain the science behind it.

Experimental: An experimental demonstration requires physical equipment. While finding the right equipment may not always be possible, some examples require materials as simple as a paper clip or piece of paper. For instance, the factors affecting the aerodynamic drag and lift forces on an object can be demonstrated with a simple piece of writing paper. Hold a flat sheet of paper parallel to the floor and drop it observing its rate of decent. Then take the same sheet of paper crumple it up, drop it and observe its rate of decent. In both cases you have the same material, the same mass, and the same gravitational force acting on the system. Therefore, these parameters can be eliminated from consideration. By further eliminating other parameters, the students can be lead to understand that the important parameter is the aerodynamic drag acting on the two different objects.

Similarly, important governing parameters in other systems could be deduced. For instance, tests could be run with the same object shapes but with different projected areas. By observing how the time of fall depends on the various parameters, the students could arrive at the main governing parameters.

Mathematical: The purpose of a mathematical demon-stration would be to explain, using the theory developed in class, the science behind some phenomena that the students have seen or heard of. This can be particularly enlightening if the phenomena is such that everyone knows about it, but few realise what really is happening. For instance, the term valve float in an Internal Combustion engine can be explained by modeling the valve as a train of solid links and springs, and then writing the equations of motion for the valve.

Sensing

Sensing examples are designed so that students can "feel" the science behind the phenomena. The goal here is to have the students carry out experiments that allow them to sense the different parameters that enter into the theory. An excellent example of this would be to study the relationship between speed and torque for a gear system using a ten-speed bicycle. The students' assignment would be to flip their ten speed bicycle upside down, switch through all the gear combinations while pedaling it by hand, and physically sense how the speed and torque for a particular gear setting are related. Clearly, the emphasis in this technique is not to teach or explain a new concept but to give a known concept more meaning by having the students sense it.

Secondary Effects

Secondary effects demonstrate the fact that sometimes the explanation of an engineering phenomenon is not obvious. The purpose here is to get the students to really consider all the possible explanations besides the most obvious one. A classic example of this would be the observation of the direction of movement of a helium balloon tied to the floor of a car when the car accelerates. Typically one would expect the balloon to move backwards when the car accelerates due to the inertia of the balloon.

This would be the case if a steel ball were to be suspended from the ceiling of a car. In reality, the students will notice that the balloon moves forward as the car accelerates. An investigation of the forces acting on the balloon can be done either as a homework assignment or as a class discussion. By doing so, the students should eventually come to realise that the balloon is pushed forward by the buoyancy force acting on it.

As the car accelerates, the air in the back of the car is compressed slightly, resulting in a density gradient from the front to the rear of the car. The helium in the balloon is lighter than air and therefore experiences a buoyancy force in the horizontal direction.

Show and Tell: Reversing Student Roles

The "Show and Tell" technique is another form of the "Practical Examples" technique. However, in this technique the role of the student is reversed to that of a teacher, thereby changing their perspective of the problem. The basic premise of the "Show and Tell" technique is that if one can explain a concept to someone else then he/she truly understands the concept.

Scope

A typical "Show and Tell" project would require a student or a group of students to explain a given theory or phenomenon to the rest of the class and also demonstrate a physical example that helps visualise the phenomenon. Almost any example that you can convincingly demonstrate in a classroom would be appropriate for a "Show and Tell" project. However, it should be remembered that as with the case of the "Practical Examples" technique, the concept to be explained by the students should be relatively simple and straight forward.

The purpose of this exercise is to challenge the students to come up with a creative solution to the problem at hand without overwhelming them. In order to avoid embarrassing situations and to ensure that the demonstrations are useful to the entire class, it is also important for you to know before hand what the students plan to present.

Example: Explain and Demonstrate the Magnus Effect

The magnus effect is a fluid dynamics phenomena observed when a projectile in flight is spinning. The spinning projectile moves in a direction perpendicular to both it's main path and rotation axis.

Goal

The student or group would be given the assignment to both explain and demonstrate the magnus effect in class. The level of the expected explanation would depend on the level of the course and the philosophy of the teaching assistant. This particular example could be explained using potential flow theory (mathematically) or more intuitively using the ideal of streamlines and Bernoulli's principle without rigourous proof.

For the demonstration the students use whatever equipment or apparatus that they can access. In the present case, one possible idea would be to use a cardboard tube from a paper towel or toilet roll and a piece of string. The student would wrap the roll with the string, stand on a chair holding the free end of the string and let go of the roll, causing it to unwind from the string and move down. In addition to imparting a downward velocity, the unwinding of the roll also causes the roll to spin.

When the string is completely unwound, the roll will tend to move perpendicular to the spin axis (horizontal to the floor) as it falls to the floor. The horizontal direction of movement of the roll will depend on the direction of rotation of the roll. The students could demonstrate this by starting with the string wound in clockwise or anti-clockwise directions. Other variations of this demonstration would be to bring in a ping pong ball and paddle and demonstrate the magnus effect by hitting the ball with different types of spin and watching the trajectory of the balls. The same idea could be demonstrated outdoors by pitching a baseball.

THE POWER OF ATTRACTION OF THE AUDIO-VISUAL LANGUAGE

The remarkable power of film fascination is probably the first thing we notice in considering mass media. This fascination is not merely a kind of diffuse moment of interest, but a very specific effect arising from the technological depiction of the world. In addition, we must remember not only the visual aspect but also the auditory components, which possess their own brand of fascination, principally of an emotional type.

This relationship of photography to our reality bound consciousness acts most powerfully through the fully-developed dynamism of film photography and television, in which it raises fascination to its ultimate level. In his research, Herbert Wölker proved empirically that the film multiplies the intensity of experience many times over, and thus facilitates identification with the matter shown. The influence of identification on the social process of learning has been made clear to us by Karl Heinrich's latest work on the effect produced by ñims.

The intensification of experience depends essentially on the visual and acoustic impact of photography. For that reason, in an age of increasing abstraction, increasing intellectuali-zation and declining sensibility, as Gehlen calls it, film and television, through their power of making things concrete, have a compensatory function. By attracting audiences to the images and the stark graphic descriptions of commercial cinema and television, this function sometimes has a very negative effect; but it nevertheless retains an authentic and indispensable therapeutic quality. Moreover, the relationship of photography to the world is not confined to this power of making things concrete. The subjects photographed have their own authenticity and documentary value. Photography always relates to facts, to something that has actually happened or really existed. This enhances its fascination, but weakens its power of symbolism. According to Cassirer's theory of symbols.photographs is never symbols used to express an intnnsically spiritual concept. They are signals pointing to some concrete fact. Therefore, the weak point of photography as a means of conferring reality and exercising fascination lies in its dubious relationship to abstraction.

Here we come to an argument applicable to ail mass media and one which recurs in a variety of shapes. Photography makes possible a maximum of what English theorists call involvement, an entering into contact with the outside world; but it holds the mind captive in concrete situations. By drawing on real situations, it promotes what might be called emotional commitment, but at the same time weakens thought by making an assault on our senses. This sometimes appears in a crude form in popular science broadcasts, where lavish visual display, an abundance and complexity of pictorial matter, very easily gives the illusion of understanding, though in reality it merely builds up visual dummies in our consciousness. The intellect is frequently quite untouched by such visual exploits. Educational responsibility and imagination must not capitulate in face of this dilemma. Indeed, they must use it consciously and even orient their educational activities on that basis, *e.g.*, by using films and broadcasts in teaching. Through their power of fascination, these are particularly suitable in the initial stages of a learning process, where the great thing is to give a powerful motivation and awaken interest from the start. The mass media are 'magnificent gateways', as the English publicist Hoggard once called them. However, they may prove to be a hindrance where abstractions and generalizations are concerned. In such cases, they may almost act as barriers. On the other hand, visual barriers of this kind can be set up deliberately, to goad pupils into using their brains.

Where an accurate observation of detail is the prerequisite for the correct training of perception, as in geology and geography, the use of films can be exceedingly profitable. It is also must valuable in the 'deepening stage', in the sense in which the term is used in Herbart's theory of phases. On other grounds, it is also valid for the teaching of politics and civics which, because of their abstract nature, are difficult to present in visual form. Here the mass media are absolutely essential.

The effect of the visual attraction of photography, as a means of realistic presentation and information, upon the film consumption of young people is best known to those who use films in teaching. A profit hungry industry exploits photography's power of attraction and conviction mainly to lend the unreal world of mediocre authors a semblance of reality and to draw the imagination of the audience into a dream world clothed in the garb of reality. We realise that there is at present no way of overcoming this evil except by preventive educational methods designed to immunize pupils against this form of mental poison. The ability to illustrate is transformed into the power to seduce. The basic meaning of the Latin word fascinare is 'to bewitch'. This conveys an echo of the assault on our senses and, let us be honest, is not this power of enchantment present to some extent in every film and in every radio or television programme?

FACILITY OF MANIPULATION

The adaptability of mass media is a property which makes of them well-forged and efficient tools in the hands of experts. It gives them their wealth of expression and ensures their suitability for all purposes. However, its values are neutral and it may serve either truth or falsehood.

The concept itself is used here in a very broad sense, which makes it possible for us to penetrate to the reality underlying every phase of film and radio production. Facility of manipulation is a universal phenomenon in the mass media and is displayed in a great variety of ways. Perhaps the clearest way of demonstrating it is by reference to the work of the film cutter, whose sole function is to cut and re-join single parts of film into intelligible sequences.

The purpose in this case is to create sense. Cutting and mixing images in film and television are primitive forms of manipulation. They may be used to tell the truth, to lie, to camouflage, to excuse or anything else.

The early Russians were well aware of the power that lay in cutting and had good reasons for regarding it as the fundamental principle of film art. But manipulation begins as early as the shooting stage, in focusing, in lighting, in camera angles. No photography is possible without perspective. Even a snapshot is a form of interpretation. Nowadays, the problem of manipulation also appears on an entirely different level in television, in the person of the interpreting speaker. Speech within the framework of a visual medium has in this way become a manipulatory power of the first rank. The oral description given in a visual broadcast establishes a very pronounced emotional accent. This is a very effective form of primitive manipulation.

It must however be granted that, on a higher level, television is nowadays campaigning for a new word picture relationship. This takes the form of an extremely interesting process where idea and observation are fused in a single simultaneous act. Words become concrete in picture sequences and images are intellectualized by the medium of the interpreting word. This cultural phenomenon is of great importance and novelty and is rendered possible only through the medium of television. This experience gives an indication of educational resources which are still untapped but which will one day radically alter the educational style of television. On the highest level, again, the manipulation process is relentlessly carried through in radio programming and in the planning centres of the film industry. Here, decisions about spheres of influence are made, and whole populations are exposed to the magical influence of planned films. In this regard, everything depends on the personality of those who occupy these posts of command. At this point, the phenomenological method of examination ought to make way for a true sociological analysis of the balance of power in the 'brains trusts' who control the broadcasting organizations and the film industry.

In any event, a study of this power of manipulation at every stage of film and radio production might well provide a most valuable contribution to our knowledge of the inner educational structure of these systems. Manipulation is also important at a much humbler level, *e.g.*, in the preparation of our educational films. Here the problem is one which causes us great concern. Should we take as our model the perfect educational film, which traditionally constitutes a system of knowledge so compact and as completely adaptable as almost to render superfluous both the teacher and any further work on the material? Or should we produce open fragments of film, where the subject matter is accompanied by questions, so that pupils are placed in a working situation which in terms of modern teaching theory is educationally ideal? Here we come up against the same ambivalence and qualitative difficulties as were encountered in considering the problem of fascination. In this case too, the search for truth or falsehood, the encouragement of sense or nonsense, the offer of an opiate or a challenge, are effected by the same method-the power of manipulation- and by that alone.

What educational maxim can we derive from this? Manipulation must always be uncovered. This must happen in two directions. In the first place, the manipulation of sense in the cinema must be discerned, *i.e.*, we must learn how to understand films. In the second place, it must be exposed. Whether we are concerned with exposing a dream structure or with seeing through the visual perfection and manipulation of the newsreels of the Third Reich and laying bare its ideology, we should be constantly engaged in an effort to uncover the serious consequences of manipulation.

5

Learner Variables

LACK OF SPECIFIC LANGUAGE KNOWLEDGE

Many reading textbooks for the ESL and EFL learner suggest higher level cognitive reading strategies or learning strategies that can benefit the student who is trying to learn to read. For instance, a prereading examination of the text for organization, headings, summaries, and so on, will help the reader make predictions about the content and locate sources of help within the text. Learning to pick out the topic sentence in each paragraph will allow the student to get most of the essential information in the text, taking full advantage of the predictable and formulaic nature of English written organization. Acquiring a repertory of reading skills like reading in depth, skimming for the gist, and scanning for specific information, permits ESL and EFL readers to adjust their reading to the task that they need to perform.

However, lack of vocabulary remains one of the major obstacles for the ESL and EFL reader. As a result, many ESL and EFL textbooks offer valuable learning strategies for vocabulary. Students learn to distinguish and look up the words that seem most essential to the meaning of the text, such as those that are repeated four or five times. They are shown how to look at morphological cues within the word that might indicate something about its meaning or part of speech, although students seem to avoid this strategy because of the cognitive load involved in it. Students may be encouraged to keep a vocabulary journal while reading so that they can use their new words actively in speaking or writing. Students become adept at finding cues in the context of the sentence or paragraph to guess what the word means. Students can also apply a cognate strategy, that is, they look for similarities between the English word and a word in their native language. Because cognates may be understood and acquired with support from the L1 lexical knowledge store, L2 readers seem to apply this strategy automatically. In the case where the student's L1 has many cognates with English, a valuable vocabulary strategy might be to "be wary of false friends," which are those words that are cognate but have very different meanings in L1 and L2.

Many teachers teach students to use these word identification strategies in reading, but they do not consistently advocate vocabulary building during reading for comprehension. Instead, some teachers commonly advocate one reading comprehension strategy at the expense of vocabulary building, that is, to "skip the words you don't know and get the gist of the meaning." Although no reading textbook promotes this strategy outright, many teachers adopt it in the classroom, as I, myself, did at one time in my life. The idea seems to stem from conclusions drawn from a number of sources in the reading literature in the past 30 years, some of which have been discussed elsewhere in this book: for example, "readers are just guessing anyway," or "readers just sample the text and don't fixate on every word." In addition, some common assumptions inadvertently have led some teachers to accept the idea of skipping over unknown words in hot pursuit of comprehension.

Coady, 1979, said the following:

Since the various process strategies interact among themselves, the ESL student should take advantage of his strengths in order to overcome his weaknesses. For example, greater background knowledge of a particular subject could compensate somewhat for a lack of syntactic control over the language.... The proficient reader learns to utilize whatever cue systems render useful information and to put them together in a *creative* manner, always achieving *at least some comprehension.* This weakness in one area can be overcome by a strength in another.

Readers do not need to understand everything in the text

Clarke and Silberstein, 1979, said the following: Students must be made aware of the number of language clues available to them when they are stopped by an unfamiliar word. They should realize that they can usually continue reading and obtain a general understanding of the item.... Most importantly, they must be taught to recognize situations in which the meaning of the word or phrase is *not essential for adequate comprehension* of the passage.

Been, 1979, said the following:

The readers should be given cues which lead him to ignore linearity, help him to exploit redundancies, and demonstrate *that meaning can be apprehended even though he does not understand every word*.

Day and Bamford, 1998, said the following: Part of fluent and effective reading involves the reader *ignoring unknown words and phrases or, if understanding them is essential, guessing their approximate meaning*.

Vocabulary Instruction Takes Up Too Much Time in the Reading Class

Gaskill, 1979, said the following:

Many instructors ask their students to learn vocabulary items which are found in their reading selections. This can be helpful if the number of words is held to a reasonable ten to twenty words per selection and if the list of words is accompanied with contextualized examples and practice. Preparing lists of vocabulary items and contextualized practice requires *additional preparation* on the part of the instructor.... Discussion of and practice with such lists takes a *lot of class time.*

Clearly, it is impossible to argue against these commonsense assumptions for the reading comprehension classroom. They have validity, but the conclusion that some teachers have drawn seems to be that, given that the goal of the reading class is improvement in the comprehension of a message, and not word learning, and that background knowledge can make up for lack of vocabulary anyway, and that readers don't need to understand every word, and that vocabulary learning is not an efficient use of reading class time, a good strategy is for ESL and EFL readers to skip over words they don't know.

Again, there is some merit in the suggestion. Lack of vocabulary is a serious problem for ESL and EFL students in reading independently. Many ESL and EFL students, especially those in higher education, are required to read stories, articles, or books that are too difficult for them to read because there are too many words they don't know. It is frustrating to read something incomprehensible, so the natural inclination for the reader is to stop reading and do something else. If readers don't read, they don't improve. It is equally frustrating for most people to consult the dictionary for every unknown word. Dictionaries are fallible, the definition may be unclear or incomplete, and by the time the reader has found the definition he has lost track of what the sentence was about anyway. Teachers don't want students to be frustrated; they want them to read extensively because that is the one sure way to improve reading.

It is a common impression among teachers I have talked to that students will learn words automatically while they are reading, that they will at least acquire some new vocabulary while reading, even if they skip over unknown words. And anyway, teachers are cognizant of the fact that the goal of reading is to get meaning, not to read and remember words. So, it was probably inevitable that reading teachers at one point began to advise students to skip the words that they didn't know to focus on getting the overall meaning of the text.

The strategy was designed to keep reading interesting and fun so that readers would read and, as a short-term task-limited procedure, it probably accomplishes its goal. One problem, however, is that it can become a long-term task-unlimited procedure for students. Some students adopt this strategy for the long run because it is easier than learning new words. They get into the processing habit of disregarding words that they fixate on as soon as they decide that it is not a word in their L2 mental lexicon. Once this habit is formed, it is hard to break. Students also apply this processing strategy to all of the reading that they must do, even the reading in which it is essential to get more than just the gist. Rather than a strategy they can apply to challenging but relatively unimportant reading, it becomes their exclusive reading policy.

Rather than applying it to the preliminary reading of a text which they are going to read more carefully again, they use it as the one and only "careful" reading they do. The simple truth is that if readers skip the words they don't know, they don't learn them, and often, they don't understand the texts they need to understand. The conclusion is that the short-term reading comprehension strategy is very detrimental to long-term vocabulary building. Even Day and Bamford (1998) cannot report substantial and consistent vocabulary gains through extensive reading programmes.

(To provide a more personal example, an ESL student of mine was once involved in volunteer work that required him to read a short training manual. He took it home overnight and read it, but the next day, when the volunteer coordinator asked him a few questions, he couldn't answer. She was peeved and expressed irritation to me. I was surprised, because he was a serious student. When I asked him about it, he told me that he had just skipped the words he didn't know. He didn't realize that he should have read any differently because this is what his teacher had advised him to do to cope with difficult reading. This is probably an extreme case but I think of it every time I hear employers, teachers, and professors complain that their non-native speaking students can't understand what they read.)

The purpose of this chapter is to suggest additional word learning strategies for ESL and EFL readers to use to read efficiently at the same time that they improve vocabulary. We have seen that reading familiar words depends on low-level processing strategies and specific linguistic knowledge of writing systems, spelling patterns, morphemes, and so on. It turns out that learning unfamiliar words depends on the same sorts of knowledge, as well. It follows that improving low-level processing strategies and linguistic knowledge might help students retain more vocabulary words from their reading and vocabulary exercises.

In Vocabulary Acquisition

First of all, what makes a person a better word learner? Ellis and Beaton gave us some ideas. There is a lot of evidence that a better word learner can repeat new words easily and repetition ability depends on the short-term memory (processing strategies) and the long-term memory (knowledge store) of the learner. To repeat a new word (a sequence of graphs) that the learner has read, he or she must access (at least some of the) graphemic images stored in long-term memory and hold them in short-term memory while they are matched to a phonemic image from the inventory of phonemes stored in long-term memory. Then the graphemic and phonemic image is held or rehearsed in short-term memory while the motor commands to the mouth are formulated and executed. If the learner's shortterm memory or long-term memory is not adequate to the task, the learner cannot repeat the unknown word and cannot store it as easily. The storage of words in the mental lexicon in long-term memory is an important part of the knowledge base.

The reader's abilities to repeat new words is part of an interactive cycle as noted by Gathercole, Willis, Emslie, and Baddeley. Repetition ability and existing vocabulary knowledge "bootstrap" on each other. Phonological skills influence the learning of new words, but also, the larger the storage of words in the mental lexicon, the easier it seems to be to come up with phonological analyses. From the point of view taken in this book, it is clear that this supports the idea that readers use probabilistic reasoning and analogy to known spelling patterns to read unknown words, and the better able readers are to do this, the better they can retain a new word, as well.

These findings come from the study of what has come to be called the phonological "loop" in vocabulary acquisition. The phonological loop, comes into play in listening comprehension and in reading to allow the listener or reader to learn unknown words. After the word is heard or read, a phonological image is formed. The loop allows for the retention of the phonological image for short periods of time in short-term memory.

The loop consists of a phonological store, which stores the image, and a rehearsal process, which serves to refresh decaying representations that might disappear from short-term memory. The function of the loop is to store unfamiliar forms in short-term memory while permanent memory structures can be constructed in the mental lexicon, thereby leading to word learning. Repetition ability is taken to be an indicator of the loop. People with poor short-term memory have a hard time repeating words. Likewise, vocabulary knowledge is also related to repetition ability. These findings are consistent for both L1 and L2 word learning.

An ingenious type of experiment shows the effect of the phonological loop in reading (at least the reading of single words). In reading, the graphs on the page are matched to graphemes in our head and these, in turn, are matched with a phonological image of the phonemes associated with the graphemes. This is die phonological "loop. " The functioning of the loop can be disrupted in reading by having readers say a nonsense syllable (like "bla bla bla") while they are reading. This method, called *artkvlatory suppression,* has a "clearly deleterious effect on die acquisition of foreign language vocabulary". The idea is that if the reader does not, for some reason, form and retain a phonological image of an unknown word which is being read, he or she will not form an entry in the mental lexicon, and therefore will not recognize the word when it is read again. Baddeley et al. offered a dynamic model of word learners as active processors of new words through phonological storage and rehearsal to add to their knowledge base in the mental lexicon. Why is it that many ESL and EFL learners fail to learn much vocabulary while they are reading? One reason might be that they are overwhelmed by the sheer number of new words in some of the texts they are asked to read. Other reasons may be found if we look at the lexical variables in word learning: acoustic similarity, word length, pronounceability or other phonological factors, orthography (script, direction of script, sequential letter probabilities, familiarity with grapheme-phoneme mappings), and word class or part of speech.

Acoustic Similarity

Papagno and Vallar found evidence that acoustically similar words confused the phonological loop in the L2 learner even in visual presentation. In the phonological loop, the phonological image in short-term memory may be confused with similar words already learned, and the confusion may impede or prevent storage of the new item in long-term memory.

Word Length

Word length affects storage and retention in the phonological loop. Cheung found this to be an important factor for Hong Kong seventh graders whose vocabulary size was smaller than the median for all the students studied. The longer the word, the harder it is to store and retain in the loop so that it can become permanently stored in the mental lexicon.

Pronounceabilities

The more pronounceable a word, the more easily it is learned. Ellis and Beaton made the point that the more a word conforms to the expected phonological forms of the language, the more pronounceable it is. In matching graphs-graphemes-phonemes, the more knowledge about the typical phonological structures of the language, the better the reader can predict the sound of the word and the easier the storage and retention in the phonological loop. In this book, we have already considered the problem of pronounceability elsewhere. We saw that there is a tendency for Japanese readers of English to use a visual strategy to remember words, that is, they try to match the visual appearance of the word with a meaning concept, as if the English word were a Kanji or logographic symbol. I think this explains some unusual findings by Saito, who was investigating the effects of pronounceability and articulatory suppression on phonological learning in Japanese learners of Japanese nonwords presented in Katakana or syllabic writing. In this study, participants were shown easy and difficult-to-pronounce "nonwords" under a control and an articulatory suppression condition. Then they were asked to recall the words in a free recall task in which they were asked to write down the words they remembered. Then there was a cued recall task in which the participants were given the first syllable of the word and had to complete the word. The prediction would be that pronounceability of nonwords would result in better word learning, and it did. Articulatory suppression, however, was expected to inhibit word learning for the nonwords.

In contrast, Saito found that in both the free recall and the cued recall, the unpronounceable nonwords were learned better in articulatory suppression than in the control condition. I think that articulatory suppression inhibits phonological storage in short-term memory and favours visual or graphemic storage, which could be expected to be well-remembered in recall writing tasks. In other words, the Japanese participants reacted to the articulatory suppression condition by treating the unpronounceable Katakana nonwords as Kanji, just as they seem to do with unpronounceable English words. This strategy led to success in the experiment but is less useful in actual reading tasks or in learning new words productively, as we have seen.

Orthography

In Ellis and Beaton's study of English learners who knew no German, the degree to which the German word conformed to the orthographic patterns of English affected their ability to translate from English to German. It is obvious that these individuals who knew no German had no knowledge of German letter-to-sound patterns and could only learn words based on their similarity to English. This study does, however, reinforce the idea that LI orthography can help in reading L2 to the extent that there is overlap between the two systems. Where there is little or no overlap, L1 interferes or does not facilitate.

Problems with English orthography may be significant contributors to the lack of vocabulary acquisition in reading generally. If ESL and EFL learners cannot match graphs to graphemes to phonemes quickly and automatically, the phonological loop may not be able to function to store and retain the word in long-term memory. If the phonological loop is not able to function, students may fall back on visual strategies for reading, which, we have argued, are not the most efficient way to read English words.

Word Class

Ellis and Beaton found that nouns are easier to learn than verbs, and this finding is consistent with other psychological literature for first language acquisition. It is unclear why nouns should be easier to learn than verbs, but one reason given is that their meaning tends to be more imageable or easy to visualize. In the case of English and German, probably the nouns and verbs correlate highly with each other because the two languages are closely related in syntax. For other languages, however, part of speech differences may be a cause for confusion in reading, because it is necessary for the reader to understand parts of speech to assign the correct syntactic structure to a sentence. Correct comprehension of syntactic structure is an important precursor to correct comprehension of meaning. The quote from Coady, cited earlier, which said that background knowledge can make up for a lack of syntactic knowledge, must be tempered with a consideration that, as one of my linguistics professors used to say, syntax was made so that we can talk about things that are contrary to our expectations about the world. How else could we understand the sentence, "A man bit a dog," if it weren't for the dominance of syntax over background knowledge.

Part of speech information is opaque in English. A fusional language like Spanish marks part of speech clearly because it marks nouns with (generally) either an -a ending or an -o, and adjectives and pronouns carry corresponding markings with the nouns they match. The Spanish noun and adjective system of marking is different from the system which marks verbs, a three-way (-ar, -er, and -ir) series of conjugations in different tenses, persons, and numbers. Because of the noun, adjective, and verbal inflections, many words in Spanish, even in isolation, are unambiguous as to grammatical category, there are many languages with even stricter marking of grammatical category information than Spanish; in these languages there is no ambiguity at all between different parts of speech.

The nouns are often clearly marked as to their function in the sentence (e.g., subject, direct object, etc.) and verbs are clearly marked with their inflections of person, number, and tense. For students from these languages, the scarcity of overt marking in English causes uncertainty in attributing a part of speech to an English word, and therefore phrasal structure is hard to compute and accurate meanings are difficult to comprehend. Further, any factors which favour noun learning over verb learning will not operate if the student cannot identify a word as a noun.

On the opposite side of the spectrum, some isolating languages have even fewer consistent markings of parts of speech than does English. Although spoken Chinese words have different categories, the written sinograms don't reflect grammatical parts of speech at all; they are invariable. Students whose L1 is like this may also have problems with English parts of speech because they may be unable to take advantage of the morphological information that is present in the English text.

Most native English readers don't have conscious or learned knowledge of the part of speech of each word in each sentence as it is being read, but they have unconscious knowledge which allows them to compute phrasal and sentential structure quickly, then discard it as soon as the meaning is clear. Given the incomplete marking of English grammatical categories and given how common conversion is as a word formation process in English, perhaps it is more accurate to think of parts of speech as weighted probabilities or frequencies from which we form grammatical expectations. For example, from our experience with language, we form the expectation that floor will be a noun, say, 95% of the time and a verb 5% of the time, except in certain registers (such as the carpet installer).

Expert English readers use these lexical expectations, the cues from the text like word order and grammatical function words like the, of, or to, and their knowledge of typical English syntactic structures, to determine the syntactic structure that they are reading. English speakers intuitively know that the subject of an English sentence is most typically a noun phrase, they know that floor is most likely going to be a noun, and they know that nouns are often preceded by the, so when they see the following sentence, The floor the man swept was clean, they will take the subject to be the first noun phrase the floor.

In addition, words themselves place requirements on the words that can or must go with them and this is part of the knowledge that readers must have about words. It is often called *collocational knowledge,* the stored information in memory about the lexical, phrasal, or clausal requirements of a word. For example, the verb put might occur in the predicate of a sentence. If so, there are certain collocational requirements placed on the verb phrase that forms the predicate. Put requires two other types of phrases within the verb phrase, a direct object, and a location phrase, as in the following sentence: He put the car in the garage. Taking away either the direct object the car or the location phrase in the garage would yield an ungrammatical sentence. The verb remember can take an infinitive or V + ing (I remembered to go/going), a that + sentence (I remembered that he went), or an OBJECT PRONOUN V + ing (I remembered him going). Each of these structures is associated with a certain semantic interpretation.

LEXICAL VARIABLES IN READING ENGLISH WORDS

Languages can be isolating, agglutinating, polysynthetic, or fusional, so even the concept of "word" is different from language to language. Words can be formed through different processes: for example, prefixing, suffixing, infixing, concatenation of morphemes, compounding, and so on. The processes typical in a student's L1 may not prepare him or her for the variety of word formation processes in English: acronym, blending, coining, generalization, back formation, clipping, conversion, and compounding. Students may benefit from direct assistance from teachers to learn processing strategies for these new words.

Another problem for students is that even if they know words, they may not have all of the necessary semantic information to understand the word and its meaning if they read it. They may lack knowledge of meanings other than the most common or the most literal. They may lack knowledge of the social, political, or religious connotation that words have. They need to be able to process and understand metaphor, discard inappropriate meanings for polysemous words, and resolve lexical ambiguity problems. They may lack knowledge of the grammatical requirements that words place on their syntactic contexts. If semantic and syntactic information about words is not automatically available to readers from their knowledge base as they process the text, comprehension of meaning is compromised.

Borrowing is a word formation process because it does result in a new word in the lexicon of a language. English has no problem borrowing words from other languages (e.g., taco, patio, Wiener schnitzel, glasnost), which has given English a very extensive, heterogeneous, and unruly vocabulary compared to languages which resist borrowing, whose lexicons are very homogeneous and rule-governed. Because of borrowing in English, there can be more than one word to refer to similar objects (e.g., sausage, bratwurst, chorizo, pepperoni). In most borrowings in English, the written word is copied letter by letter closely, but it is pronounced more or less as an English word with perhaps some concern to authenticity, depending on the speaker. ESL and EFL readers can benefit if the borrowed word happens to be from their own language, but otherwise, recent or uncommon borrowings are probably all going to be new and unknown.

Besides derivation and borrowing, English frequently uses *compounding* to form new words. Compounding is also common in German, which allows long compounds of many free morphemes put together, and in Chinese, which prefers short compounds of two free morphemes. It is not as common in some other languages. For instance, many speakers of Romance languages like Spanish, French, or Italian, prefer possessive structures instead of the more typical compounds in English. For instance, they might say the leg of the table or even the table's leg instead of the more correct the table leg. When they read this compound they might wonder about the relation between the two nouns. They might lack an interpretive strategy for these words because of their structure. The strategy is that the second noun is the object and the first noun is descriptive.

Long compound nouns made up of a number of words can be very confusing because the interpretive strategy must be applied over and over again; the English Department Curriculum Committee Summer Retreat Planning Committee requires quite a bit of mental gymnastics to understand. To understand what this compound means, first the student must realize that this is a compound and not a sentence or clause. The capital letters in this compound indicates that this is not a sentence, but if the compound is not capitalized, students may not understand that such a long group of words is a compound noun and not a sentence. Then the student must apply the interpretive strategy first to the individual two-word compounds and then to the four-word compounds and then to the eight-word compound. There are other types of compounds also, among them, compound adjectives (e.g., red-hot, candy apple red, etc.) and compound verbs made up of a verb and a particle (e.g., pick up, pick on, pick out, etc.) Compound verbs require an interpretive strategy that differentiates them from verbs with prepositional phrases. (This is often treated as a grammar issue but not necessarily a reading comprehension issue. However, syntax and reading comprehension are intimately connected.)

Common word formation processes in English besides derivation, borrowing, and compounding are blending, coining, generalization, acronym, back formation, clipping, and conversion. *Blending* is a process where two separate words are reduced and combined. For example, brunch is a blend of breakfast and lunch. In the case of brunch, it might be hard for ESL and EFL students to apply a strategy of breaking up the two parts to combine the meaning, because they might not recognize it as a blend. Other blends are more recognizable; reaganomics or chocoholic come to mind. *Coined words,* or words "minted" out of thin air, are harder to detect. Many are trademark names like kleenex or xerox, so they might, in fact, be multinational. Sometimes trademark names or other proper names become common nouns or verbs through a process *of generalization,* as in kleenex or a quisling.

Another much-used word formation process in English is *acronym.* The words radar, AIDS, and NATO are formed by taking the first initial of each word or main part of a word in the originating phrase and pronouncing them together as one word. This is distinguished from an *abbreviation,* where the initials are pronounced as letters, as in FBI or CIA. (Another type of abbreviation is a shortened form of the original word which is written with a period at the end. This is not really a word formation process, that is, Dept. for department is not a different word.) It may be my imagination, but it seems like acronym and initial abbreviations are becoming more common in some other languages, possibly due to U. S. influence. One strategy for dealing with these might work for students from Romance languages: reverse the direction of the letters and translate them. In Spanish, for example, NATO is OTAN and the UN is La ONU. Other students should recognize them as acronyms or abbreviations and look in the text for cues as to what they represent.

Back-formation and clipping are similar processes which yield different results. Edit is a back-formation from the word editor. In *back-formation,* the original word (editor) is analyzed as having a derivational morpheme at the end -or, which means "one who does X. " The suffix is removed to form the new verb (edit) on analogy with pairs like act-actor and bake-baker. Thus, usually the word that is formed through back-formation has some kind of grammatical difference from the original word. Often, its part of speech is different, as with enthuse from enthusiastic. If students know the original word enthusiastic, they can use it as a cue to meaning, but they should also notice the change in part of speech. Back-formation explains the neologism echolocate from echolocation that was mentioned earlier. Prof is a clipped version of professor. *Clipping* means shortening a multisyllable word either from the end or from the beginning without much regard for the morphology of the word. Clipping doesn't really derive a new word with a different meaning and part of speech, but rather a different word that is just shorter than the original. Prof and professor mean the same thing, math and mathematics mean the same thing, and golf pro and golf professional mean the same thing. Clipped words differ from abbreviations (of the second type, mentioned earlier) because clipped words can take on a life of their own. They are easier to pronounce and usually slangy or informal. The strategy for reading clipped words is to recognize them as such and relate them to the longer word if it is known. Alternatively, students may be more familiar with the clipped word; if so, they can relate the longer word to it when they see it.

These word formation processes may cause the ESL and EFL student some difficulty in reading, especially authentic materials like academic texts or articles, magazines, and newspapers because acronyms, new blends or coinages, back-formations, clipped forms, and abbreviations may not be in the dictionary and their meanings may not be self-evident.

The use of metaphor to refer to an object, although technically not a word formation process, can also create challenges for readers. *Ametaphor* is a figure of speech in which a word which denotes one thing is used in place of another to suggest a likeness or similarity between the two things. Using the word ice instead of diamond is a metaphor drawing on our awareness that diamonds and ice have similarities in appearance. If a waitress uses the term ham sandwich to refer to a customer in the sentence, "The ham sandwich left without paying, " she is using a figure of speech drawing on the associated concepts of the individual customer and what he ate. This example of *metonymy,* where a word meaning an attribute or a part (the sandwich) is used in place of another which is the whole (the customer), is a specific type of metaphor.

Understanding a metaphor requires reasoning by analogy. To understand the use of that old goat in reference to an elderly character, students must first know that goat is being used to refer to the character and not some extraneous animal in the story. They must know what a goat is and what properties could be shared by a goat and an elderly man (e.g., smelly, shaggy, stubborn, reclusive, bossy, stringy, and thin) to successfully understand the analogy. Native-speaking readers can usually understand figures of speech because the meaning associations stored in semantic memory are not self-contained and isolated one from another.

Rather, they are widespread networks of interconnected concepts and associations (called schemas) which have been built up through the years as we have learned about words, culture, and the world. Thus, when native-speaking readers come across a figure of speech, the associations evoked allow the readers to understand what the writer is trying to say. ESL and EFL readers may not have the stored cultural concepts and associations to understand common metaphors in English, or they may understand them in an unintended way. In addition, comprehension of metaphor is not universal. It is learned and developmental, and as such, it is reasonable to expect cultural variation in its use and interpretation.

Metaphors can, through repetition, become so conventionalized that they lose their special status as a figure of speech and become merely cases of polysemy. *Polysemy* is not a word formation process, but it can be confusing. It refers to any words which have more than one meaning. In some cases of polysemy, the meanings of the word are clearly related to each other and yet we are quite sure that the meanings are different. An example of this would be the use of the word mouse, which began as a metaphor to describe the computer part because of its resemblance to the animal in colour, size, and shape, and possession of a tail. Now, many would probably say that the word mouse has two clearly different meanings equal in importance: the small animal and the computer part. It is ceasing to be a metaphor and becoming a case of polysemy.

In cases with a longer historical background, the meanings may seem more distant from each other, but we would agree, still, that they are related. An example is the word point:

He sharpened the point of the knife (sharp end). He wasn't sure of the point of the story (purpose). He made an interesting point (an important detail in his argument). He walked to a point 10 feet from the outhouse (specific location). He made a point for his team (a score). The decimal point is in the wrong place (a mathematical punctuation).

The problem with polysemous words for English L2 learners is that the commonest words tend to have the most meanings and the students only know one or possibly two of the main definitions for a word. Because the word is common, teachers may overlook the difficulty students have with polysemy because they think that students must already know the word.

Polysemous words must be distinguished from homonyms, homophones, and *Homographes* are different words which happen to have the same pronunciation. There are two types of homophones: those that have different spellings (e.g., through-threw, bear-bare, eight-ate, you-ewe) and those that have the same spellings (e.g., bear-bear, bank-bank, quail-quail). *Homographs* are different words which happen to be spelled the same. Again, there are two different types of homographs: those that are pronounced differently (e.g., bow-bow, lead-lead), and those that are pronounced the same way (e.g., bear-bear, bank-bank, quail-quail). The words in Column II, which are both homophones and homographs, are called *homonyms,* two different words which have both the same form and the same pronunciation. We can rule out metaphor in these cases because there is no similarity in meaning and we can rule out polysemy in these cases because it seems quite clear that different words are involved, not different meanings of the same word. Homophones, homographs, and especially homonyms, present some of the same decision-making dilemmas as polysemous words. Students may know only one word from a pair, so the meaning they assign is wrong and they won't detect it. If the readers know both words, this can still cause problem-solving nightmares for the reading processor that is developing in the ESL and EFL students because they create lexical ambiguity. If students are aware of two different homonyms, how do they know which one is the intended one for this context? If their comprehension of a text is already shaky, lexical ambiguity could sabotage it completely.

Top-down schema-activating strategies can help with polysemous words and homonyms because they will prime the reader to understand the text the right way from the beginning. Other than that, one strategy is for students to acquire as extensive a semantic memory as possible in L2 and to use syntactic cues to narrow down the part of speech of the word in question.

Any teacher, no matter how novice, will agree that ESL and EFL readers face challenges with vocabulary acquisition, word recognition, word meanings, and grammatical information. This is, of course, supported by research. For example, Schmitt and Meara (1997) found that L2 learners did not have extensive mastery of the word associations even for verbs they reported they "knew." They were only able to produce 50% of the word associations possible as compared to native speaker norms. This indicates that the meaning associations for the verbs they were tested on were only half as elaborated as they were for native speakers.

In an earlier paper, Meara found that L2 learners gave more varied responses to test words than native speakers did and that their associations are often nonrelated words that sound similar instead of words that are related in meaning. This tells us that students' intuitions about words are not conventional. Their associations are simply from phonemic image to the similar phonemic image of other similar words. Their associations between words may not be through meaning at all. Fragmentary knowledge of word meaning has an impact on comprehension. Ying (1996) found that adult English learners' incomplete knowledge of certain types of verbs (e.g., psychological verbs like think and perception verbs like hear) prevented them from processing sentences like the native speakers did. ESL and EFL readers also lack syntactic collocational information about the phrases and clauses that the word requires. Lennon found that advanced learners of English have a broad concept of verb meaning for simple verbs, but their knowledge of contextual and collocational restrictions is not precise. If this is the case, then even advanced ESL readers may have difficulty interpreting syntactic structures and this may influence their ability to comprehend what they are reading. Lennon concluded that even advanced learners may require classroom vocabulary work on simple verbs within their common lexical and syntactic contexts.

Word Learning and Recognition

When the participants in Ellis and Beaton's 1993 study repeated the unfamiliar L2 word, their ability to produce the unfamiliar word later was enhanced, presumably because the phonological loop was used and an entry in the mental lexicon was constructed. When they used a keyword strategy, their ability to translate the L2 word to the L1 word was enhanced. Translation of the L2 word to L1 is considered to be a receptive skill, but probably appropriate to reading. A keyword strategy was one where the foreign word is associated with the L1 word by means of a mediating word which is similar to the foreign word in sound. For example, the Spanish word for bread is pan; English-speaking learners of Spanish might visualize a loaf of bread in a pan.

The Spanish equivalent (pan) for one word (bread) is learned by mediation of a similar sounding English word (pan). The keyword in this case is the English word "pan." The keyword strategy in some ways might be similar to a visual or Kanji strategy for word identification, but there are some important differences. First of all, Ellis and Beaton found that acoustic similarity enhanced the association between the target unknown word and the native language keyword. This means that the target word is being processed phonologically and a phonologically similar (but not orthographically similar) word is chosen as keyword. In the Kanji strategy, the target word is not processed phonologically. The keyword strategy is also different in that the mediating image or sentence probably improves memory for meaning over a purely visual strategy in which an English word is associated by rote with a sinogram.

According to sources cited in Ellis and Beaton (1993), the keyword method of learning vocabulary is superior to rote rehearsal or presenting vocabulary in context; however, they pointed out the following:

However, theories of FL vocabulary learning and the role of phonological memory systems typically fail to make the important distinction concerning direction of translation. The present study's finds suggest that phonological factors are more implicated in productive learning when the student has a greater cognitive burden in terms of sensory and motor learn. Ellis and Beaton (in press) demonstrate from individual differences analyses that *although keyword techniques are efficient means for receptive vocabulary learning; for productive learning they are less effective than repetition* (at least for learners naive to the pronunciation patterns of the foreign language). MariCarmen and Despina can supplement their natural tendency to use L1 to L2 cognates to identify new words with these methods. Mohammed and Ho especially need these methods to increase their productive and receptive vocabulary for reading and writing. They will be a lot better off in the long run than if they just skip the words they don't know. Certainly, at the early stages of English L2 reading, all new words should be learned productively through repetition, because the words common in early reading are likely to be common in listening, speaking, and writing, as well. Even in later advanced reading, most words should be learned productively so that they can transfer from reading to writing. However, there might be occasions, in very advanced stages of reading acquisition that readers might wish to apply the keyword strategy to remember some unfamiliar words which they will not be using in writing.

These findings suggest that teachers should teach vocabulary in reading class in certain ways to empower students to become active human word processors:

- To the extent that it is possible, choose readings that contain only a limited number of new words. Readings should be considered comprehensible input, that is, just slightly above the student's true reading level at present.
- Provide ample opportunities for students to read on their own for pleasure outside of class.
- Continue using the top-down reading strategies to prepare students to read effectively.
- Teach vocabulary and reading in the context of English phonology, orthography, morphology, word formation processes, and grammar to make more new words more pronounceable, repeatable, and comprehensible to the students.
- Teach vocabulary items with their part of speech and teach words, especially verbs, in collocations.
- Teach students different word learning and recognition strategies to apply on their own while they are reading, to be proactive about increasing their overall vocabulary and comprehension and to decrease reliance on ineffective visual strategies.
- Teach students to distinguish between words to be learned productively (most words) and words to be learned receptively (a few words).

6

Online Teaching and Learning

An instructor's degree of comfort in using different Web technologies has a direct bearing on classroom practices as well as the decision to teach even part of a course online. When instructors are hesitant or lacking in confidence, there is less likelihood for innovation and risk taking.

Therefore, we asked these early Web adopters about their degree of comfort with the following Web skills:

- Creating HTML pages,
- Hosting an online chat,
- Sending and receiving file attachments,
- Using Web-based courseware systems, and
- Moderating a Web-based asynchronous discussion.

The responses were interesting. For instance, over 90 per cent of these faculty members felt a high degree of comfort sending and receiving file attachments in e-mail. Fewer than one per cent of respondents were uncomfortable with this skill. Somewhat surprisingly, 62 per cent were highly comfortable with creating HTML pages and another 20 per cent had a medium level of comfort.

However, this acknowledged degree of comfort likely includes a range of skills from using standard software options such as "save as HTML" to actually being facile with HTML and other programming code. The degree of expertise with HTML remains a question for future surveys. These early adopting faculty were somewhat less comfortable moderating a Web-based asynchronous discussion forum or bulletin board. Still, nearly 50 per cent rated their degree of comfort as high, while another quarter of them reported a medium level of comfort. Similarly, 44 per cent were highly comfortable with Web-based courseware systems and another 34 per cent felt moderately comfortable.

On the low end was comfort with hosting an online chat session. Perceptions of online chat tools were roughly split across low, medium, and high comfort categories. These results indicate that these faculty members possessed at least some basic technology skills. Perhaps, as the NEA survey of traditional and distance learning higher education members revealed, workshops and training sessions on teaching via distance learning are now readily available. While such a skill base and comfort level may be expected of these early Web adopters, many of these faculty members are either taking advantage of university training and support or are engaged in a heavy amount of self-teaching in regard to Web-based teaching tools. Or perhaps they are overstating their skills. In fact, latter parts of this report reveal a somewhat different picture.

OBSTACLES TO WEB-BASED TEACHING

There certainly are a myriad of obstacles to utilizing the Web in higher education instruction. Issues of time, training, experience, ownership, costs, confidence, technological infrastructure, administrative support, and interest are often mentioned.

In this study, the main obstacle to effective use of the Web was time; more specifically, the amount of preparation time required for Web-based course development and delivery. Sixty per cent of the college instructors in this survey reported that preparation time was a major issue. What other obstacles did our respondents face? Contrary to findings from the NEA study, nearly 4 in 10 found the lack of technical support to be a major deterrent.

Slightly fewer, 37 per cent, indicated that a lack of time to learn to use the Web was an obstacle. Along these same lines, a quarter of the respondents lacked training on how to use the Web. And even if they did receive proper training or time allocation, nearly 30 per cent felt that they lacked the equipment or software to display the Web in the classroom. Of course, such findings contrast with what was reported earlier about fairly abundant technology access. Perhaps it indicates that technology is available in their buildings for utilizing the Web in instruction, but it is not yet found in their particular classroom settings.

What were not viewed as major obstacles? Fewer than 20 per cent of the faculty respondents cited lack of hardware or outdated equipment in their office as a barrier. Even fewer, 15 per cent, indicated that the lack of software or outdated software was a problem. And amazingly, fewer than 2 per cent had no interest in using the Web in their teaching. Keep in mind, once again, that the respondents were generally early Webbased teaching adopters who would be expected to be interested in using the Web in their instruction.

Still, the nearly unanimous interest in using the Web indicates that this is a technology with the potential for transforming higher education. Around 17 per cent of the respondents remarked on other problems holding up their adoption of the Web in their teaching. In open-ended responses, these early Web adopters focused on issues of administrative support, time, student interest, pedagogy, vision, funding, incentives, utility, reliability, motivation, and bandwidth.

Administrative support comments included:

- "Lack of administrative vision."
- "Lack of incentive from administration and the fact that they do not understand the time needed."
- "Lack of system support."
- "Little recognition that this is valuable."
- "Rapacious U intellectual property policy."
- "Unclear university policies concerning intellectual property."

Pedagogical comments included:

- "Difficulty in performing laboratory experiments online."
- "Impossible to teach drawing and lithography."
- "Lack of appropriate models for pedagogy in content-based instruction."

Time-related comments included:

- "Lack of incentive."
- "More ideas than time to implement."
- "Not enough time to correct online assignments."
- "People need sleep; Web spins forever."
- "Time to grade/interact."

Cost also appears to be an issue as the following comment notes, "Institution supports because it is the cheapest...is too hard for students and faculty to learn." The following comment from one respondent summarizes many of these issues:

- "...The lack of time to develop materials and add to what is already developed. Little recognition that this is valuable and thus hurts promotion and tenure decisions which seem to be primarily based on publications in juried journals not on stuff on the Web."

When comparing obstacles encountered at private and public institutions, two important differences emerged,

- The perceived lack of time to learn to use the Web and
- Other obstacles faced by faculty at private institutions.

First, faculty members from public institutions were significantly more likely to indicate that time to learn to use the Web was a problem than those from private institutions. It is unclear, however, whether this is due to differing teaching and research expectations, support structures, or Web-based learning initiatives at their institutions.

Second, 30 per cent of the faculty respondents from private universities noted that they faced other obstacles not listed as compared to just 14 per cent of respondents from public institutions. On several other items, faculty members from public institutions were more likely to indicate problems than those from private ones. For instance, faculty respondents from public institutions were slightly more likely to complain that Web-based learning required too much preparation time and that they lacked the proper equipment to display the Web in their classrooms. An interesting finding emerged when comparing differences in the number and type of obstacles by the size of the institution. While faculty respondents from smaller institutions perceived a lack of Web training, computer hardware, and technology support compared to those from larger institutions, only the perceived lack of support for technical problems and courseware development was significantly different.

More specifically, 47 per cent of those from institutions under 3,000 students viewed this as a problem, 53 per cent of those from institutions between 3,000 and 9,999 noted it as a major obstacle, and only 31 per cent from institutions over 10,000 indicated that this was an obstacle. When combining the responses for those in institutions under 10,000 students, the differences remained significant with 51 per cent of those in the smaller institutions indicating a need for such technical and courseware support versus only 31 per cent in larger institutions.

There were also some modest indications that the lack of Web training and inadequate technology in the classroom and office were also obstacles in the smaller colleges and universities. We also explored obstacles to Web-based teaching as reported by gender. The only item that approached a significant difference here was a lack of software or outdated software that was noted by 19 per cent of the males compared to only 9 per cent of the females. However, females pointed to such obstacles as time to learn to use the Web, lack of classroom equipment to display the Web, too much preparation time, and a lack of technical and courseware development support. Apparently, there are more perceived barriers for female instructors in college settings than for males. While male instructors might recognize outdated software tools, females seem to be seeking additional training and support. Overall, time for course preparation and delivery as well as technical and administrative support are among the major obstacles for college instructors attempting to teach online. Equipment and software tools are less significant factors. All findings vary, however, by type and size of institution.

Support for Web-Based Teaching and Research

The survey also addressed the type of support required by college educators to utilize the Web in their teaching, research, and administrative duties. Given the answers regarding online teaching obstacles, it was not surprising that release time was the most popular form of support selected here.

In addition, each of the following three forms of support were desired by nearly 7 in 10 respondents:

- Recognition for use of the Web in tenure, promotion, and salary review decisions;

- Technical support staff to assist with online course development and associated technical problems; and
- Instructional development grants or stipends.

Given the lack of differentiation in responses, universities may want to embed aspects of a few of these key support preferences in their distance education policies and initiatives. For instance, they might offer options between release time, instructional development grants and stipends, additional salary, and designated technical support.

They might also adopt policies and practices wherein online teaching and research activities would be more fully recognized in college professor tenure and promotion cases. Nearly 60 per cent of respondents felt that it would be valuable for instructional designers to assist faculty members when needed. The same per cent asked for time to learn about and utilize the Web. In addition, 45 per cent thought that additional training on how to use the Web in teaching would be beneficial. Around thirty per cent of these faculty respondents suggested that greater student access to computers as well as online resources would also be helpful, while slightly over one fourth of them considered e-mail notification of technology changes or updates to be valuable.

In contrast, a mere 13 per cent thought that chat room help for Web-related problems was a support they needed for effectively using the Web in teaching, research, or administrative duties. A few respondents suggested additional ideas for online teaching support. Among the advice was for "better equipped classrooms for demos," "really specific examples of 'good courses' so we have some idea what we are trying to achieve," "more money," and "assistance with routine office tasks, grading objective tests, etc., to free up my time to create Web lectures and other course materials." Others argued for outcome data and useful learning research, clearer royalty definitions, and administrators who believed in the priorities of student learning and could articulate the importance of Web teaching.

These support needs correspond closely with the perceived obstacles including the need for greater technical support. Given these findings, it appears that a multi-pronged approach to online instructor support and training is warranted. Respondents at public and private institutions expressed some significant differences in the types of support they needed.

Those in public institutions were significantly more likely to ask for online resources to use the Web effectively in their teaching, research, and administrative duties compared to those in private institutions. They were also significantly more likely to suggest that they needed instructional development grants or stipends to support their online teaching efforts than those at private institutions. Along these same lines, they were significantly more inclined to ask for release time than those in private institutions. Perhaps faculty members at public institutions are simply more demanding.

For instance, other areas wherein faculty members in public institutions indicated that they needed more support to effectively use the Web in their scholarly pursuits than those in private institutions included the need for instructional design help, time to learn about and utilize the Web, greater training regarding how to use the Web in teaching, greater access to computers for students, and recognition for tenure, promotion, and salary review decisions.

Technical support staff was identified as necessary by about 68 per cent of both public and private institution respondents. It is clear that those in public institutions have higher expectations of the support structures required before adopting the Web in their teaching and other duties. Whether they have differing instructional standards, course loads, or support histories and experiences is not known and is an open question for further investigation. In exploring the data by size of institution, there were no significant differences in Webbased teaching support.

However, from a descriptive standpoint, faculty members at institutions with enrollments under 3,000 students pointed to the need for instructional design support and training on how to use the Web in teaching. Instructors in medium-sized institutions were more likely to select time to utilize the Web and student access to computers. Instructors at the medium and large institutions favoured recognition for tenure, promotion, and salary review decisions, development grants and stipends, and release time.

While none of these differences were significant, they do provide an interesting picture of Web-based teaching support needs at different sized institutions. When comparing those in institutions larger and smaller than 10,000 students, respondents at the smaller colleges and universities were more likely to select technical support and student access to computers as important issues, whereas instructors at the large institutions were focused on having more online resources, recognition, and development grants or stipends. Gender differences in terms of perceived supports were minimal.

TIME COMMITMENTS

In terms of overall time investment, these college instructors almost unilaterally agreed that teaching online is more time-consuming than traditional classroom-based instruction. More than 4 in 5 faculty agreed that teaching online courses requires more time than traditional courses.

Fewer than 10 per cent disagreed with that statement. Once again, this is consistent with the NEA report finding that more than half of college faculty teaching via distance learning spent more time on their online courses than their traditional ones regardless of the number of students or times they had previously taught the course. Such findings point to a need for greater course support and incentives that could ease time pressures felt by instructors involved in online teaching.

Attrition

Some reports and media releases contend that students are more likely to drop online courses than traditional ones. Those utilizing a mixed mode or blended approach—traditional and online in the same course—were less likely to experience significant student attrition than those teaching completely online courses.

In fact, only 29 per cent of those utilizing a blended approach experienced more than 10 per cent drop the their courses, whereas 44 per cent of those teaching completely online courses had more than 10 per cent drop their course. Perhaps more strikingly, only 2 per cent of blended courses experienced more than a 50 per cent attrition rate compared to 10 per cent of the completely online courses with such huge attrition rates.

Internet Access

Computer access does not appear to be a problem for these early adopters of Web technologies. Seventy-eight per cent of these college instructors had Internet access in their current or most recent classroom. Computer lab accessibility was even higher with 93 per cent indicating that they had access to an Internet-connected computer lab for class use. Even more, 97 per cent, had Web access from home.

This is more than double the 47 per cent of Americans who are users of the Internet at home as reported in a recent UCLA study. Such high level of technology access is not too surprising given that the majority of the respondents were early Web adopters who had a high level of education. In effect, these findings indicate that access to computers and Internet resources is no longer an obstacle for many college faculty.

Platform Choices and Preferences

The delivery platform for online courses is a significant factor in faculty online teaching experiences. Eighty-three per cent of the respondents to this survey indicated that their institution provided a Web-based platform or courseware system for developing online courses or enhancing on-campus courses with online features. Our survey data also indicated that many institutions are utilizing more than one courseware package.

In fact, 22 per cent of the respondents worked at institutions that provided access to more than one Web courseware or conferencing platform; when excluding those having yet to adopt a Web courseware system, this increases to 27 per cent. Moreover, 10 per cent provided access to three courseware systems or conferencing tools, and 5 per cent had four or more systems or tools available. When asked what is missing from the courseware tools that they use, slightly over half of the respondents at institutions supporting at least one courseware platform offered some ideas.

The specific features mentioned in their open-ended responses included:

- Ability to annotate documents and visuals in real-time,
- Better grade reporting systems,
- Collaborative white boards,
- Collaborative working tools,
- Drawing software,
- Easy ways to create animations,
- Effective drop box tools,
- Efficient ways to display mathematical notation,
- Electronic library resources,
- Good real-time chat tools,
- Improved quizzes,
- Options for chatting and using PowerPoint at the same time,
- Private asynchronous rooms for group work,
- Proctored testing,
- Streaming video,
- Three-dimensional concept visualization tools,
- Tools for tracking student statistics, and,
- 24/7 support.

Of course, many of the tools already exist in the common courseware platforms used in higher education. Other features, such as "options for chatting and using PowerPoint at the same time" are available in various synchronous presentation and collaboration tools often found in corporate training settings. Some general design features requested by these respondents included simplicity, ease of use, user friendliness, enhanced speed, less ugly designs, less cumbersome interfaces, customizability, integration across areas of campus, and flexibility to organize content. In general, there appeared to be a call for more professional appearance, easy to use features, and functional or usable tools. When asked what they liked about their present courseware tools or system, 56 per cent of the respondents offered ideas.

Instructors preferred:

- Ability to link in lectures with PowerPoint presentations,
- Assignment parts for students to pick up homework,
- Chatrooms,
- Comprehensive tools,
- Consistent course appearance,
- Customizability,
- Data and course security,
- Detailed statistics on bulletin board use,
- Ease of use,
- Flexibility,
- Good online help,

- Internal e-mail systems.
- Online discussion boards,
- Password access,
- Posting of assignments on the Web,
- Posting of deadlines and due dates,
- Randomized test banks,
- Reliability,
- Student drop boxes, and,
- Versatility in quiz types.

USEFULNESS OF WEB-BASED TOOLS FOR TEACHING AND LEARNING

USEFULNESS OF WEB-BASED TOOLS FOR TEACHING AND LEARNING

We were also interested in the attitudes of these college instructors about Web-based instructional tools, resources, and activities.

As a result, the respondents were asked to rate the degree of usefulness for items categories:

- Online Class Tools.
- Collaboration and Sharing Tools.
- Instructional Activities.
- Web Resources.

After rating each item as low, medium, or high usefulness for online teaching and learning, the instructors were also asked whether they in fact used that item in their courses.

Useful Online Class Tools

In general, these college educators perceived high utility for most of the online class tools considered in this part of the survey. Perhaps more importantly, at least one-third of the respondents actually used each of the items in this category. Not surprisingly, respondents tended to rate the tools that they actually used as more useful.

The highest rated tool was for posting syllabi online. Not only did 72 per cent of the faculty respondents report this feature as highly useful, 85 per cent actually used such a tool in their courses. These findings also match the Web-based Education Commission report, which documented the increased posting of course syllabi to the Web and incorporation of Web resources within college instructor syllabi. Of course, many of our survey respondents were selected for this survey because they had already posted their syllabus online. The fact that more use this type of tool than rate it as highly useful indicates it is relatively easy to do. The large number of respondents using tools to post their syllabi online reveals an initial area of penetration for the Web in college teaching and learning. For example, the University of Michigan School of Information has compiled a list of faculty course syllabi and placed it online.

Similarly, the UCLA Humanities Department created the E-Campus for syllabi, assignment announcements, and other course related links. However, as indicated earlier, the most complete listing of college syllabi to date is located at the World Lecture Hall. This site hosts syllabi across disciplines for college instructors worldwide. A tool for posting cases, questions, or problems corresponding to course material on the Web was the next most valuable courseware feature of these early Web adopters.

Not only did 70 per cent rate this survey item as highly useful, but nearly 70 per cent also had engaged in such online activities. In fact, only 4 per cent rated this item as low in perceived usefulness. These college instructors also valued file uploading and downloading tools. Sixty-five per cent of the respondents felt they were highly useful, and 71 per cent had used such tools in their teaching. The next highest rated item in terms of usefulness was an online lecture notes utility, which was rated as highly useful by 57 per cent of the respondents and actually used by 69 per cent of them.

Once again, this indicates that while faculty members might view different tools as more useful, they generally rely on readily accessible tools that perform a useful function. Such findings also signify that online tools for posting lecture notes, cases, and syllabi are among the first wave of Web-based instruction courseware. In contrast, online databases received high ratings for usefulness from 51 per cent of the respondents but only 44 per cent were using such a tool. Perhaps such tools are not yet available to the degree that college instructors would like. Once a course is on the Web, there must be some student evaluation and assessment. Indeed, some scholars advocate the use of the Web for online testing and evaluation as a means for reducing costs and increasing speed.

In addition to quick and cost effective feedback, online evaluations provide more organized, individualized, and plentiful course feedback. Despite these benefits, Hmieleski and Champagne report that 98 per cent of the most wired schools still use pen and paper course evaluations. Among the early Web-adopting faculty members of this study, however, 52 per cent rated student online evaluation tools as highly useful and 48 per cent were actually using such tools. Online quizzes or tests were deemed highly useful by 47 per cent of respondents and nearly the same per cent were actually using online exams in their teaching. One in five respondents gave a low usefulness rating to such tools, however.

Receiving even lower support was online student evaluations of course materials. Only 41 per cent rated these as highly useful, while just 36 per cent used such tools. Most of the findings are consistent with the research from

Peffers and Bloom which found that online instructors tend to rely on common software such as e-mail, file uploading and downloading, and asynchronous conferencing as well as simple tools for posting static or dynamic syllabi, Web links to course material, and lecture notes. Significantly fewer instructors used chatrooms, multimedia lectures, online examinations, animation, and video streaming.

However, this research also revealed that the instructional impact of Internet media tools in college settings is expected to dramatically increase in the next few years. Firdyiwek's review of courseware tools indicates that few such tools support pedagogy in an integrated fashion. As tool development proliferates, so, too, does resulting confusion about how to effectively use these online tools.

Interestingly, in this study, only 49 per cent of respondents were highly supportive of tools to place their entire courses on the Web and 47 per cent were using such tools. Could such modest numbers among early Web adopters be due to the lack of pedagogical support in these tools? Or does it reflect a lack of time or training? Perhaps these early Web adopters simply do not want to give up traditional instruction. Or perhaps they rely on customised courseware tools. Whatever the answer, this seems a ripe area for additional research.

Useful Collaboration and Sharing Tools

There are decades of research studies detailing the clear advantages of cooperative and collaborative learning over more individual and competitive formats. Fortunately, many collaborative pedagogical strategies have relevance in Web-based instruction. In fact, a proliferation of collaborative learning technologies have recently emerged for both work and educational environments. In higher education, technologies are becoming more interactive and distributed, enabling learners and instructors to participate in an incredible array of information, resources, and instructional experiences.

The blending of technological and pedagogical advancements presents new opportunities for both research and teaching focused on online dialogue, information sharing, and facilitating learning. In part, such collaborative tools have come on the scene to meet the needs of an older and more diverse student population than in the past. Perhaps this survey will help educators design more powerful e-learning environments for Web-based collaboration and sharing. Collaborative Web-based learning tools offer unique ways for learners, instructors, and experts to interact.

There are now Web tools for student collaborative enquiry, problem-based learning, articulation and dialogue, debate, and personal reflection. Some research indicates that effective use of these new tools can actually foster communities of practice. To create a learning community, the tool or system must bring people together for some initial common interest or quest. There not only is a need for a common reference point or issue for the online group, but members also need multiple ways to become informed about events of that community. Sharing information online often involves conferencing and computer-supported collaborative learning tools.

Fortunately, such tools have begun to infiltrate online learning courseware. In addition, communities such as the World Lecture Hall, MERLOT are now available for visitors to locate and share learning materials within specific discipline or interest areas. But what were the views about such resources and tools among the respondents to this particular survey who already had been involved in online information and resource sharing?

Surely, they would understand and promote collaboration and sharing tools more than the rest of the population. As research from Peffers and Bloom predicts, the respondents to this survey perceived less utility for collaborative and online sharing tools than for test, lecture note, and syllabus tools. For instance, when asked about the utility of tools to share success or failure stories with other instructors, only 27 per cent had done so and only 30 per cent listed this as a highly useful item. Another 51 per cent, however, rated the degree of usefulness as medium.

Hence, more than 80 per cent would find some use for such tools; perhaps they simply are not yet available. Similarly, only 26 per cent used online tools to collaborate and form partnerships with other instructors. Still, 40 per cent saw this as a highly useful idea. Another 44 per cent saw it as of medium utility. Slightly more college instructors used Web-based tools in their courses for students to share success or failure stories with other students.

Forty-one per cent listed this as highly useful and another 45 per cent felt that it was of medium utility. Slightly higher, 46 per cent of the respondents used tools for students to collaborate and form partnerships with other students. In fact, 56 per cent felt that this was a highly useful endeavor and another 34 per cent found it of medium usefulness. The fact that 90 per cent perceived value in student online collaboration is of significance.

Asynchronous discussion forums, synchronous chats, and annotation or feedback tools are common means for electronic collaboration. Sixty-one per cent of faculty members in this study utilized bulletin board or asynchronous types of discussion in their courses. While 60 per cent rated this type of tool as highly useful, another 31 per cent saw it as having medium utility. There was a significant drop in perceived utility and actual use in terms of synchronous collaborative environments compared to asynchronous environments.

Only 32 per cent of the instructors in this survey had used real-time chats, and only 37 per cent rated this item highly. In fact, 28 per cent of the respondents rated this item low in utility. In contrast, tools for interactive feedback, commenting, and annotations fared much better in terms of usefulness among these respondents. Forty-six per cent of the faculty respondents had used interactive feedback or annotation tools in their classes. Even more, 56 per cent perceived them as highly useful, while only 6 per cent rated this type of collaborative tool as low in utility. Perhaps software developers might want to target annotation and feedback tools; they are highly valued and yet not everyone is using them.

Personal profile tools are another means to share information online with peers and other instructors. Whereas 52 per cent claimed to use instructor profile tools in their courses, only 34 per cent utilized student profile tools. Such a finding seems odd. Perhaps there was misinterpretation on this item or perhaps it is easier to reflect on tools one is personally using. Only 30 per cent considered instructor profiles important, indicating that they are using such a tool simply because it is there and it is easy to use. Even less, just 25 per cent, found student profile tools useful.

In fact, 35 per cent rated the degree of usefulness of student profile tools as low. Online guestbooks were even less appealing. Only 6 per cent used them and just 7 per cent rated them highly. In fact, 66 per cent of the respondents—the largest of any item—rated this type of tool as low in usefulness. Related to our findings about online evaluation and testing, only 7 per cent used the Internet for collaborating with other instructors for test-making.

Still 22 per cent rated this as a highly useful item, while another 40 per cent felt it was of medium utility. Similarly, few instructors collaborated with other instructors on class tasks, activities, and discussion. Only 18 per cent had engaged in such collegial activities, while 34 per cent rated this as highly useful and another 41 per cent consider it of medium utility. Perhaps these are two immediate areas wherein universities and software development companies might partner together to develop and test new Web-based teaching and learning tools. Finally, online technology demonstrations received fairly favourable reactions from our respondents.

Thirty-one per cent of the faculty members had used this type of tool in their classes. In addition, 42 per cent rated this item as highly usable in their classes, while 38 per cent rated it of medium utility. Despite these findings, college instructors perceived a need for more collaborative tools. Tools with more than a 10 per cent gap between actual use and perceived high utility included tools for instructors to form collaborations with other instructors, tools for students to share stories with other students, tools for interactive feedback and annotations on student work, tools for instructor test-making collaboration, tools for instructor task collaboration, and tools for online technology demonstrations. These large gaps between teaching practice and perceived utility indicate a need for more collaborative tools in e-learning environments. They may also point to the current direction of Web-based teaching and learning practices.

Useful Online Instructional Activities

Instructional activities that these instructors found useful were also of interest in this study.

The first four online activities asked about were:

1. Scientific simulations;
2. Data analysis;
3. Lab activities; and
4. Performance activities.

Examples of the latter activities might include band or music tasks as well as online decision making in any discipline including counseling, finance, or teaching. These four activities were all infrequently used by the survey respondents. The actual use of these tools ranged from 23 to 26 per cent, with lab and performance being used slightly more often than scientific simulations and data analysis. All of these types of activities were deemed highly useful by approximately 45 per cent of the respondents. Such are interesting since the percentage of respondents who rated these items as highly useful was nearly double the percentage of who actually used them. When combining those who rated activities moderately or highly useful, more than 75 per cent of the respondents indicated utility for each of the four tools. Such data clearly indicate that there is a market for such tools, but college faculty members currently do not have access to them. A fifth and final instructional activity was online critical and creative thinking activities. This item was rated more favourably than the other four.

Forty-five per cent of these faculty members used such activities in their online teaching, and even more impressively, 62 per cent rated them as highly useful for their teaching discipline. An additional 28 per cent rated them of medium usefulness. Only 10 per cent considered their degree of usefulness low. Such results are further indication of the need for better pedagogical tools in online learning environments.

Useful Web Resources

The Web is highly touted as an online resource. Some suggest that it is a gigantic library sprawling in front of students and instructors alike. But in what ways do early Web adopters actually view it as a resource for teaching? Questions were asked about the utility of such Web resources as search engines, glossaries with links to examples, Web link suggestions, article and journal links, book recommendations, newsgroups, collegial Web sites, and general and discipline-specific online resources.

Given that research has revealed that college instructors tend to rely on easy to use tools, it is not surprising that search engines were the most commonly used Web resource with 83 per cent of these faculty members utilizing search engines in their teaching. Equally impressive, 70 per cent ranked search engines such as Yahoo or Lycos as highly useful and only 6 per cent ranked them low. The next most favourable ranking was for online article and journal links. Seventy-four per cent of the respondents used such tools and 70 per cent rated them as highly usable.

Only 3 per cent rated this item low. Sixty-one per cent of these college educators used discipline specific resources in their teaching and 63 per cent found them highly useful. Along these same lines, 59 per cent had used Web sites created by colleagues in their teaching. Such collegial Web site use included syllabi and lecture notes. This is not surprising given where the sample was derived. In fact, only 8 per cent rated the utility of this item as low. Similarly, 58 per cent had used general teaching and learning resources or instructional strategies that had been posted online. Once again, only 8 per cent viewed this item as low in utility.

Online glossaries are another emerging Web-based teaching resource. In fact, 57 per cent of the survey respondents had used online glossaries with links to examples on the Web in their teaching. Similarly, 55 per cent viewed this Web resource as highly usable, while another 35 per cent gave it a medium rating. In effect, the use of online glossaries, colleague Web sites, and general as well as discipline-specific online teaching and learning resources indicates that the Internet has spawned a new type of teaching—one that is reliant on the Web for a significant part of college instruction. Online teaching in an online world is different, and new faculty, as well as experienced ones, need to be prepared for it.

The three lowest rated areas, which were the only items used by less than 50 per cent of the respondents, were student Web link suggestions, online book reviews, and newsgroups. Slightly under half of the faculty members in this survey had used tools where students made Web link suggestions. Still, 45 per cent of the survey participants viewed this item as having high utility, while another 42 per cent rated it as medium in degree of usefulness.

Book recommendations received roughly the same ratings; 47 per cent had used such a tool and 44 per cent deemed it as highly useful. In contrast, newsgroups were used by only 18 per cent of these faculty members, while just 17 per cent rated them as highly useful. Our findings suggest a relatively high and diverse use of Web resources in teaching. Web resources are highly valued by college educators since they can augment lecture notes with visual depictions of concepts, replace the need for textbooks with online articles and glossaries, and provide more current research and professional news. Tools to search, share, and evaluate online course materials are vital parts of one's Web-based teaching arsenal.

When asked to share URLs of Web resources they found particularly useful in their teaching, 15 per cent of these college instructors responded with extremely diverse suggestions. For instance, they listed course-sharing Web sites such as MERLOT, professional organization sites such as the American Psychological Association, textbook publisher Web sites, locations for instructional design models, and university teaching and learning centre resource listings. Only MERLOT was listed more than once. The findings denote many areas wherein improvements in online teaching and learning could occur. The numbers reveal that tools for collaboration and resource sharing are highly valued by college faculty members but are not yet part of their typical online teaching life. Tools for annotation and feedback, article or journal linking, and online discussion were considered highly valuable. Additionally, activities for student labs, simulations, and critical and creative thinking have not been as prevalent as college faculty desire.

Nevertheless, the number of tools and activities that were of substantial use already, as well as the high usefulness ratings that many additional tools received, was striking. Such ratings are signs that online teaching and learning is not going away in higher education settings, but, instead, is about to be enhanced, extended, and perhaps even transformed.

INSTITUTIONAL MOTIVES AND DECISION MAKING

PRIMARY INSTITUTIONAL MOTIVES FOR ONLINE EDUCATION

As Ron Owston pointed out, during the past few years, perhaps nothing has captivated and excited the minds of administrators and educators more than the notion of teaching courses on the World Wide Web. He then argued "Before we introduce any new technology into our classrooms we must be able to justify its contribution".

The three key areas wherein Owston suggested that Web-based learning might be evaluated were improved access to education, student learning, and cost efficiency. While he detailed many improvements to educational access as a result of online technologies, documenting learning outcomes and costs proved much more difficult. In order to establish the level of college instructor agreement with Owston's key areas, our study participants were asked whether profit, improved learning, or access to education were among the primary motives behind the development of online education across institutions of higher education.

They could select all three. As Owston had documented, there appears to be more support among these early Web adopters for the use of Internet technology to increase access to education than for improving profit or learning. Of our respondents, 93 per cent agreed that access was a primary motive for developing online education. Only one person strongly disagreed with that statement. Additionally, 61 per cent agreed that improved learning was a primary motive. In contrast, only 41 per cent felt that profit was a primary motive. Hence, those in the Web-based learning trenches put the emphasis on access and learning over profits. When asked the same questions about their own institutions, these general patterns hold. However, these instructors were slightly less likely to agree that each of the three motives were applicable to their particular institution; only 29 per cent agreed or strongly agreed that profit was a motive while 53 per cent agreed that learning was a motive and 81 per cent felt that their own institution was concerned about access. The reasons for the lower agreement levels were unclear.

Reasons for Institutional Investment

These early Web adopters were asked to rate the level of importance of five key reasons why colleges and universities, in general, might be interested in investing in Web-based teaching and learning. Access to an external universe of libraries, information resources, and databases was the most important reason cited by respondents to explain university investment in Web-based teaching and learning.

The second most important reason, just as to these faculty members, was to support improved efficiency and effectiveness in teaching and research. Offering distance education to a potentially unlimited audience was rated third, while fostering closer inter-institutional cooperation, consortia relationships, and resource sharing within the higher education community was rated fourth. Finally, some respondents felt that building partnerships with private businesses and the government was a critical reason for investing in Web-based teaching and learning. Fewer than 10 per cent of the respondents offered additional reasons why higher education institutions should invest in Web-based teaching and learning.

Most of these reasons concerned student recruitment, student access to education, student skill development, contributing to the economy of the state, revenue enhancement, and staying up to date. Quotes from some respondents included, "to offer equal opportunity of high quality education to students in more rural areas," "we are under a mandate to increase the number of students we serve. We cannot do it on campus, so we are trying distance learning...," "to recruit and retain tech-savvy students," "It's a new revenue source, that's #1," and "because Web-based activities are becoming ubiquitous in ALL workplaces." One person simply stated, "Students will demand Web-based courses or go somewhere else."

Web-Based Teaching Technology Decision-Makers

We also asked about the organizational level in which decisions regarding Web-based teaching, including system purchases and policies, were made. Surprisingly, faculty governance also appears to play a key role in these institutions as 40 per cent of our respondents indicated that technology decisions regarding Web-based teaching were made at the faculty level. Similarly, 39 per cent indicated that it was a departmental responsibility or decision.

There were other key players here. For instance, 36 per cent of respondents thought that the technology support unit on campus made these decisions, while 27 per cent considered it a function of the Chief Technology Officer. Twenty-two per cent selected the teaching and learning centre director level as responsible for these decisions. Four per cent listed others as responsible including the office of distance education, grant administrator, board of regents, or college provost.

Finally, only 5 per cent did not know who made these decisions. There were no statistically significant differences in instructional technology decisions across size and type of institution. However, there were some interesting trends. For instance, in institutions with fewer than 3,000 students, facultylevel decisions are made regarding courseware slightly over 50 per cent of the time, whereas this drops to 32 per cent in medium sized institutions and 41 per cent in large institutions. In comparisons of public and private institutions, we found that college instructors have a role in instructional technology decisions in nearly half of the 45 private institutions, whereas in this survey just 34 per cent of the faculty members in the 151 public institutions in this study helped formulate such decisions.

Besides asking for faculty input, smaller institutions also seem to rely on campus technology support units and the chief technology officer slightly more often than medium and large institutions. Larger institutions have a slight preference for learning centre and departmental-level decisions compared to smaller institutions.

Still, most institutions appear to rely on highlevel administrators to make the technology decisions that impact Web-based teaching and learning. Next, we looked at differences in the organizational level at which instructional technology decisions are made between institutions with fewer than 10,000 students and those with 10,000 or more students. At the larger institutions, the department or school is more involved in these instructional technology decisions than in smaller institutions.

Teaching and learning centre directors are also more involved in making these decisions in the larger colleges and universities than in smaller ones. This is not unexpected since larger institutions are more likely to have campus teaching and learning centres. Administrators are involved in Web-based teaching technology decisions at roughly the same rate at both types of institutions. None of these comparisons were statistically significant, however. That differences in the organizational level of technology decisions between public and private were minimal. Public institutions more often involved teaching and learning centre directors in their decision-making about the use and support of instructional technology than private institutions whereas private institutions more often involved faculty members in these decisions than public institutions. Administrative-level decisions were made at over 60 per cent of both public and private institutions. Once again, none of these differences were statistically significant.

FUTURE ONLINE TEACHING SITUATION

PREDICTED INSTRUCTIONAL TIME ONLINE

Given that many of those surveyed were likely among the technology leaders at their respective institutions, it was important to ask about the per cent of time they anticipated teaching online in the next 1, 2, 5, and 10 years. Interestingly, while just under a third of these faculty members anticipated teaching more than one-fourth of their teaching load online one year from now, this increased to 43 per cent of the respondents in two years, 61 per cent in five years, and 59 per cent in 10 years.

The reason there was a drop-off in the 10 year data was due to a dramatic increase in those not anticipating to be teaching a decade from now. Once again, the age and experience level of these instructors would indicate that many of them plan to retire before the decade is out. When excluding the data related to those retiring or not teaching, the predictions regarding online teaching commitments were even more striking.

The per cent of respondents who anticipate devoting more than one-fourth of their teaching load to online activities increased as follows: 27 per cent in one year, 44 per cent in two years, 64 per cent in five years, and 73 per cent in ten years. Those predicting that at least half their teaching load would be online increased from 13 per cent in one year to nearly 50 per cent in ten years. And those expecting 75 to 100 per cent of their teaching to be online increased from 5 per cent a year in 2001 to 17 per cent at the end of the decade.

Hence, the college instructors responding to this survey expect the Web to become an even more vital instructional tool during the upcoming decade. Though most respondents do not view it as a replacement for all of their teaching activities and requirements, this finding indicates that Web-based teaching expectations will soon be common.

Freelance Instruction

In addition to predictions of increased online teaching loads within university settings, many college faculty members will likely encounter a myriad of new opportunities to teach for other institutions online. Whether "star" faculty members will be hired guns within the online teaching world is not yet known. Instead, what is occurring already is the use of college instructors as freelance instructors in online institutions. These faculty members might work for multiple institutions, teach online during breaks or in the summer, or perhaps even take a leave from their institution to attempt to earn an income teaching online. Other freelance instructors might include practitioners in the field wanting to keep one foot in academia, recently minted Ph.D.'s struggling to find tenure-track positions, and graduate students seeking relevant teaching experiences. Fueling such freelance needs, many institutions are offering new online courses or programmes without expanding their faculty lines, thereby forcing them to find adjunct faculty or add to present faculty teaching loads.

The scenarios leading to freelance instruction are certainly complex. The 16 per cent of the faculty respondents in this study had experience as freelance or adjunct online instructors. However, in the next five years, 75 per cent of these respondents indicated that they believed that they would be interested in teaching as freelance or adjunct online instructors. There definitely is potential here for someone to help coordinate and manage freelance instructor services. Perhaps pending retirements of our respondents factor into these predictions, but other considerations may include additional online course opportunities and expected increases in Web tool availability and reliability.

EMERGING THEORIES AND ONLINE LEARNING ENVIRONMENTS FOR ADULTS

As our world embraces technology, the way instruction is delivered to students is evolving from face-to-face instruction to online formats. Creating effective interactive learning environments for adult online courses is important to the success of students. Online learning is a relatively new format for teaching, but as a growing field, it is important for educators to understand the best methods for creating learning environments with available technology. Technology can enhance or defeat the building of community learning environments.

Social constructivists understand that learning takes place in a community setting, where instructors and students interact to construct meaning. Connectivists realize knowledge is increasing at such fast speeds that it is important for learners to know how to find pertinent information. Transformative learning theory is also grounded in communication, with reflection as a key component. Instructors must incorporate these key components when creating their online courses.

Learning Theories Reviewed Many learning theories have similar components and can be blended together to provide the best online learning environment. Online learning communities should help students feel more connected to their peers and instructors. Social constructivist learning environments create opportunities for students to develop meaning by dialoguing, discussing, and debating with other learners. This social interaction creates meaning from current and prior knowledge, thus deepening understanding and extending knowledge for the students. The learning activities are authentic. Learners are actively involved in constructing knowledge of a topic using communication and social interactions with peers.

Connectivism starts with an individual's personal knowledge that is organized and used as needed. The speed at which information is doubling and becoming obsolete has created the need for new ways of providing instruction. George Siemens (2005) discusses how the acquisition of knowledge is changing from what is known to how to find the information when it is needed. This leads to continual learning for an individual based on one's ability to find the correct information, to connect it with past and current information, thus increase his or her knowledge.

Transformative learning theory has been around more than 25 years. Edward Taylor (2007) looks at the data available from 1999 to 2005 on the subject of transformative learning theory. Taylor states it is a theory that is "uniquely adult, abstract and idealized, grounded in the nature of human communications". Reflection is a big part of the transformative theory. Some researchers say that transformative learning is the adult constructivist theory.

Creating Online Learning Environments Loyens and Gijbels (2008) state a key component of a constructivist learning environment is self-regulation. Students will not be successful in a constructivist learning environment if they are unable to set goals, develop a plan of action, and complete necessary steps to solve the problem. Problems should be complex with the possibility of multiple solutions. Students need opportunities to build deeper understandings when taking an online course. Learners build deeper understandings of the subject while working through a problem.

Dede (2008) discusses the changing epistemology of online interactions with the advent of Web 2.0 tools. These tools have changed learning from one right answer, which traditionally comes from experts via textbooks, to the creations by and interactions of learners using Web 2.0 tools like Wikipedias. This new media requires teaching learners how to be smart consumers who, for example, can discern whether the information is from a credible or non-credible resource.

This shift of learning from traditional materials to using Web 2.0 tools should cause teachers to rethink how they deliver content, and to seek ways to incorporate the tools students use for recreation to further their interest and education. In a perfect world, educators would be able to take the best from traditional and online formats to create a superior system for building understanding and knowledge. According to Dr. Ruth Brown (2001) there are three stages to building community in online courses. First, students become acquainted. Second, students begin, through longer interactions, to discover similarities and differences between themselves and their classmates and begin to interact with the course content. In the third stage, students begin supporting one another and taking their friendship outside the course requirements.

Some even begin to plan the courses they will take together in future semesters. Students new to online classes will need more support from the instructor than veteran students. Beginning students are happiest with short assignment and timelines. They also prefer frequent feedback from their professor. Veteran online students do not need as much hand-holding by their professor and quickly make connections with past classmates. Their conversations show connections from shared past points of view and from courses they have taken together. The effectiveness of the learning community can be seen when all members share ideas and reflect on the process together.

Online communities work best when members enter into relationships by getting to know each other, by participating in online discussions about the learning material, and by supporting one another's learning and understanding. Silvers, O'Connell, and Fewell (2007) identified several strategies for building community. Some of the strategies are journaling, responding to discussions, e-mailing, creating digital presentations, and collaborating. The above formats, along with blogs and Wikipedias, provide places for adult learners to reflect on what they learn, to make connections with past knowledge, and to construct meaning. Barriers to Constructivist Online Learning According to Huang (2002) there are seven barriers facing online educators trying to provide a constructivist learning environment to distance learners. The first barrier is the learner's isolation from classmates. Adult learners learn from their peers as well as their instructor. Second, the instructor must understand their learners' characteristics and their individual situations.

Adult learners come from a variety of backgrounds, living situations, jobs, family situations, and have different reasons for taking an online course. All of these differences will influence their online interactions. Accommodating these differences can be difficult when all interaction takes place online.

Fourth, instructors must not pre-authenticate learning. This conflicts with the constructivist learning theory, which asserts that learners need to construct their own learning. A fifth barrier is the extensive time required to evaluate online learning activities. Sixth, adults are used to learner-centered teaching. Online formats will be new to some of the learners. The seventh barrier is the ability of instructors to effectively create and evaluate collaborative learning opportunities for adult learners. These barriers can cause social isolation in opposition to what social constructivism learning environments should be providing its learners.

Teaching and Design of Online Learning

When instructors are aware of the barriers online students face, they can take steps to address them when designing their course materials. According to Heinecka, Dawson, and Willis (2001) the following six principles can be used with constructivist-focused, online teaching: interactive learning, collaborative learning, facilitating learning, authentic learning, learner-centered learning, and high quality learning. Petraglia (1998) acknowledges learners draw on prior knowledge and experiences when approaching learning tasks. Since individuals learn and work collaboratively in their everyday lives, instructors can use similar interactions between learners to build knowledge of content.

Students may enter into either synchronous or asynchronous discussions throughout the course via chats, blogs, wikis, threaded discussions, or e-mail. This collaboration leads to shared knowledge and higher critical thinking skills. The instructor of the course must maintain the accuracy of the learning. The instructor's role is to facilitate learning, support learners, monitor their learning, and to provide directions and guidelines for learners. Adult learners need authenticity in activities that directly relate to their work experiences and real life.

This authenticity creates meaningful knowledge and adults value the learning process. Huang (2002) stresses adult learning must be learner-centered. Adults need to take ownership of their learning, but not all adults know how to do this, as they have grown up in an era where instruction came from the "sage on the stage". As Cercone (2008) points out some adults need help learning to be self-directed. Instructors can support adult learners by providing assignments early in the course that are short and directed to help the reluctant learner see the value of an online course. The sixth learning principle is high quality learning. Huang (2002) states "online learning should involve high-order thinking skills to learn how to determine the authenticity and quality of information by assessing the authority of the source and validating it from other sources". Constructivism and connectivism encourage high quality learning by having learners engage in constructing knowledge from multiple sources while using their life experiences. Reflecting on what is learned is used in transformative learning theory to develop higher order thinking skills.

Students Role in Building Communities

How students approach learning is changing due to the explosion of technology. Technology increases the speed at which we obtain knowledge and how fast it becomes obsolete, making it even more important for instructors to provide opportunities for learners to make connections with their prior knowledge using available technology tools.

Siemens (2004) discusses how learning has changed in the last twenty years. Just a couple of decades ago, people learned a trade and remained in their chosen field for the rest of their lives. This is not true anymore. Today learning is a continual need as most individuals will hold more than one job in their lifetimes, not all of which may be in the same field as their original training.

Ultimately, learning is constructed by the learner based on their past knowledge and experiences. Rikers, Gog, and Pass (2008) state "an important goal of constructivist learning environments is to engage students in deep and meaningful learning".

Teachers may need to help students understand how to learn and how to become comfortable within the online learning community. Many students come from traditional classroom settings where assessments are based on the reading of the chapter in the textbook, completing a couple assignments, and then taking a test; therefore, they find it difficult to embrace the different kinds of assessments associated with social constructivist teaching. Adult learners will need support and extended opportunities to practice different assessment methods that are new to them before they are comfortable and before instructors see changes in students' assessment behaviour.

Training of Instructors

Online instruction should not look the same as instruction in a traditional course on campus. It can be helpful for instructors to experience online learning before teaching a course. Sanford Gold (2001) analyzed a two-week workshop taken by professors who were beginning the transformation from teaching in a traditional classroom to teaching an online course. The workshop was based on constructivist teaching methods. The creators of the workshop felt that an effective online teacher needed to experience an online course first lest they continue teaching the same way online as in their traditional face-to-face courses. One result of taking the workshop was that professors shifted to more of a constructivist learning environment approach and reported feeling the online environment was actually more interactive than their traditional classrooms.

Instructors are moderators in online courses. Gold (2001) identified three key fundamental roles that online instructors have as they serve as organization, social, and intellectual moderators. Instructors organize the course materials, create the timeline, provide social interaction opportunities, and ensure high quality instruction. As in a traditional classroom, the online instructor's role is to provide an environment that is friendly and welcoming to students. It is essential that instructors provide time in the beginning of a course to set up the format for discussions. Gold (2001) states, "good moderators often send out welcome messages, using a personal tone, and seeding their feedback with specific examples and references". The effort in the beginning of a course to build the social aspect of a class leads to deeper understandings through interactions with peers and instructor for students later in the course. Huang (2002) identified the importance for instructors to address the problem of social isolation of the online learner to ensure quality learning environments.

The third role of the instructors is to maintain high intellectual content of course materials. The instructor doesn't disappear from the scene, leaving instruction to students, but rather, effective instructors monitor what is happening online, clarify important points, ask questions to help students move towards a deeper understanding, and provide ways for students to synthesize and summarize key points. Instructors may summarize information for the students (Gold, 2001).

The effectiveness of a learning community is seen when all members participate together to share ideas and reflect on the process. Silvers, O'Connell, and Fewell (2007) found online communities work best when members enter into relationships by getting to know each other, participating in online discussions about the learning material, and supporting one another's learning and understanding.

Individuals have different learning styles; therefore, it is important to create online learning communities that include a variety of learning activities. Snyder (2009) presents ways to help create an online environment that take into consideration adults' need to be active learners. She reminds readers that all adult learners come to a course with different backgrounds, needs, and goals.

Adult learners have different learning styles, so instructors should develop courses to include multiple learning styles thus giving learners an opportunity to learn in their preferred style and the opportunity to experience other learning styles. Effective instructors provide ways for learners to share their work publicly.

Public sharing helps all community members gain deeper understandings. Some formats for public sharing include wikis, blogs, and peer reviews. Petraglia (1998) states "most educators easily accept constructivism's central premise that learners approach tasks with prior knowledge and expectations based on their knowledge of the world around them, leading educators to attempt to create authentic learning environments".

Authentic learning environments must correspond to what the learner needs versus what the teacher has predetermined is the need of the learner. Adult learners especially want to know the value in completing requested tasks. Online communities should take input from learners to help determine the direction of the activity. Learners will be more engaged in activities when they feel it has some connection to their job or is what they want to learn.

Delivery of Course Materials

Course Management Systems (CMS) in higher education and the tools within the systems are growing and becoming more robust each year. With the advent of open source systems such as Moodle, course management systems are offering more flexibility for instructors when designing their online curriculum. The perfect system does not exist yet, but CMS are evolving each year better meeting the needs of teachers and students. Another unique characteristic of the adult learner is their reduced memory. Providing charts and graphic organizers help adult learners organize the content and retain information. Use easily read fonts and use bold colours to promote the readability of online course materials. Consistency in menus on the course management system will help adults navigate easily within the course material.

Appalachian State University professors Bronack, Riedl, and Tashner (2006) developed a 3-dimensional virtual world, AET Zone, for their courses. Although many colleges were offering distance education at the time they wrote their paper, very few instructors were utilizing virtual worlds for student learning and for interactions with their peers and instructor. Virtual worlds allow opportunities for students and instructors to interact synchronously, providing a richer social interaction for learning. The authors state, "learning environments are most effective when they reflect the nature of the community in which they occur".

Learners should be encouraged to participate in creating the learning community, drawing on their experiences to create new meaning from their current studies. AET Zone helps students feel as if they are in a class interacting with their peers and instructor. AET Zone has students select an avatar to travel within the virtual world at the student's direction, while using other tools in the virtual world to interact with other students and instructors. Virtual worlds are becoming more common in educational settings.

Online Learning Environments and Their Applications to Emerging Theories of Educational Technology

The 21st century is fast becoming known by its nickname of the 'digital age' which does a good job of describing what daily life is like in modern day society. Through the use of technology, information is being developed very rapidly and connections between this knowledge and the individuals that interact with it are virtually instantaneous. Theories of learning need to address this new pace of education today.

There is a positive correlation between the increase in new technology being integrated into society and the development of new theories on how to use technology as a catalyst for learning. The most prevalent of these new leaps in technology is the use of the Internet in teaching and learning. Online learning environments (or e-learning) have changed the dynamics of the traditional classroom. E-learning provides an opportunity to bring together individuals into one community that surpasses physical space and time to unite and engage them in purposeful learning. The theories of socio-cultural constructivism, transactional distance, cognitive theory of multimedia learning, and connectivism will be discussed by providing a description of their defining principles. Then a correlation will be made on how they can be integrated successfully into online learning environments. Some foundational definitions of the terms theory, learning theory, and learning environments need to be given before a valid argument can be made for these learning theories and their online applications. Studying theory and what constitutes a strong theory often results in more confusion. The word "theory" is used for such a wide range of contexts that warnings have been made to prevent it from becoming meaningless. Often the use of the word theory creates an obstruction rather than an understanding. For this chapter a basic meaning of what constitutes a theory will be proposed in an attempt to help bypass the natural debate as to whether the concepts presented in this chapter are actually or even potential theories of learning.

Koetting and Januszewski (1991) use the definition of theory established by the Association for Educational Communities and Technology (AECT) to help establish a definitional foundation. The AECT defines theory as, "a general principle, supported by considerable data, proposed as an explanation of a phenomena; a statement of the relations believed to prevail in a comprehensible body of fact". It is easy to see that this definition contains problematic terms such as "considerable data" and "comprehensive body of facts." These terms are subjective and open for interpretation. It is noteworthy that the AECT definition establishes the notion that a theory attempts to explain something through establishing relations between proven facts.

Ketterling and Januszewski (1991) go on to discuss different types of theories and use learning theory as an example of a descriptive theory. They state that, "through learning theory we identify the process of learning in such a way that through the application of that theory we can control the learning process, and through that control, we can predict the outcomes of learning". As theories of learning evolve so does the definition of what a learning theory is and the "control" and "prediction of outcomes" as described in the above definition loosen and provide for a more non-restrictive definition.

The learning theory then no longer takes on the role of the box that holds instruction but the basis for expanding and redefining the box as an agent for change, not restraint. Learning theories would have no contextual meaning if not for the existence of a setting that supports such learning. These settings are called learning environments. When the learning environment takes place on the World Wide Web, it is known as an online learning environment. E-learning (electronic learning) has been used to define different concepts. One of these is to address online learning which is how it will be defined for the purpose of exploring the above mentioned learning theories and how they apply to online education.

Sociocultural Constructivism

Credited for major contributions to the sociocultural constructivist theory is L.S. Vygotsky. A Russian psychologist, Vygotsky is well known for his Zone of Proximal Development (ZPD) theory. The ZPD is often defined as the relation between what a learner knows and the knowledge that exists within the social context. Sociocultural constructivism uses this relationship and continues it with stating that through this social interaction a new level of knowledge is acquired. Emphasis is on dialogue that participants engage in as a means of collaboration and negation of meaning to reach a new understanding.

This process allows the learner to internalize what is being taught, and thus, they become an active part in shaping the learning environment. Sociocultural constructivism defines learning as a sociocultural dialogic activity. Therefore instruction needs to provide opportunities for participation in a community of learners that learn through authentic tasks.

Zeina Nehme (2000) describes how a sociocultural learning environment would work in a synchronous online community of learners. She states that, "the synchronous online tool is the mediator and the social area is achieved through the different types of communication, collaboration, cooperation and interaction that happen among the moderator and the learners online". The use of online learning environments brings with them the availability of an extremely complex network of information and personnel that enrich the learning community.

Other principals of sociocultural constructivist theory that can be enhanced through e-learning are the need for a mediation tool and distributed intelligence (Bonk, 1998). There is a need for a learning environment to facilitate the development of a culture in which participants learn and grow. This community of learners must be diverse and utilize an array of knowledge. Online learning environments provide the framework for creating such mediation as well as the ability to bring together a limitless perspective on any subject imaginable.

Transactional Distance

Transactional distance (TD) theory was developed by Michael Moore around 1997 (although it has been in the works since around 1972). This theory has been the basis for argument among many scholars including Grosky and Caspi (2005) who argue that TD might not be an actual theory at all. They do, however, agree that it is valuable in that transactional distance is viewed as a framework for understanding distance education and cited that the reduction of TD is a needed factor. This theory has also been supported and studied in universities as vital to understanding how distance learning affects individuals who participate in such learning environments. Moore (1997) uses Dewey's concept of transaction as describing the role between individuals and the learning environment to establish a theory based on the unique learning environment created by distance education. When learners and teachers are separated by time and physical space (as in distance education), the potential for misunderstanding between these individuals is increased. This increase in the potential for miscommunication that can occur in distance education is what Moore (1997) defines as transactional distance. TD is a relative variable and its degree is ever-changing based on the unique circumstances of each particular situation. The principle factors that determine the degree of TD with a particular learning environment are the amount of dialogue, structure, and learner autonomy present.

Moore (1997) goes on to declare that distance education programmes "with little transactional distance receive directions and guidance regarding study through dialogue with an instructor in a programme that has a relatively open structure designed to support such individual interactions". Online education by its very nature has the potential for a less predetermined structure or "open structure" thus allowing for the flow of dialogue between learners and instructors to increase and in turn lessen the amount of transaction distance present.

The effect of transactional distance on online learning environments was addressed in a study conducted by professor Yau-Jane Chen from the National Chung Cheng University in Taiwan. Chen (2001) studied a web course offered by the university for the purpose of gaining learner's perspectives in regard to the different factors of TD. The conclusion showed support for the existence of transactional distance in online learning and the need to address it as a factor of student learning when instruction for e-learning is being designed.

Online education has the ability to adapt instruction based on the third factor of TD which is learner autonomy. Learner autonomy is described as the "extent to which... the learner rather than the teacher determines the goals, the learning experiences, and the evaluation decisions of the learning programme". Other media sources do not have the ability to create the needed dialogue for learner success. For example, the use of a prerecorded video programme as a media source for a distance education course must contain a highly structured programme since all content is designed and produced prior to the actual instruction. Since predesigned structure drastically decreases the amount of learner autonomy available in the course of study.

Cognitive Theory of Multimedia Learning

Cognitive Theory of Multimedia Learning (CTML) was designed by professor Richard E. Mayer (cite?). Professor Mayer is well known in the field of educational psychology and has made it his goal to develop a theory based on researched-based principals that explain how people learn from words and pictures in multimedia learning environments. It is based on the assumptions that people process audio and visual input differently, that people only process limited elements at one time, and that learning occurs when learners are presented with the right kind of cognitive processing.

Five cognitive processes are presented in CTML that examine how people learn from words and pictures. Selecting words when verbal material enters through the ears, selecting images when visual materials enter through the eyes, organizing the words and the images, and integrating and building the connections between the visual, audio, and prior knowledge. This understanding of how people learn was experimented with and research-based principles created. These principles focus on eliminating processing that is not related to the goal, managing basic processing related to the goal, and providing a deeper reflective processing of the goal.

Online learning environments can be designed with these principles in mind so as to promote more effective learning. It is easy to present large amounts of material in an online learning environment since so much knowledge is accessible in a digital format and easily uploaded to present to learners. According to the CTML theory, learners can only process limited amounts of information and therefore e-learning should limit the amount of information that a learner is asked to process. Digital media can also become extremely complex and information jumbled in a format that looses the focus of the related goal. Information needs to be simplified, focused and presented in a format that is easily understood and clearly delivered. Simplified and precise information is the focus of CTML along with taking this focus and extending it out into a deeper reflective understanding of the content. Reflective learning is not a new idea and online learning environments have the potential to create a framework for reflection through activities such as personal learning journals, wikis, and discussion board questioning. Cognitive theory of multimedia learning is a research-based theory that can be applied to improve the level of online education available.

Connectivism

Connectivism is a learning theory established in 2005 by well known theorist George Siemens. He explored the theories of chaos, network, and self-organization to formulate this theory. Siemens (2004) proposes the need for a new theory to address the change in how people think and handle knowledge as a result of the increased uses of technology in all aspects of daily living. He argues that the "know-how and know-what is being supplemented with the know-where (the understanding of where to find knowledge needed)". Principals of connectivism explore new ideas in learning and data transfer. The theory states that due to the fact that information has now become digital, its flow has increased to a point of becoming too complex for an individual to keep up with it all. The learner thus finds a need to create an external network of valid sources such as people or content of information called nodes. These nodes create places for the individual learner to organize up-to-date knowledge that can be accessed when needed. Thus putting the value on the external environment in which knowledge is filtered and transferred as opposed to how it is internalized by the learner. Epistemological principals of connectivism are unique in that learning may occur outside the individual. In this view, knowledge is made up of connections that emerge and adapt based on the context thus giving connectivism its epistemological framework for its grounds as a learning theory. Siemens verifies this new belief of how learning occurs in a post on his web site, www.connectivism.ca, when he writes that, "the learner aggregates related nodes...and relies on each individual node to provide needed knowledge. The act of learning is offloaded onto the network itself –i.e. the network is the learning". By their very nature online learning environments have a structure consisting of networks where information is gathered. This information is then retrieved by the individual participant and studied and sorted. Connectivism provides the needed shift in learning skills and activities to provide a successful and up-to-date learning environment through the use of online tools and resources.

Predictors of Success for Adult Online Learners Predictors of Adult Students' Success in E- learning Environments E-learning has become an expected part of higher education in recent years. In fact, more than a decade ago Moore and Kearsley (1996) found that an overwhelming majority of distance education students were between the ages of 25 and 50. Since online enrollment continues to grow, so does the scholarly interest in students' educational motivations in such courses. However, to be successful in an online only learning environment, students should be well-motivated, autonomous learners, who are able to self-regulate their learning experiences. A motivated student may be defined as one who seizes the opportunity to learn—the opposite of a procrastinator. The motivated learner will stick with the class even in the face of adversity.

Autonomous, self-regulated learners committ to controlling their own learning experiences. Some of the ways that this self-regulation may be displayed is by seeking help when they lack understanding, believing in their own capabilities, rehearsing the material to be learned, organizing the material to be learned, and holding an intrinsic belief in the value of learning. Many active, self-regulated learners use their past experiences and the context of their present virtual classrooms to set goals for their learning. Their goals become a standard against which they compare their progress. Highly motivated and autonomous, self-regulated learners are needed in e-learning environments because of the autonomous nature of the online classroom, in comparison to a traditional classroom.

Graduate vs. Undergraduate Motivations

Differences have been noted between undergraduate and graduate distance learners and their motivations. Even though many graduate students are less experienced with online learning and technologies, they were more likely to be self-motivated, to utilize critical thinking skills, and were less likely to procrastinate when compared to their undergraduate counterparts. In contrast, undergraduate students were more likely to procrastinate and less likely to use in-depth critical thinking skills. Age as a Factor in Online Learners' Success The literature supports the idea that because adult learners are not as technologically savvy and have more responsibilities towards work and family, online learning is more difficult for them. However, Ke and Xie's (2009) study showed that regardless of an adult learner's age, students self-reported the same amount of effort put into learning tasks and reported comparable levels of satisfaction.

Artino and Stephens (2009) saw differences between undergraduate and graduate online students: even though undergraduates were more likely to procrastinate, they were also more likely to show greater continuing motivation to enroll in further e-learning courses and reported valuing and benefiting from online classroom tasks. The majority of the undergraduates in the study were non-traditional students—working adults between 25 and 50 years old. Their age and circumstance may have played a part in the outcome. On the other hand, Hargis (2001) points out that age alone will not predict online learning outcomes. Since more and more online students are between the age of 25 and 50, further studies that explore differences in non-traditional versus traditional learners may be beneficial in helping instructors and universities to better understand the motivational differences of these demographics and compensate practices and design accordingly.

Design Model Characteristics and the Impact on Performance and Learner Satisfaction

Understanding the nature of online learning helps educators and schools implement online courses. High-quality course designs should include certain features within their makeup. Cercone (2008) suggests that course design models:

- Connect new knowledge to prior learning
- Maintain collaboration and social interaction between students
- Promote a self-reflective environment
- Include current or immediate applications
- Advance self-regulated learning.

These components in the design of a class lead to deep learning as opposed to just surface learning. Deep learning proves successful and provides satisfaction by engaging the whole learner in the learning process, socially, cognitively, and affectively. Deep learning permeates across all age groups and all types of learners. Distance learning should be desirable to all adult learners, regardless of age, and promote lifelong learning.

Implications for Online Instructors: Practices to Promote

In light of the findings, it would be wise for instructors to implement practices that cultivate self-regulation and critical thinking in their students.

Teachers may need to provide varying levels of support and guidance for their undergraduate and graduate students. Undergraduates, for example, may require more explicit support that will help them self-monitor. Providing reflective prompts is one way to support all online learners (Davis and Linn, 2000). Making specific and clear syllabi and assignments with progressive calendar deadlines may encourage task completion and improve self fulfillment.

Other strategies that have improved self-efficacy in both undergraduate and graduate learners, are to provide students specific performance feedback on a timely basis (Bangert, 2004; Wang and Lin, 2007), as well as assist students in identifying and setting challenging yet reachable goals. In regard to online discussions or discussion board prompts, undergraduates in particular may benefit from instructor assistance, or scaffolding in such a way that promotes critical thinking.

Some examples of instructor-enhanced scaffolding within the prompts includes modeling a response to the prompt, requesting clarification, reinforcing students' ideas, correcting misunderstandings, and asking for consensus within areas of disagreement. These practices may improve learner interaction; increase satisfaction; increase retention; and facilitate critical thinking and self-regulation in students.

Implications for Online Instructors: Approaches and Techniques

Instructors should consider different approaches and techniques that they may utilize to maximize students' success. Online learning models may incorporate both asynchronous and synchronous communication tools. Asynchronous tools include applications such as e-mail, discussion boards, newsgroups, and conference rooms where users are allowed to contribute at their leisure, but are not required to be online at a specific time. Asynchronous forms of learning lend more to self-reflection and deep learning as posited earlier. Synchronous tools include chat rooms, webcasts, desktop video, and audio technologies. These tools are used to simulate real-time teaching strategies, like meeting with groups of students or delivering lectures or presentations. The synchronous activities may help foster a sense of community to facilitate learning a complex body of knowledge. Three different types of learning experiences may be fostered within an online community. These approaches are

- Expository learning,
- Active learning, and
- Interactive learning. The type of learning provided may determine the way the learner acquires knowledge.

Expository learning is a conventional approach to learning where the information is given to the student through a lecture or via written material. Active learning involves the learner having control over how and what she learns. Learning is enquiry-based, such as working on manipulation of artifacts, simulations, web quests, or games (Zhang, 2005). Interactive learning emphasizes collaborative learning activities where the learning develops from interaction with others or other knowledge sources within the course. Teachers may be facilitators in such learning.

In determining which approach to use and when, the instructor should 1) remember what has been said thus far about learning and best practices, 2) consider the student group to be served, and 3) consider how the learning should best emerge. Think of using technology as a tool to foster deep learning and critical thinking skills.

With expository instruction, the technology is conveying the content. With active learning, the technology is allowing the learner to be in control of the learning by investigation of information or of problems. With interactive learning, the technology is mediating the interactions of learners and allowing learning to emerge (USDOE, 2009).

Implications of Findings for Online Instructors

The U.S. Department of Education (2009) says earlier online programmes typically utilized either asynchronous or synchronous applications within their courses. The Department suggests that combining these types of forums in online classrooms is catching on. It has also become more of a common occurrence to provide a blended model of instruction where, in addition to the online format, an occasional face-to-face class will take place. However, a U.S. Department of Education study (2009) found that when comparing an online-only versus a blended classroom, the learning outcomes are similar. Thus, learning will emerge and provide a similar success rate in online-only classes with or without a face-to-face component.

With the convenience of distance learning, I see the trend pushing more towards the online-only realm, especially since the study showed comparable learning gains. Additionally, the study found that active learning strategies enhance learning and foster self efficacy and intrinsic motivation, as Shea et al. (2005) and Whipp (2003) say are necessary for critical thinking and deep learning. Interactive learning is another trend that will prompt learner reflection and assist with developing a sense of community, as noted by Schwen and Hara (2004) and Vrasidas and Glass (2004). Instructors should focus on this trend to promote the community feeling that students tend to express they feel is lacking within online courses.

Students say online learning is what they turn to for flexibility and because of their busy lifestyles. As a result, instructors should change their teaching styles to be just as flexible and accommodating to all learners by incorporating the various strategies discussed and by being easily accessible to students. National University's (NU) School of Education, where I am an adjunct professor, has a 24 hour "return policy": If a student contacts a professor, the professor should get back to the student within 24 hours by e-mail or phone. In regard to student satisfaction and retention, I suggest that instructors and universities consider promoting an environment of continuous improvement by allowing students to anonymously complete a survey at the end of the class to assess their learning and improvement and the instructor's teaching and course management. The quality of an instructor is an important determinant of an effective learning system. If measured, it will get attention.

NU has a policy of asking students to complete course evaluations, and instructors ratings are reviewed by deans and heads of departments. Instructors' ratings play a part in whether they are asked to teach that class again. About half of my students complete the evaluations for my course, but this only gives me and the other faculty a partial picture of my effectiveness as an instructor. I'd suggest universities give students an incentive for completing course evaluations to increase the likelihood of a higher return.

The studies reviewed suggest that students are using their past experiences and the context of their present online environment to set goals for their learning where the goals set become a standard against which to compare their progress. Thus, instructors should look to mirror this idea within their own teaching of future classes. Instructors should also use evaluations or other student feedback to drive their future instruction. Just as technology is always changing and evolving to meet the students' needs, so too should the instructor's teaching and management of the course.

WEB-BASED LEARNING

As the Internet technology is introduced it makes a new revolution in information technology. The wide use of Internet also affected the methods of education. It is a global network and gives the concept of global classroom where any number of students can interact with each other at any time. Goodbye classes, goodbye books and Goodbye teachers' is possible with the webbased education.

The WWW gives attractive features to Web Based Education, which are:

- The ability to have multimedia documents
- The hypertext/hypermedia capability
- WWW network basis, allowing for distance learning.

In web based education we have two different types, asynchronous and synchronous learning:

- In asynchronous the educational module is to be installed from a particular web site and then you can unpack it offline on your machine. In this case there is no mutual interaction of student with teacher.
- In synchronous type there is synchronization among the students and teacher on-line. This synchronous Web based education provides the

most emerging concept of E-learning. E-learning is not a web delivered a common misunderstanding.

E-Learning is an interactive experience with access to on line tutors and can be done from any computers once you have your password. Access is through web browsers such as Internet explorer and Netscape Navigator. With ELearning training is organized in the form of modules. The modules are approximately onehour session that focuses on specific subject of training. Using E-Learning the training can be brought right to your desktop. This makes technical training more convenient. During the live E-Learning module, participants will have the ability to ask the instructor questions, get answers and interact with other students — all on line.

We have discussed problems, considerations and approaches to WBL in India along with important Features of Web-Based Learning Environment.In what follows, part second explains the scope for improvement in school education by using Information Technology, third part explains tools of Information Technology useful for school education, fourth part explains

Web Based Education: Considerations and Approaches, fifth on problems to be faced while implementing IT in school education in Indian context sixth part explains important Features of Web-Based Learning Environment and finally last part gives conclusion.

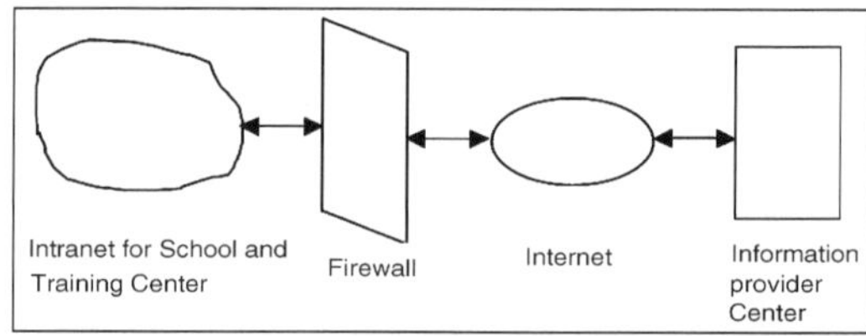

TOOLS OF INFORMATION TECHNOLOGY USEFUL FOR SCHOOL EDUCATION

SYSTEM IMPLEMENTATION STRUCTURE

To implement the WBE we propose the system implementation structure. The school classrooms, office and training centers are connected through Intranet. This Intranet is connected to the Internet by using network operating system. Firewall is introduced between Intranets and Internet in order to provide security.

SYSTEM DESCRIPTION

In initial stage of school education the students are not expert in reading and writing. Subject understanding increases if they learn the things through visualization. With the help of multimedia or Rich Media, which includes, Audio, video, graphics and Java Applets have made WBE very effective. We propose

Multimedia content database scheme as shown in fig. In this database contents the data about educational centers, courses, tutors, students, examinations as well as some story books and games in the form of html pages, audio and video files, Images and Java Applets. Student and teachers can access this database for learning as well as for teaching.

In the primary stage students don't have good knowledge of English. Therefore the presentation should be available in their mother tongue for the better understanding, which is also helpful in improving their pronunciation. This is possible by developing Natural Language Interface to database. One important device called, as "Tech Commander" is also useful for teachers to identify students potential by viewing any students computer display on his own monitor. If he finds something that everyone should see he could set everyone's monitor to display it.

Web Based Education: Considerations and Approaches

- *Conversion of Existing Material*: In order to shift from traditional education to WBE we have to convert the existing school educational material to the Web. The important points to consider are bandwidth, design, usability, and the necessity of high quality media elements and consistency of material across the mediums.
- *Authoring for Multiple Delivery Environments*: We have to provide consistency of interface and ease of authoring and design of an effective multi platform course.
- *Using the Web for student/Teacher Interaction*: Web site can be used for posting of assignments, student work and marks, along with the ability to submit work on-line through the site, also JavaScript and JAVA applets to demonstrate course concepts interactively. This means that course delivery on the Web must be dynamic and truly interactive between the instructor and the students.
- *Faculty Support and Training:* We have to provide centralized support and training resources for training the teachers initially.

Problems to be faced while implementing WBE in school education in Indian context: Looking at how to use Information Technology in school education, its different tools, the system structure as defined and described it is obvious that we will face some problems while implementing WBE in school education in India.

The major problems we will be facing are:

- Intensive Training to Schoolteachers: Schoolteachers are not introduced to the web based education. Therefore training should be given in order to create a learning environment that will itself train and spur students on the one hand to turn the learning experience into useful, practical and personal knowledge.

- WBL awareness and Workshops: In rural area parents are not much knowing about WBL. So the demonstration, seminars and workshops needs be conducted for society in order to understand the importance of it.
- *Bandwidth Limitations*: Limited bandwidth of Internet connection gives slower performance for sound, video and intensive graphics, causing long waits for downloads that can affect the ease of the learning process. Improved bandwidth will help the teacher to solve his problem.
- *Effect on Teachers*: WBL will lead to reduction in manpower as per as teachers are concerned. This will lead to agitations by teacher's organization.
- *Effect on Students*: Although the students will be benefited by WBL there will some part of students opposing this introduction of technology in education.
- Infrastructure: WBE will primarily require free access to Web to all the learners and hence government of India will have to setup nation wide Fibre Optic Cable network.
- *Access*: Every school will not have equal opportunity to information because of access issues. The schools with fewer budgets will always face this problem. This is the major problem as per as India is concerned, as there is big gap between poor and rich communities in India.
- *Download*: The learning material that appears on web needs to be downloaded will require more time. The speed depends on the transmission methods and bandwidth, which is problem as per as India is concerned.

Important Features of Web-Based Learning Environment

While designing Web-Based Learning sites the following important features should be kept in mind:

- *The Online Syllabus*: An online syllabus provides the instructor with a way to change course material easily and as per the requirements in industry, and the student will have a complete and up-to-date picture of the course requirements. Hypertext links to sample relevant disciplinary web sites may be helpful in giving students (and also prospective students) a sense of the disciplinary context for the course.
- *Personal Home Pages*: Personal home pages can be used to foster the sense that the class is not just a collection of isolated individuals but a community of learners who can profit from interacting with one another. Home pages encourage students to learn about each other so as to encourage contact and mutual interests. This helps the learners to create a group with common interest.
- *Interactivity*: Adding discussion forums and chat sessions to your

online course is a common way to add an interactive component to a web-based course. There are many implementations of bulletin board and chat session software to choose from. A second method of interactivity is, of course, e-mail. It's a good practice to have an online list of the e-mail addresses of all registered students, the professor, and teaching assistants. This is possible with an e-mail subscription mechanism included in your Online Syllabus.

- *Assignments*: The web page listings of homework assignments, upcoming events and exams can be more interactive than the familiar print counterparts. If some homework assignments, for example, are based on online materials, they can be directly linked to the class schedule. This helps the students to plan the preparations for the examination in systematic way.
- *Announcements*: To be effective, announcements need to be read; for that to happen, students need to know when a new announcement has been posted. Alert sounds or perhaps a blinking link added to a page can let students know of new announcements, or perhaps, even a mass e-mail to all students in the course. For a home page, or a long life syllabus, various software tools can be used for the subscribers announcement about page changes. All these techniques will attract the learner's attention towards announcements.
- *Testing*: Online drill or practice testing can be used to reinforce material, even if the results are not used as part of a grade. Reading comprehension questions, for example, in short answer or multiple choice formats can provide students with an assessment of their level of understanding of text. This facilitates the students to measure his level of understanding and through continuous assessment he can try to improve his performance.
- *Course Management*: Software should be available to add or delete students from the course, assign user Ids and passwords, create or edit home pages, and manage any open discussion groups. This helps to keep up to date records of students admitted for various courses.
- *Content*: Perhaps the most difficult part of developing a web-based course is creating the online contents. You can begin by transferring your basic lecture materials to the web and integrating media such as sound, images, and video. Remember, to experiment with incorporating some of the new web-based learning paradigms. And finally, come back and rebuild the lecture building its graph structure and using more html facilities.

Other Features of a Web-Based Learning Environment

- Managing cognitive load — the amount of information people can process — is essential to effective teaching or training. Bombarding learners with too much information at once, called cognitive overload, is one of the chief obstacles to learning. This indicates that we should provide only required information in order to avoid cognitive overload.

- Dividing each tutorial lesson into segments (Classroom, Quiz, Lab, etc.) and then further subdividing these segments into a manageable number of chunks allows users to digest new concepts and skills in a manner that prevents overload.
- *Web-based tutorial*: Users will also enjoy a great deal of flexibility in managing their cognitive load, selecting instructional tasks from a menu of lessons, depending upon the amount and kinds of skills they bring with them, and once engaged in a lesson, selecting which portions of that particular lesson they wish to complete. This allows the students to learn the topics in proper sequence and according to his ability of understanding.
- Because the limited capacity of working memory is rapidly overwhelmed by large amounts of new information, frequent opportunities to practice are important. Rehearsal encodes or moves information into long-term memory. The practice assignments can be presented with practice opportunities throughout the classroom portion of the lesson and is also encouraged to complete the practice portion of each lesson. This allows the student to find out how much he has understood at the end of learning a particular module.
- Finally, online testing is used to reinforce material. Elaborative rehearsal involves presenting questions, which allow the user to apply knowledge in an appropriate context, thus encoding it into permanent memory.
- Quiz questions are designed to provide an authentic assessment of user skill levels by calling on the user to apply the appropriate techniques and practices from the lesson.

WEB BASED EDUCATION

If Information Technology is used in school education it provides:

FLEXIBILITY, ACCESSIBILITY, AND CONVENIENCE

With a very short period of training the student can access the learning material when their schedule allows. No separate distribution mechanism needed (WBL), can be accessed from any computer anywhere in the world, keeping delivery costs low, this leads to cost saving.

ENHANCED LEARNING

Cognitively, active and context-based ("real world") learning activities, the highly interactive nature of well designed online learning, flexibility to review course material at any time, all improve learners abilities to synthesize and retain information. Many learners also find it easier to ask questions via E-mail because they have the privacy of direct contact with the instructor and avoid the classroom fear of "exposing" ignorance.

EASE AND SPEED OF UPDATE

WBL allows for efficient and quick updates to course material for frequently changing information. The changes are made on the server programme. Everyone worldwide can instantly access the update.

CONSISTENCY OF LEARNING MATERIAL

Each learner gets identical instructions to ensure the consistency and quality of the message by using WBL.

CROSS PLATFORM

WBL can be accessed by web browsing software on any platform Windows, Mac, UNIX etc. All these factors contribute to improve the quality of school education by overcoming factors like social background of students, parents, different standards of teaching and teachers training programmes, all teachers cannot deliver the same message to all learners. Also by using WBL students can do their self –assessment and management has access to progress reports and assessment data of individual learner.

EVALUATING ON-LINE LEARNING AS A PROCESS

This chapter describes the kinds of evaluation employed in the creation and management of a credit course in technical writing developed at the University of Waterloo. From September 1995 to April 1998, sections of this course have been offered entirely on the Web to students across Canada at 4-month intervals. The course uses SGML converter technology in the creation and maintenance of its materials and in students' preparation and submission of assignments. Evaluation includes examination of students' records of system use and access, assignment preparation and a variety of electronic communications, as well as the electronic marking and measurement of their course assignments. We attempt to assess group performance against perceptions and to incorporate student requests into our design and expectations. In addition to the above methods, we present students with a series of optional on-line evaluations after significant assignments and at the conclusion of their final report at the end of the course. All student responses in this process remain anonymous.

University Community and their On-line Variations

Generally, the University of Waterloo distributes course evaluations to students to obtain responses on the success of every course. Instructors distribute evaluations to on-campus students during the last scheduled class, while distance-education students are mailed the evaluation at the end of the term. In both cases the responses are anonymous, and the professor does not receive the evaluation results until after the final marks are registered. Each faculty administers a variation of the form specific to its academic needs. Both the number and the range of the questions are limited.

For example, the distance-education evaluation is made up of nine questions dealing with presentation of course material, the course's ability to maintain student interest, the course organization, value of readings, fairness in grading, instructor feedback, and an overall evaluation of both the instructor and the course. Students may respond to these questions in the five categories of 'excellent', 'good', 'satisfactory', 'fair', and 'poor'.

In addition, there are three 'comment' style questions dealing with the strengths and weaknesses of the course, and a general view of the course. In this way, this form is specific to distance-education needs. By comparison, our on-line technical writing course incorporates the evaluation process throughout the course, allowing for a two-way dialogue to which the instructor can react, and the students witness responses to their suggestions.

Instead of a single evaluation at the end of the term, students have the option to complete several evaluations throughout the course. These occur at times when their new skills and our grading of their work enable them to understand both their performance and our learning objectives in light of applied instruction. In total, the students can respond to over one hundred questions. They receive the evaluations after each assignment is submitted but before the return of their graded work on-line. Such timing provides for more honest responses because the students are not influenced by their assignment marks. Evaluation responses are completely confidential. They are sent via e-mail to a designated computer account from which authorship cannot be traced. These evaluations solicit information on most aspects of users' learning experience, participation, support and their sense of what the course provides, with its relevance to their expectations about their own training and understanding of the processes of technical documentation. We have synthesized the ranges of questions from five faculty models and resolved them to the new conditions of the electronic version of the course. We have developed these evaluation procedures to elicit a comprehensive view of both real activity and student opinion about their learning process. We make modifications in content, course administration and requirements in light of the results of each term's survey and we try to show students the immediate good effects of their responses by announcing changes to procedures and materials.

These have given us clear evidence that students:

- Deem the on-line learning process to be highly effective as an academic exercise

- Perceive it to be comprehensive and integrated in application
- See its technology and theory as integrated into a useful set of tools for their scholarly and applied writing.

Structures for the Evaluation Process

The 4-month university course in technical writing, which we offer entirely on the Web as credit and certificate learning through the Department of English at the University of Waterloo. Our colleague, Dr. Katherine Schellenberg, has provided the extensive statistical planning and analysis which now form the bases for our evaluation methods.

The course consists of a web site with:

- Extensive content on technical writing techniques and standards.
- Integrated internal communication methods-e-mail, chat, newsgroups, Instructor Comments, on-line marking and the evaluation procedures which are the topic of this chapter all available at the course site.
- The course's delivery engine, an SGML editor and converters, which enable students and instructors to create the entire range of course content on any topic or subject area.

We use these same tools to develop on-line materials for this and other courses and we incorporate appropriate student materials, (with their permission), in new aspects of the work. Students complete five technical documents in a sequence of increasing complexity. They provide all other members of the course with a current resume and proposal letter, from which, by a process of enquiry and selection, all members form themselves into groups of three to complete the central 50 per cent of the exercise. They work together to produce portions of a manual, on which they then conduct usability tests.

They complete the course with an extended Report on an aspect of their learning experience, often related to the application of on-line techniques to other areas of their training and work. Students create all assignments in SGML and then convert them into HTML for on-line display to classmates and markers. A graded version of each assignment is returned to the student under a password for privacy.

Members are encouraged, in chats and by tutorials, to look at their own work in the contexts of others' submissions and the instructor's remarks internally in their documents. Students retain and may distribute their materials as proof of their abilities in SGML and the creation of interactive learning. We provide references on students' request to potential employers and recommend members to companies seeking technical writers with these skills. By the completion of the course each participant has experienced the major communications tools used in the creation and exchange of Web-based technical documents. Each has worked with and understood the mark-up and conversion issues surrounding SGML, RTF and HTML displays. Most have dealt with some of the requirements for full multimedia expression on CD-ROM, the Web or on Intranets for internal distribution. This is 'Technical Writing' in a very current and complete sense and our students have been trained in it, individually and in groups, with all the resources our databases and course layout can provide. In the near future we plan to add optional services in audio and video interchange, XML document creation and Java authoring.

In effect, we have made a course in which the course materials and techniques are learned and used by participants even as they complete their writing assignments.

By the conclusion of the course many members have the full capacity to create SGML-based interactive projects for inter- and Intranet expressions. for their own and their employers' uses. Most course materials have been available to the public at our web site and we continue to respond to enquiries and applications from individuals and companies on the Web. At the time of writing we are preparing a commercial version of our work, with certificate status for participants and an extended range of topics related to on-line learning and information exchange, to launch in fall of 1998.

ON-LINE ADULT LEARNING

Covering on-line adult learning in a short article is a little like trying to see a city in a day—a whole lot of running around with brief, and hopefully meaningful, visits here and there. That being said, the focus here is to take the broad span of adult learning and apply it to an on-line environment. Ideally, he will reduce the "running around" and provide you with a few meaningful "visits" to adult learning in on-line environments.

His searches on both the WWW and Proquest revealed little that was directly applicable to adult learning on-line. There is lots on adult learning generally (both on-line and print based) and a growing literature base on on-line education and web based training generally (again, on-line and print based), but little that linked the two in a meaningful way for people who are actually taking a course on-line. So what follows are my observations - first as an academic and practitioner in adult education, and second, as a learner and facilitator on-line since 1995. He views this course as a way to build the theory and practice in learning and facilitating on-line. We are pioneers in this area and can contribute a tremendous amount to future on-line learners! Through our discussions and your assignments, we can create a set of valuable resources and "publish them" on the net for others to see. This is probably one of the most exciting aspects of on-line education to me - it is relatively easy to create and share our knowledge as a class and leave a legacy for others! How often in traditional face-to-face classes have we been able to do this in a relatively easy way?

Definitions and Perspectives

There are hundreds of articles and books written about adult learning and hundreds of definitions. In a class devoted to adult learning, one might spend the first two weeks alone defining learning and exploring it from a multitude of perspectives and another two weeks defining adult. For me, adult learning is about change-change in attitude, change in knowledge, change in behaviour, change in a skill, change in how we think about things. He used to get into more complex definitions and models but have found that less useful as time has gone on. The perspectives on adult learning vary according to the context or discipline in which one operates. Some businesses and industries appear to view adult learning as a commodity that, once mastered, will lead to efficient workers. Some entrepreneurs in the "workshop business" view adult learning as a golden opportunity to make money.

Some self-help groups view adult learning as a transformational process that empowers people to live healthier, happier lives. Some futurists view adult learning as central to our transition into the knowledge age. Some psychologists view adult learning as a cognitive process, while still others focus exclusively on behaviours. Some adult educators, view adult learning as a lifelong process of discovery and have committed their lives to exploring it and facilitating it for others. If you are interested in exploring adult learning in depth, try Merriam and Caffarella's book as a start (listed in the bibliography at the end). It orients you to the literature and is an excellent reference.

Types of Learning

The most useful categorization I've seen is one offered by Saljo in Candy (1991)

- Learning as an increase in knowledge. (eg. You now know what emoticons are, for example.)
- Learning as memorizing. (eg. You may have memorized how to post messages in the bulletin board area.)
- Learning as acquisition of knowledge that can be retrained and/or utilized in practice. (eg. You have learned how to use WebCT and could apply this skill to other forms of on-line conferencing.)
- Learning as the abstraction of meaning. (eg. You are exploring your own understanding of adult learning and on-line education and what this means to you.)
- Learning as an interpretive process, aimed at understanding reality. (eg. You will probably engage in speculation and interpretation about how the Internet/WWW are going to affect how people work, live, learn in a broader sense.)

Dialogue and discussion with others are central to any type of learning, but most especially for the type of learning concerned with meaning and interpretation. That is why the main activities of this course involve discussion and the assignments involve working with others.

Learning Capabilities

A writer who has influenced him the most in thinking about different learning capabilities is Virginia Griffin (1988). She suggests that he has six learning capabilities comparable to the six strings on a guitar. Most of our education has focused on one string—the rational—and excluded the other five. As with playing a song on a guitar using six strings instead of one, tapping into the six capabilities of learning enhances our learning. The six strings are:

- Rational (The one we are familiar with and have the most experience with. We assume that learning is a rational, intellectual activity.)
- Emotional (Instead of denying that emotions play a role in learning, they are acknowledged, accepted and considered valuable in aiding the learning process.)
- Relational (Learning is enhanced through relationships with others.)
- Physical (Learning can be enhanced or inhibited by our physical state.)
- Metaphoric (Learning can be enhanced through symbol, metaphor, intuition.)
- Spiritual (A deep sense of connection with everyone and thing.)

Griffin suggests that if the rational, emotional, relational, physical, and metaphoric capabilities are facilitated, the spiritual will evolve. My own significant learning experiences have always occurred when more of the "guitar strings" were activated. Knowing about Griffin's framework has allowed me to analyze why a particular learning experience is not meaningful, and what I can do as a learner to make it better.

I would say that Griffin's framework is especially important in an on-line environment. When I first started as a learner myself in an on-line course, I was concerned with the emotional and relational aspects of learning. I didn't feel that such a high tech approach could facilitate these dimensions of learning. As in face-to-face classes, however, it is the design of the course, the learners themselves, and the approach the facilitator takes that make the difference. The tone of an e-mail, together with the use of emoticons, can convey much - both expressions of joy or frustration and anger!

The relational aspects of learning can occur to a certain extent in main list discussions, but it is the small group activities, both synchronous and asynchronous, that facilitated my getting to know someone. I learned much through my e-mail conversations (asynchronous) and webchat sessions (synchronous) with individuals in the course and, as with face-to-face sessions, I am still in contact with some of these people. The physical capability of learning was most striking for me as an on-line learner. I work best very early in the morning. I am awake, alert, and do my best work. Afternoons are my down time and right after dinner is especially low for me. As a face-to-face learner and facilitator, most of my classes have occurred in the time slots when I'm most tired. It was a real joy to tailor my participation in the on-line class around the times of day I was most awake and, if need be, not participate at all when I was tired. This is not a luxury we have in face-to-face classes!

I make use of metaphors a great deal in my learning, especially so when I'm encountering a completely different subject or content. Such is the case with on-line learning. It was so new to me that I needed to find ways to attach the "new" to an "old" framework. For example, taking an on-line class for the first time is similar to taking a class for the first time at a university. How much time do we spend trying to find the place to park, the building, the classroom? It's overwhelming and confusing. A first time experience in an on-line class can be the same. I tried to find metaphors like this for helping me to become used to the on-line environment.

The spiritual capability of learning is something I've not experienced to a great extent in face-to-face classes, but one that I've actively sought to develop in myself. There are some Internet users who believe that e-mail communication (and some synchronous chats) are a more direct "experience" with others, a connection to their consciousness or true essence, as opposed to the usual distractions we read into face-to-face communication. A lengthy discussion on cyber relationships took place on a list to which I subscribe—the wisdom at work list.

While there were certainly those who believed that there is more fiction on the net (that people may create characters and misrepresent themselves), there were also those who felt that the internet was the vehicle that would move our society to a higher level of consciousness and spirituality. As Let Davidson, moderator of the Wisdom at Work list so eloquently stated on April 5, 1996:

I agree that at this point there is no obvious revolution in interpersonal relations... yet. But I definitely agree with Susan that something is afoot and that the technology has a tremendous potential to affect the way we relate, in both directions: towards avoidance and escapism, as well as towards greater spiritual intimacy. I think it helps to recognize that cyber communication is a different form and shouldn't be expected to accomplish what face-to-face experience yields. It will be very frustrating to expect it to carry the freight of sensuality or physical intimacy.

Electronic communication seems to me to be more suited to conveying consciousness or spirit, and is much closer to the way consciousness operates than it is to physicality. We could say that basically what you see in front of you is consciousness— code—translated into subtle on-off pulses of light transfigured into virtual pixels on the screen. It is all light taking virtual forms in the same way that all colours are refractions of the same light. In the same way that what we call physical reality is varying speeds and frequencies of light energy. (E=mc2)

It seems e-relating is a more subtle, intermediate technology, somewhere between physical relating and pure mind communication (ESP, clairvoyance, telepathy, etc). I think cyberspace represents a step in the evolution of consciousness which seems to be moving many people beyond strictly egoic bodymind identity to a greater sense of our true identity as spirit, consciousness or light energy, and eliciting our ability to commune with this underlying reality. Let, Some challenging ideas.

Let captures the real essence of Virginia Griffin's coming together of the five capabilities of learning into the sixth - the spiritual. This is food for thought for those of us who have thought (and maybe still do) that high tech cannot be high touch.

Adult Learning Principles (A Selection)

The following adult learning principles are compiled from many sources. Most are ones he feels most represent his own experience as an adult learner, while others are included because they raise many questions for me. What do you think?

- Increasing and maintaining ones sense of self-esteem and pleasure are strong secondary motivators for engaging in learning experiences. (Zemke, 1988)
- New knowledge has to be integrated with previous knowledge; that means active learner participation. (Zemke, 1988)
- Adult learning must be problem and experience centred. (Gibb, 1960 as quoted in Brookfield, 1986)
- Effective adult learning entails an active search for meaning in which new tasks are somehow related to earlier activities. Prior learning experiences have the potential to enhance or interfere with new learning. (Knox, 1977 as quoted in Brookfield, 1986)
- A certain degree of arousal is necessary for learning to occur, whereas stress acts as a major block to learning. (Brundage and MacKeracher, 1980)
- Collaborative modes of teaching and learning will enhance the self-concepts of those involved and result in more meaningful and effective learning. (Brundage and MacKeracher, 1980)
- Adults will generally learn best in an atmosphere that is non-threatening and supportive of experimentation and in which different learning styles are recognized. (Smith, 1982)
- Adult learning is facilitated when the learner's representation and interpretation of his own experience are accepted as valid, acknowledged as an essential aspect influencing change, and respected as a potential resource for learning. (Brundage and MacKeracher, 1980)
- Adults experience anxiety and ambivalence in their orientation to learning. (Smith, 1982)

- Adult learning is facilitated when teaching activities do not demand finalized, correct answers and closure; express a tolerance for uncertainty, inconsistency, and diversity; and promote both question-asking and -answering, problem-finding and problem-solving. (Brundage and MacKeracher, 1980)
- Adult skill learning is facilitated when individual learners can assess their own skills and strategies to discover inadequacies or limitations for themselves. (Brundage and MacKeracher, 1980)
- Adult learning is facilitated when the teacher can give up some control over teaching processes and planning activities and can share these with learners. (Brundage and MacKeracher, 1980)

Group Development in On-line Education

There has been much research on group development in educational settings. The most well known one is Tuckman's (1965) who suggests groups move through four sequential phases—forming, storming, norming and performing. He also like Cog's Ladder (sorry, he can't find the full reference!) which suggests the phases are the polite phase, why we're here, bid for power, constructive phase, esprit phase and the grieving phase. He has noticed the same type of group development in on-line education as he has observed in hundreds of face-to-face classes. Similar group development occurs in listserves as well. While every class may not go through every phase in the same manner, sequence or to the same degree, there are definite predictable commonalities. In on-line education, it goes something like this:

Polite Phase (forming)

- People send out introductions and are excited about working with people from all over.
- People usually make welcoming and polite comments about other people in the course.

Why We're Here Phase (forming)

- There are always a few individuals who question their participation in the class. Some may send notes to the instructor individually clarifying expectations or asking to participate at another time or even drop out.
- Others may post to the whole group asking clarifying questions about either the content or process of the course.
- Most experience some type of "imposter syndrome" (Brookfield, 1992) which they may or may not express to the entire group. The syndrome goes something like - everyone else is smarter than I am, I am not qualified to be in this course, someone will find out (most likely the instructor!) and ask me to leave!

- He finds the imposter syndrome especially prevalent among people very new to the Internet/WWW. Even though others in a group may have announced their own inexperience, everyone feels like s/he is the "ultimate newbie among newbies". They may also be quite hesitant to post notes.
- Everyone is trying to get a feel for how the course will run and what they can expect.

Bid for Power Phase (storming)

- People may start to voice dislike or opposition at some aspect of the course process or content.
- People may start to openly disagree with one another—sometimes politely, sometimes not so politely!
- Groups or cliques may develop as people start to seek out those with similar opinions.
- People may start to openly (or in private e-mail to one another) question the instructor's competence and authority.
- Some "flaming" (strongly voiced criticism, personal attack or insult) may occur, although I've seen this only rarely in the courses he has taught.

Constructive Phase (norming)

- People will start to ask that personal criticism be left behind to be replaced by the task at hand-the course.
- People will come to terms with their concerns about the course-sometimes, a person may even apologize for a hastily sent note to the group in the storming stage.
- People remind each other of the reason they are there and restate some fundamental norms about how the course should run.
- People start to own their own reactions to the learning process.
- Discussions about the course content and process resume, but at a more sophisticated level than before.

Esprit (performing)

- Real group synergy takes place. This may happen in the whole group or in smaller groups that have developed in the class.
- Discussions are initiated by everyone and people build on each other's comments.

Grieving (sometimes when a group ends)

- May occur with a whole group but more likely among individuals who have worked together and come to know one another.
- Sometimes, the group (or subgroups) are extended beyond the conclusion of the course.

The role the instructor plays during this group development is central to how quickly the group moves through stages (or even skips stages) on their way to a productive learning experience. Instructors who are aware of group development anticipate the stages and use techniques to facilitate a smooth transition. They also learn not to "personalize" notes of frustration or even anger from participants at certain points in the class, as very often becoming used to the on-line world can be intimidating and alienating for some learners. Understanding these stages from a learner's perspective is also helpful. For example, sometimes the "storming" stage can be particularly stormy and for people like myself, quite distressing. Understanding group development gives one another perspective from which to view things.

Group Work in On-line Education

For the most part, he had favourable experiences with group work in an on-line environment, again a surprise to him. He assumed that the lack of face-to-face contact and nonverbal cues would limit the "human touch" of working cooperatively with people in groups. My experience was just the opposite, an observation made by researchers in the computer-mediated communication (CMC) field. As pointed out by Rob Higgins (1991):

Without encompassing the full range of human sensory and expressive capabilities, text-based interaction is often thought to be an impersonal medium devoid of social context cues and nonverbal communication. Experience and research, however, are demonstrating that socio-emotional content can be communicated in text. Steinfeld (1986) states that: "Evidence continues to mount showing that CMC will be used for emotional interaction. People seem to work around the nonverbal cue limitations and actively provide their own text-based translations of nonverbal cues" (p. 176). Tracz (1980) bears out this perception in a comment on his experience: "I was pleasantly surprised, nevertheless, that most users of electronic information exchange system (EIES) attempt to incorporate many little expressions to compensate for the lack of face-to-face contact, and on the whole, gentleness prevails." (p. 17). (p. 40-41)

Group methods or cooperative learning are widely written about in both adult and youth education. A common belief is that such approaches to learning are more human and productive than competitive approaches. Also, such approaches are held up as facilitative of the construction of knowledge (see for example Belenkey et. al.. (1988) and Vygotsky (1978)), a focus of many adult educators, myself included. Links have been made between cooperative learning and educational computing as pointed out by Higgins (1991).

Those involved with cooperative learning have not missed another growing innovation: educational computing. Johnson and Johnson (1986) discuss the complementary strengths of cooperative learning and computer-assisted instruction (not including Educational CMC). They cite their research involving cooperative, competitive, and individualistic learning in conjunction with the use of educational computer programmes featuring drill and practice, simulation and discovery, and word processing (pp. 16-17). Their data confirm the general effects of cooperative learning:

...computer-assisted cooperative learning promoted greater quantity and quality of daily achievement, more successful problem solving, and higher performance on factual recognition, application, and problem-solving test items than did computer- assisted competitive and individualistic learning (p. 15). Another interesting finding was that the computer-assisted cooperative methods had an especially positive impact on female students in terms of their attitudes towards computers. Conversely, the competitive methods had an especially negative impact on their attitudes towards computers. Competitiveness also reduced the female students' confidence in their ability to work with computers (Johnson & Johnson, 1986, p. 15). (pp. 31- 32)

Concepts from cooperative learning, computer-assisted learning, and CMC are particularly relevant to educational classes being delivered using Internet/ WWW technology. Again, Higgins (1991) clarifies the role of synchronous (simultaneous) and asynchronous (flex-time) in cooperative learning:

In the realm of educational computer-mediated communication, there are many studies that cover issues of social psychology and deal with socio-emotional factors, but nothing that addresses the cognitive foundations needed to help establish a theoretical and practical model for computer supported cooperative learning (CSCL). A variety of research efforts and numerous descriptive, or anecdotal reports appear in the literature. Some address issues relating to the use of computer conferencing (CC) (Harsim, 1989; Hiltz et. al.., 1990; Mason, 1990; Phillips et. al.., 1988) in asynchronous mode. Others report on the application of synchronous communication via local area networks in the classroom (Foster, 1991; O'Kelly, 1991; Peyton, 1989; Wilton, 1988)....

Those involved with computer conferencing seem particularly resistant to the notion of an important role for synchronous CMC. This is not surprising in view of the fact that the features and capabilities provided by computer conferencing software have not changed significantly over the past 10 years, and appropriate synchronous capabilities have not been readily available. Another reason for lack of attention to the potential of synchronous CMC is that the asynchronous nature of computer conferencing is regarded as one of its most valued attributes in terms of intellectual activity. Levinson (1988) notes, "'Asynchronous' or nonimmediate communication...may produce exchanges of richer intellectual quality than those resulting from immediate face-to-face dialogue" (p. 115).

In an on-line seminar, Turoff (1989c) took the extreme position and challenged the participants to produce examples to counter his proposition, "that there is no human group problem solving activity that would not be better served by asynchronous communications..." (conference note C1295 CC4). Further, he stated that, "...a pure synchronous system is worthless as far as I am concerned" (conference note C1295 CC16).

Obviously, then, an important debate exists. Synchronous interaction may be a critical feature of peer interaction and an important component in the developing theories of the social construction of knowledge as they pertain to cooperative learning. Asynchronous interaction, on the other hand, may improve group problem solving and lead to richer intellectual quality in the communications. (pp. 6-7) Higgins research with nursing students working on a nursing case study demonstrated that *...the synchronous mode of text-based CMC are more likely to include verbal elements reflecting important cognitive activities such as problem formulation, interactive arguing, and task management than similar discussions in asynchronous mode.*

...greater focus on, and accuracy of outcomes are possible with synchronous text-based CMC than with asynchronous.

...greater mutual facilitation occurs in synchronous text-based CMC than in asynchronous mode. This facilitation is reflected in verbal elements demonstrating attempts to establish interpersonal ease, support, understanding, and encouragement.

... the novel and unique modes of interaction possible through CMC (synchronous and asynchronous) can have a motivating effect for learning activities undertaken in dyad or group situations. (p. 19)

His own experience as a learner in an on-line class and anecdotal reports from learners in previous classes I've taught confirm the importance of synchronous communication in collaborative learning. This course is designed around these considerations and, thus, group work is considered essential to the overall success and enjoyment of participants, and synchronous chats are encouraged as a way to address the human element.

Creating a Learning Community in an On-line Environment

One of the best papers he has read on creating an on-line learning community is Sally Fox and Don Comstock's Computer Conferencing in a Learning Community. Their "Summary of Processes that Build a Learning Community" provide a number of suggestions and points to ponder for anyone either taking or facilitating a course on-line. He has tried to build in a number of their strategies. Another interesting paper is Creating Community On-line. The authors of this paper discuss their "learnings" in terms of converting a face-toface class to on-line delivery. Of particular interest, is their rethinking of the instructor's role in a classroom and how instructors may (unknowingly) contribute to learners looking to them for approval, instead of thinking about things themselves. The on-line environment challenged this perspective.

7

Multimedia Web-based Textbook Learning

Recent advances in computing technology have provided convenient and powerful tools for the interaction and visualization of information from large data sources. Through an appropriate CD-ROM or web-based technology it has been possible to provide a rich environment for the retrieval, visualization, interpretation, and querying of the knowledge base that comprises any technological discipline. Course instructors and students can use the system at home, in the office, and in the classroom/laboratory. Access is made available on instructor's and student's personal computers, and in the computer laboratory.

Such a facility provides a much richer tool for instruction and reference than conventional textbooks and traditional classroom presentational media.

Key features of the facility are as follows:

- Presentation of animated diagrams and charts, audio, and video information, with related information viewed in concurrent windows.
- Interaction between the user and the knowledge base–a user could control and direct the sequence of presentation of information, as well as ask questions.
- Guided walkthroughs of user-selected topics, acting as a Virtual Tutor that takes the user through subject matter in a structured manner, but also answering questions and anticipating user questions and misunderstandings. The walkthrough may be formatted as a lecture, case study, or a tutorial session for solving any problem from a set of in-built examples. The user could progress at whatever pace desired, backtrack, and make lateral explorations of the knowledge base.
- Random walkabouts exploring the knowledge base. This is analogous to flicking through the pages of a textbook but is supported by sophisticated query/keyword search and cross-reference tools, as well as backtracking capabilities.

- Interfacing to the Internet with distance learning and conferencing capabilities, allowing the establishment of a virtual classroom in which students and instructors can interact from remote locations, submit class assignments, and return graded material. Also, interfacing with the Internet allows direct reference to external supplementary sources of information through the World Wide Web, as well as greatly facilitates the education of people with physical disabilities.
- A choice between in-depth, intermediate, and abridged presentations of information.
- Assisted exam/test/assignment compilation for instructors, using pre-written questions a la carte, with automated production of model answers.
- Assisted course and lecture compilation for instructors, with preassembled a la carte course structures and lectures.
- Report generation facilities to enable a student to compile and output reports for class assignments, etc., calling on information generated during a session with the system.
- Automated note taking, whereby the user could search information and demonstrations provided in the system, and collate the points of interest into a notebook for future reference or hardcopy output.
- Student self-examination through interactive tests/examinations.
- Simulation facilities allowing users to monitor and control the behaviour of various processes operating under different conditions.
- Gaming facilities operating in single and multiple-user environments. This allows users to interact with each other within simulated environments, and could be used as the basis for class exercises and/ or class assignments.

Although virtual reality tools have computational demands beyond the capabilities of most current personal computers, the proposed system is structured to permit future inclusion of this technology. Virtual reality techniques would greatly enhance the simulation and gaming components of the system, enabling, for example, walkthroughs of buildings at various stages of construction.

COURSE ADMINISTRATIVE TOOLS

ON-LINE SYLLABUS

An on-line course syllabus provides the instructor with a way to change course material easily, and inform the student with a complete and up-to-date picture of the course requirements. The format need not (and probably should not) duplicate the print version. Hypertext links to sample relevant disciplinary web sites may be helpful in giving students (and prospective students) a sense of the disciplinary context for the course.

The Syllabus should include the following:

- Course name, number, and prerequisites
- Class time and location
- Instructor
- Instructor contact information
- Teaching assistance
- Teaching assistance contact information
- Course description
- Course objectives
- Required course materials
- Assessment methods course schedule
- Grading
- Late policy.

CLASS SCHEDULE

Class schedule provides students with a clear idea of the course timetable so they know the specific lesson for each given date.

FREQUENTLY ASKED QUESTIONS (FAQS)

A FAQ is a list of commonly asked questions and their answers. Posting FAQs provides ready answers to the student. FAQs also reduce the amount of time spent in answering questions piecemeal.

Some of the items that may be posted are:

- FAQ concerning course content.
- FAQ concerning technical help (computer support, internet, how to use the web site).
- FAQ concerning the course in general (registration, important dates, instructor, TA).

STUDENT ACCESS TO GRADES

It is common practice at many universities for teachers to post grades, sorted by student ID, in a common area, *e.g.* on an office door. It would be easier, faster and more convenient to post the entire list in the course web site.

TESTING TOOLS AND OTHER RESOURCES

ON-LINE EXAMS, QUIZZES AND ASSIGNMENTS

Exams, quizzes and assignments can be delivered to the students via the WWW. The student answers are sent privately to the instructor or TA through e-mail and the results are returned privately to the student.

SELF-EVALUATION TESTING

On-line drill and practice or testing can be used to reinforce material even if not used as part of a grade. Reading comprehension questions, for example, in short answer or multiple choice formats can provide students with self-assessment of their level of understanding of the text.

QUESTIONNAIRE

A questionnaire or a survey is a rapid means of collecting opinion on a wide variety of questions. Most educators will be familiar with end-of-term student questionnaires where students will rate the course they have attended. In our project, three kinds of questionnaires were constructed, the first questionnaire aimed to measure student's computer skills to determine what type of training they will need for handling web-based education.

The second and third questionnaires are dealing with web site feedback, evaluation and assessment by students and site visitors. To construct questionnaires that are submitted and stored via the web, you can create quizzes which allow users to record the results of an evaluation, or you can use a specific survey creation tool such as Infopoll Designer. FrontPage 2000 provides a simple way to create forms (for quizzes, exams, feedback forms, or questionnaires) with the form wizard utility.

RESOURCES

The instructor provides any information resources that will help students, support their understanding and broaden their knowledge in the course material.

Such resources include:

- Old exams, quizzes and assignments;
- Related links extra readings;
- File and software download;
- University phone directory and civil engineering department staff information;
- Guides to the Internet and its components;
- Glossary containing terms defined for the course and is searchable via prefix string, which are also linked directly from the notes to the glossary.

HELP TOOLS

Finding information on the web can be challenging with the number of web servers and web pages growing rapidly. A search engine is the solution for this problem: the search engine is a programme that looks for pages relevant to the keywords the user enters into the engine and displays the results as hyperlinks. You can add a www search engine to your course web site very easily using Java scripts and Java applet. In our course web site, a Java script search engine was designed allowing the user to search the net using 1 to 12 of the most popular search engines at the same time, and the results of each engine is displayed in a different window. Calculators and plotting tools are provide the students with some help in understanding and solving problems. They are mainly designed using Java or Java scripts.

SUMMARY AND CONCLUSIONS

While many texts have been developed around the basis of the CD-ROM and webbased media, and while many more are currently under development, the application to technology education has been less developed, and the construction industry is quite lacking in this utilization. Originality of the research is largely derived from the topic that is investigated (construction education) and from the simultaneous development of shell and content. These items are not original per se; rather it is their combination which warrants such designation. Thus originality must be viewed from the perspective of applicability to setting and appropriateness to user within the increasingly complex and technologically sophisticated construction industry.

COURSE WEB SITE STRUCTURE

COURSE NOTES

Perhaps the most important and difficult part of developing a web-based course is creating the online content which begins with translating the basic lecture materials to the web and integrating media such as sound, images and even video.

The lecture homepage is divided into:

- *Title*: Lecture number, chapter number, and subject.
- *Lesson*: The main part of the page, which uses multimedia for illustration.
- *Example*: Links for any examples illustrating the lesson (problem statement, given data, required items, solution steps).
- *Pages references*: List of all information resources used to construct the lecture.
- *Assignments*: Link for the lesson assignment and due date.
- Related Links and Extra Readings.
- *Help tools*: Link to calculator, unit converter, and list of tables needed for solving the example.

COMMUNICATION TOOLS

Computer-mediated communication (CMC) is communi-cation accomplished through the use of computer and networking technologies among faculty and students. It can be person-to-person (such as e-mail) or among a group (for example, a 'listserv' or newsgroup). Although the quantity of interaction may not be as great as it is in a standard classroom, users of CMC often find that the quality of the correspondence is better and the rate of learning is higher.

CMC uses include:

- Students use e-mail to ask questions of faculty or teaching assistants at times other than class periods or office hours and even when faculty is away at professional meetings. Answers to frequently asked questions (FAQ) might be posted to a shared location.
- Faculty asks a critical question prior to class so students are better prepared for in-class discussion.
- Students share their papers, outlines, homework problems and project plans to receive feedback from other students.
- Posting important announcements.
- Creating groups and having group discussions on a specific topic.
- Posting lecture notes, sample exam questions, or study tips.
- Requiring discussion questions or homework to be turned in electronically.
- Having an on-line help desk supervised by the professor or teaching assistant.

Computer-mediated communication can be synchronous or asynchronous. Synchronous communication is the exchange of messages among correspondents who are on-line at the same time. One form of synchronous communication is online text-based chat and conferencing. Educational uses include virtual office hours and small group meetings. On the other hand, asynchronous communication is the exchange of messages among correspondents who are not on-line at the same time. The most common forms include e-mail, newsgroups (Usenet), mailing list servers, group project collaboration and course discussion groups. Whether the type of communication is synchronous or asynchronous, it can be on a whole range of levels. These different levels were implemented in the developed web-based courses.

- *One-alone*: *e.g.* one person accesses on-line resources such as on-line databases or journals, remotely executes software programmes stored on a remote computer, or downloads application software via Internet File Transfer Protocol (FTP).
- *One-to-one*: *e.g.* two people send messages back and forth via e-mail such as a student corresponding with a teacher or two students communicating.
- *One-to-many*: *e.g.* learning materials can be posted to a web site by a teacher, forming an electronic lecture which any number of students can view.
- *Many-to-many*: *e.g.* any number of participants (students or teachers)

interacts via chatting, a computer conferencing system. Debates, discussion groups and brainstorming can take place.

The following communication components were implemented in the developed web courses:

- *E-mail*: E-mail between faculty and students can be integrated into the web environment. The web page allows e-mail to be sent to faculty and classmates, and a pop mail system can be integrated for reading e-mail messages. In both cases, e-mail can include attachments of any binary file (*e.g.* word processing files, spreadsheets, graphic images, and even sound and video files). The mailing services included in the course web site were provided from Zap Zone Network. Students can access the mail login page. With this service, an instructor can monitor his or her students, send e-mail to all of them at the same time informing them about any changes in the course, or reminding them of any important dates.
- *Message board/discussion group*: A message board for communication among all course participants is a wonderful resource allowing for course discussions, questions regarding course material and assignments, and course announcements. Its advantages are tremendous including greatly enhanced student inclusion and participation in the course. Another communication facility is the discussion group that sets up a forum for site visitors to communicate with each other. A discussion group allows site visitors to post articles and reply to them. The easiest way to create a discussion group with FrontPage 2000 is by using the Discussion Web Wizard. The wizard asks for the desired features, then creates a web and sets up the pages for you. After the web is created, you can open the pages and customise them. Another way to create a message board is by using on-line free board services like inside the web service.
- *Real-time chat facility*: Allows for the holding of real-time typed conversations. Office hours can take place this way without the need for instructor, students or teaching assistants (TAs) to travel to campus. A multichat service was used in the course web page. MultiChat is a Java chat client applet service that enables you to place a chat room on your own site.
- *Feedback form*: Provides the instructor with the student's response and comments. The user should first choose the comment kind from the following: Complaint, problem, suggestion, or praise. Then he should use the pull-down menu to select the item he wants to comment about (web site, class, lab, instructor, TA, technical help, or other). The last step is to write the comment in the provided field and his contact information.

- *Announcements*: Effective announcements need to be read; for that to happen the students need to know when a new announcement has been posted. Alert boxes or running footers (using JavaScript) or a blinking link added to a page can let students know of new announcements. Such announce-ments are implemented in the web course site to remind students of exam dates, assignments due date, etc. Announcements are created with FrontPage 2000 using Marquee option from the Insert menu.
- *Yellow Shared Board*: A tool to assist chatting sessions. It lets the instructor illustrate his or her ideas to students as in the same way as with pen and paper. Meanwhile the student could participate in the illustration. NetWriter, a free shared Yellow Pad on-line service provided by ParaGraph/Vademto, was used in the course web site to implement the yellow-shared board. With NetWriter the instructor can reserve the session ahead of time and send e-mails to students to inform them with the session time and number.

DESIGNING MULTIMEDIA WEB-BASED COURSE

The design and development of a web site for any course should include all necessary educational materials that the instructor intends to give to the students as well as those materials that the students should retrieve on their own from the library or external references.

Having access to such materials on-line is not only a matter of convenience to students but also a matter of saving much of their effort and time. Such a web-based course provides an on-line interactive environment for students to obtain homework assignments and submit their solutions and for professors to grade homework and send results along with feedback to students. Several on-line course components and tools are considered in designing the course home page. The course web site structure is demonstrated in Table, and is described in detail later.

TESTING, OPERATION AND ASSESSMENT

The end product is then tested for technical functionality on the web site and simplicity of use to students. Whenever the system failed to carry out any of its functions, it was taken back to the design stage for further technical reviews and modifications.

The web-based course is incorporated into the teaching process and it has been evaluated by both teachers and students. Learner performance is assessed through quantitative indicators such as: grade scores (of exams, homework, projects) and time of student engagement with the web-based course materials. Qualitative assessment is also carried out through a questionnaire on the web site use in the learning process to students and teachers at the end of the course work. This qualitative assessment is also part of evaluating the learning environment for future improvements. Quantitative and qualitative indicators of students in the study programme are then compared to similar indicators of students who did not take part in the programme. Conclusions and recommendations are drawn based on the completion of the evaluation process.

Course Lectures:	• Text. • Animation. • Still pictures and graphs. • Audio. • Video.
Communication Tools:	• E-mail. • Message board\discussion (news) groups. • Chat room. • Comment and feedback forms. • Announcements.
Administrative Tools:	• Course and lab syllabus. • Class and lab schedules. • Faculty information. • FAQ. • Exam scores.
Testing Tools:	• Quizzes and Tests on-line • Student Self-evaluation test, • Questionnaires. • Assignments.
References:	• Previous exzms and Assignments. • University phone Directory. • Extra Reading. • Course Glossary. • Useful Links. • Files and Software Downloads.
Helping Tools:	• Search the Course Homepage. • Search the WWW. • Calculators. • Plotting Tools. • Class Mail List.

Another type of evaluation is associated with web authoring and design. Considering the enormous amount of information available on-line, web users need some criteria to evaluate the reliability of web information. In this stage, this kind of evaluation can be considered as designing criteria in web site authoring.

Web site evaluation criteria:

- Content:
  - *Accuracy*:
    - i The information source should be accurate and reliable (compare with other sources, logical information, check author background information).
  - *Authority*:

i The name of the individual or group creating the site should be clearly stated.
ii The creator should give a source for information in the site where necessary.
iii The web site author or manager should provide a way for users to make comments or ask questions.
iv The web site author or manager should be responsive to any questions regarding copyright, trademark, or ownership of all material on the site. Sites that knowingly violate copyright statutes or other laws should not be linked, listed, or recommended.

- *Up-to-date*:
  i The information should be updated when needed.
  ii Dates of last up-date should be stated.
  ii Links should be updated when needed.
- Interaction and student engagement:
  i The content should encourage students to think and interact.
  ii Evaluation ways for student's knowledge acquisition should be provided (on-line testing, self-evaluation testing, drill exercises).
  iii Ways for students collaboration should be facilitated (shared projects and assignments, student's communication tools).
  iv Students should be encouraged to continue research by providing additional hyper links. Provide communication channels with Experts.
- Nature of the content
- There should be enough information to make visiting the site worthwhile.
- Content should be appropriate for student level and background.
- Content should be unique (information and images from more than one source, adding animation, sound, links, or any other web features).
- *Quality of writing*:
  i Well-written text.
  ii The title of a site should be appropriate to its purpose.
  iii Site content should be easy to read and understand by the intended audience.
  iv Spelling and grammar always should be correct.
- *References*:
  i Appropriate references and copyright statement should be included when needed.

• Navigation:
  - Links:

i Moving around the web site should be easy.
ii Sufficient shortcut or hot buttons should be provided.
iii Links should be clearly and accurately described.
iv Navigation links should be visually obvious.
v Links are logically grouped.

- *Site organization*:
  i Homepage should contain a well-labeled table of content.
  ii Site map should be provided.
- *Consistency*:
  i Navigation buttons should be consistent throughout the web site.
  ii The type styles and background make the page clear and readable.
  ii The layout is consistent from page to page.
- *Ease of browsing*:
  i You can tell from the first page how the site is organized and what options are available.
  ii There is a link back to the home page on each supporting page.
  iii The links are relevant to the subject.
  iv The icons clearly represent what is intended.

• *Workability*:
  - *User Friendly*:
    i Easy to use web interface.
    ii Help information should be provided when needed.
  - *Required computing environment*:
    i Best-view web browser software should be stated.
    ii Required 'plug-ins' or other helper applications should be clearly identified.
    iii Links to web browser and plug-in download sites should be provided.
    iv Text only versions should be provided.
    v Printer friendly version should be provided.
    vi Easy to switch between (Frame- Non-frame) versions if needed.
    vii In case of file transfer (file name, type, size, and required time to download should be provided).
  - *Searching*:
    i Web site search engine should be included.
    ii WWW search engines should be included to assist further research.
    iii Search engine interface should be intuitive and easy to use.

• *Web site Design*:

- *Visual appeal*:
  - i The site design and style enhance information delivery.
  - ii The site design should be appealing to its intended audience.
- *Thematic design*:
  - i The design should be related to the site topic.
  - ii The design should be consistent for each web page within the web site.
- *Clarity of presentation*:
  - i Add appealing web design features like tables and graphs.
  - ii Pages should be uncluttered and cleanly designed.
- *Flexibility*:
  - i Web site should be viewed and tested by different text browsers (Lynx) and graphics browsers (Netscape Navigator and MS-Explorer).
- *Stimulation*:
  - i The web design layout should get the students' attention and maintain their attention.
- *Appropriateness*:
  - i Make appropriate use of graphics in the design layout.
  - ii The site's design should be appropriate for the intended audience.

- *Performance*:
  - *Page acquisitiontime*:
    - i Try to minimize the time needed to load web pages with the type of connection you are using in your classroom.
    - ii Offer a text-only option.
    - iii Offer a thumbnail version of large graphics.
  - *Connectivity*:
    - i Check the site accessibility (Is the site usually accessible or is it difficult to connect into?).
    - ii You can connect quickly to the page.
    - iii Site URL should be short and easy to memorize.
    - iv The page is available through search engines.
  - *Hardware speed*:
    - a. Consider your connection speed when you access a web site.
- *Multimedia Issues*:
  - *Problems of size*:
    - i Compress large multimedia files to minimize downloading time.
    - ii Provide download information (file name, type, size, and required time to download).
    - iii Multimedia files such as videos, sounds, and animations are usually very large files and can take a very long time

to download. It is recommended to download these types of files ahead of time and have students access them locally from a hard drive or mass-storage device.

- *Required applications*:
  - i Many multimedia objects on the WWW require a helper application or plug-in. Some helper applications such as Shockwave require an excessive amount of memory and time to load and run multimedia animation. Make sure you have the appropriate helper application or plug-in loaded ahead of time before using these files with students.
- Purpose of themultimedia:
  - i Sounds, graphics or video enhance the site's message.

• *Communication Issues*:
- *General:*
  - i Provide communication channels with instructor (e-mail, chat room, discussion groups, etc.).
  - ii Provide communication channels with students (e-mail list for all students in the class).
  - iii Provide communication channels with experts (e-mail, invite to chat room, specialized news groups, etc.).
  - iv Encourage collaborative projects and assignments (provide chat room, e-mail, discussion groups, etc.).
  - v Provide feedback and comments forms.
  - vi Use announcements to get students attention to important dates and issues.
  - vii Provide help and supporting material to enhance student performance (*e.g.* how to use e-mail, chat room).

• *Objective and Scope*:
- *General*:
  - i State the purpose of the web site.
  - ii State kind of intended users.
  - iii Specify the scope of the site.

In this project, the evaluation process is still in progress. Initial evaluation results of 35 students are encouraging indicating that more than 88% of the students responded with agree or strongly agree to the general evaluation questions, *i.e.* the web site is very helpful to the course instruction, and the concept of WBI (webbased instruction) is a very effective instruction tool. Students reported convenience of accessing all course materials anytime and anywhere.

Extra time and effort were devoted at the beginning of the semester getting acquainted with such a new environment of teaching for the first time compared to other traditionally taught courses. Once getting used to the web-based application, the students appreciate the time saving and the excitement of receiving educational and practical knowledge in a variety of multimedia tools at their finger tips. Currently, we are conducting further improvement and expansion of the course web site mainly to make it more interesting, attractive and useful to the students.

For example:

- Animation and visualization of construction operations demonstrating the safe movement of construction equipment and labour on site;
- Alternative efficient site layout options for a given project;
- Simulation programmes of earthmoving operations;
- Walkthrough programmes for site inspection and final testing;
- Increasing the number of self-evaluation quizzes and assignments;
- Expanding the knowledge base of the course material and enhancing the user interface allowing faster information access.

Bibliography

A Ramamurty: *Advaita: A Conceptual Analysis*, D K Printworld, 2008.

A.N. Kapoor, V.P. Gupta and Mohini Gupta: *A Dictionary of Political Thought and Allied Concepts,* Radha Publication, Delhi, 2007.

Abishek Ramesh: *A Concept Of Nothing*, Rupa Publication, Delhi, 2008.

Arun Kumar: *Age, Teaching Models and Concept Attainment*, Manak, Publication, Delhi, 2004.

B Thomas: *Teaching Skills and Classroom Management*, Pointer, Publication, Delhi, 2005.

B.N. Swami, D.C. Joshi and S.R. Choudhary: *Agricultural Organic Waste : Basic Concepts, Potentials and Characteristics*, Himanshu Publication, Delhi, 2006.

B.V. Verghese: *Management of Teaching Skills in Primary Schools*, Anmol, Publication, Delhi, 2002.

K H Makde: *Advance Concepts in Plant Sciences*, S E Pawar and A D Choudhary, Dattsons, 2005.

Makarand Madhukar Gore: *Anatomy and Physiology of Yogic Practices*, Motilal Banarsidass, 2014.

N.N. Bhattacharyya: *A Glossary of Indian Religious Terms and Concepts*, Manohar, Publication, Delhi, 2004.

Naga Raju and Digumarti Bhaskara Rao, S.B.J.R. Chowdary: *Mastery of Teaching Skills*, Discovery, Publication, Delhi, 2004.

Pramod Chandra P. Bhatt: *An Introduction to Operating Systems: Concepts and Practice*, PHI Learning, 2008.

R.K. Tailor and Sunita Tailor: *Advertising: Modern Concepts, Principles and Methods*, Aavishkar Publication, Delhi, 2010.

R.V. Prajapati: *A Hand Book of Geography : Realms, Regions and Concepts*, Cyber Tech Publication, Delhi, 2010.

Rajender Singh Yadav: *Adult Education : Concept Theory and Practice*, Associated, Publisher, Delhi, 2002.

Rajwant Kaur: *Teaching Skills Through Self-Instructional Material*, Hind Publication, 2004.

Rakesh Hooja and Ramesh K Arora: *Administrative Theories : Approaches, Concepts and Thinkers in Public Administration*, Rawat, Publication, 2007.

S Suresh Babu: *AIDS and Ayurveda : The Ayurvedic Concepts of AIDS and Its Management*, Chaukhamba Sanskrit Pratishthan, 2007.

S. C. Datta: *A New Look at Stereochemistry: Concepts and Mechanism*, Macmillan Publishers, Delhi, 2011.

S.K. Jain and Ashok K. Jain: *An Introduction to Ethnobotany : Definitions Methods New Concepts and Approaches*, Deep Publications, Delhi, 2013.

S.K. Saxena: *Aesthetics : Approaches, Concepts and Problems*, D.K. Print world, 2010.

S.P. Denisia: *Teaching Skills*, A P H, Publication, Delhi, 2011.

S.S. Kaptan: *Advertising New Concepts*, Sarup, Publication, Delhi, 2002.

Sharad Rajimwale: *A Handbook of Literary Terms, Concepts and Movements*, Sarup, Publication, Delhi, 2003.

Subir Ghosh: *Agricultural Transformation : Concept and Country Perspectives*, SBS Publication, Delhio, 2012.

T.K. Oommen: *Alien Concepts and South Asian Reality: Responses and Reformulations*, Sage, Publication, Delhi, 2004.

T.M. Srinivasan: *Information and Communication Technology Teaching Skills*, Aavishkar, Publication, Delhi, 2002.

Tapomoy Deb: *A Conceptual Approach to Strategic Talent Management*, Indus Publication, Delhi, 2005.

Tripta Sharma: *Improving of Teaching Skills*, Hind Publication, Delhi, 2006.

Vidya Bhavani Suresh: *A Comprehensive Dictionary of Carnatic Music: Dictionary, Concepts*, Skanda Publication, Delhi, 2005.